Neil M. Kay is Senior Lecturer in Economics
at Heriot-Watt University, Edinburgh. He
was previously Lecturer in Industrial
Economics at the University of Nottingham
and Lecturer in Policy at Strathclyde
University Business School. In addition he
was Visiting Associate Professor, University
of California, Irvine, 1980–82.

He is the author of *The Innovating Firm* (St.
Martin's 1979) and *The Evolving Firm* (St.
Martin's 1982).

THE EMERGENT FIRM

Also by Neil M. Kay

THE INNOVATING FIRM: *a Behavioural Theory of Corporate R & D*

THE EVOLVING FIRM: *Strategy and Structure in Industrial Organisation*

THE EMERGENT FIRM

Knowledge, Ignorance and Surprise in Economic Organisation

Neil M. Kay

St. Martin's Press   New York

© Neil M. Kay 1984
All rights reserved. For information, write:
St. Martin's Press, Inc., 175 Fifth Avenue, New York, NY 10010
Printed in Hong Kong
Published in the United Kingdom by The Macmillan Press Ltd.
First published in the United States of America in 1984

ISBN 0–312–24402–9

Library of Congress Cataloging in Publication Data
Kay, Neil M.
The emergent firm.
Bibliography: p.
Includes index.
1. Microeconomics. 2. Neoclassical school of
economics. 3. Business enterprises. 4. Economics.
I. Title.
HB172.K39 1984   338.5   83–40528
ISBN 0–312–24402–9

FOR COLETTE

Alice laughed 'there's no use trying' she said, 'one *can't* believe impossible things'.
'I daresay you haven't had much practice' said the queen.

Lewis Carroll, Through the Looking-Glass

'Economics, the science of the quantification of the unquantifiable and the aggregation of the incompatible.'

G.L.S. Shackle, Epistemics & Economics

Contents

Preface

I have a genuine affection for prefaces. In many cases they are the most interesting part of a book, often cloaking miniature dramas of frustration, tedium and disappointment. After months or years of toil the writer has to set the context to his or her work in a tone which custom dictates must be, at worst, one of graciousness and humility and, at best, one of such gratuitous servility as would shame Uriah Heep. The preface world is an idyll peopled by super-intelligent conscientious colleagues, sweet-natured understanding families, and hyper-efficient telepathic typists.* They all have a sense of humour which is 'unfailing' in the case of secretaries, and only the author ever makes mistakes.

It is curious that the standards of verisimilitude expected of scholarly analysis in general can be suspended by tacit agreement in the case of the preface. In fact, the convention defends both public and writer; raw honesty in prefaces could shatter reputations and careers, unleash a storm of literary litigation and divorce petitions, and drag academics up into the same insurance risk bracket as North Sea oil divers. Coyness and restraint in prefaces is a professional defence mechanism whose advantageous natural selection properties have helped species academia go forth and procreate throughout the known world.

At their best, prefaces are constructively disingenuous providing harmless entertainment that may be spiced by personal knowledge of authors and their true circumstances. The problem with economics is that creating unreal worlds can be infectious and economists have been notoriously reluctant to stop at the preface, frequently pursuing the theme into the body of the text. However, in this context, unreality has the air of tragicomedy. Humour may be found in a situation in which phalanges of economists have spent man-years running into man-millenia building economic worlds which do not, will not, and cannot exist. The tragedy is that much of this is bad science; technique has overrun the discipline and become an end in itself rather than a simple

* Heriot-Watt University and the University of California are the only institutions known to employ telepathic secretaries.

means. Conventional neoclassical economics is a self-sealing closed system which has successfully insulated itself from empirical reality.

Such criticism has been made before, and from a number of quarters both inside and outside the profession. Some would allege that the straw man of neoclassical theory has been put to the torch so often that further disinterment and incediarism would be an unnecessary embarrassment. It can also be argued that many objections to neoclassical theory go only halfway in this respect; they criticise and identify failings, but do not provide an alternative approach.

This book was written with both objections in mind. It is essential to conduct a critical audit of neoclassical theory, because in the reasons for its failure are to be found the clues necessary for any useful reconstruction of theory. As far as the second objection is concerned, it is true that the performance of a theory must be judged on empirical grounds. Consequently, empirical explanation is the major objective of this work just as with its two predecessors, *The Innovating Firm* and *The Evolving Firm*.

Most of the book was written in the course of a two year leave of absence as visiting faculty in the University of California, Irvine. My thanks to Charles Lave, head of the economics department for bringing me over for the first year and Lyman Porter, dean of the Graduate School of Management (GSM) for keeping me on for the second. My extended stay was also partly due to Susan Sills, GSM administrator, who thought the MBA students deserved the aural challenge of a Celtic accent, and to Craig Galbraith in GSM with whom I started working during my first year. Part of our joint work is reflected in Chapter 7 which is co-authored with Craig, and I owe Craig and the Galbraith family – Jean, Devon and godson Scott – for contributing so much to my stay.

I also took the opportunity to try out extracts from earlier drafts of the book on economics undergraduates and MBA postgraduates. I thoroughly enjoyed the teaching and the text has benefited from the exposure.

The reader is entitled to some warning as to what is to follow. It is curious that academics typically find schools of thought easy to assign in the third person, but too narrow a measure to define the richness and variety of their own thinking. It would be presumptuous to break with tradition, but some hints might be given. The basic position taken here is that all non-trivial problems in economics arise from knowledge imperfections and the form such imperfection takes is the fundamental determinant of economic behaviour. It is the antithesis of the position represented by Milton Friedman, that the price mechanism provides sufficient information for markets to deal adequately with economic problems. As a consequence, considerable attention is given to Friedman's work later in this book as the embodiment of neoclassical theory. Most neoclassical theorists qualify their analysis by recognition of various real worlds contained, usually, in footnotes. Milton Friedman is neoclassical theory unadulterated by footnotes. His approach is consistent and unambiguous, and the clarity of his vision makes it a useful reference point. It is the logical, reasoned purity of his framework which has resulted in its being cited as the antithesis to the approach developed here, not any desire to argue *ad hominem* against Friedman himself. Such a comment may be necessary given the emphasis on his work later. In fact, I use Friedman's *Capitalism and Freedom* and *Free to Choose* regularly for personal use and teaching purposes whenever I wish to find out how markets could deal with a particular issue in the absence of any extraneous information problems. It is the ambivalence of other neoclassical theorists that makes Friedman an ideal representative of the neoclassical position.

This book continues the theme of *The Innovating Firm* and *The Evolving Firm* in being concerned with bounded rationality and non-decomposability in economic organisation. Frank Stephen of Strathclyde University pointed out to me the strong affinities between some aspects of the approach in *The Evolving Firm* and G.L.S. Shackle's view of the world. This is not surprising since Shackle's philosophy heavily influenced the courses given by Brian Loasby on my undergraduate degree at Stirling University. The links with Shackle should have been more clearly spelt out in *The Evolving Firm*, and I am pleased to be able to rectify this in the present work.

Rusty Thornberg, Mary Ellen Fuellerman, Richard Rumelt, Craig Galbraith, Peter Earl and Andrew Scott read all or part of the book and provided useful advice and encouragement. Rosemary Johnston, Gillian Cannon, Jean Roberts, Joyce Spencer and Ann Dolan attempted extra-sensory typing and can now read my writing better than I can myself.

Having resolved to break with convention and write a frank and realistic preface, in review it looks disappointingly like almost any other. What conclusions can be drawn from this may be best left as an open question. In any event, chasing away unreal worlds in prefaces is the easy part. The difficult part follows.

N.M.K.

1 Introduction

'The adventures first' said the Gryphon in an impatient tone,
'Explanations take such a dreadful time'.
Lewis Carroll, *Alice's Adventures in Wonderland*

Economics is about the role of information in resource allocation. All economic problems are reducible to problems in information. In the absence of information problems there is no economic problem. In this book we discuss some implications of the above statements and attempt to justify them. It is, admittedly, an unusual way of defining economics but one which it is felt may help illuminate fundamental issues. The hard shell of mainstream theory conceals a soft yolk in the form of information problems. The inability of conventional theory to come to terms with empirical reality has been reinforced by the orientation of much economic theorising as intellectual games[1] rather than as attempts to extend our understanding of the way the world works. Here, we are concerned with the sterility of mainstream theory and with a possible alternative to it.

There is little novelty in the idea of attacking neoclassical theory. However, critiques are of limited value unless a replacement approach can be suggested; many previous critical analyses have not provided substitute theories, or any empirical analysis. Here, as with two previous works (Kay, 1979 and Kay, 1982) we hope to contribute to a framework by starting with the deficiencies of neoclassical theory. Each work – *The Innovating Firm* (1979), *The Evolving Firm* (1982), and, here, *The Emergent Firm* – identifies two critical omissions in neoclassical theory; these are the issues of bounded rationality (and associated information problems) and system non-decomposability (and associated aggregation problems) respectively. Bounded rationality refers to cognitive and language limits on the decision making ability of actors in the economic process, and non-decomposability refers to systems in which interrelationships and linkages between subsystems means that the whole cannot be treated as the sum of independently operating parts. If priority has to be accorded to either of these concepts it must be to bounded rationality. While non-

1

decomposability represents a fundamental issue in its own right, bounded rationality and consequent information problems enter into every corner of economics, including questions involving non-decomposability.

Bounded rationality is a very straightforward concept. It simply means that there are practical limits on individual ability to collect, assimilate and process information in decision-making situations. It is closely tied in to problems of information and uncertainty; the strategic planner deciding whether or not to recommend diversification, the consumer deciding whether to experiment with a new product, the multinational assessing the possibilities for a joint venture with a foreign partner, all these examples are liable to encounter problems of information and uncertainty. We shall argue that the nature of bounded rationality problems in each case is critical in shaping the form of respective economic problems.

Much criticism has been directed towards the degree of abstraction, the 'timelessness', and the role of equilibrium in neoclassical theory. The lack of 'realism' in the theory is frequently seen as its major failing. We take a rather different tack here. Directly approaching the lack of 'realism' of elegant, static, equilibrium theory has not been particularly fruitful in terms of suggesting reformulations. By focusing instead on the role of information in economic organisation we hope to both identify the congenital weaknesses in conventional economic theory, and to suggest a basis for redirection. It is not that such criticisms of neoclassical theory are regarded as necessarily invalid; the problem is that neoclassical theory occupies a dominating role that makes it difficult to dislodge. Criticising its degree of abstraction naturally suggests a more 'realistic' theory should be developed; criticising its static nature encourages the obvious notion that dynamic processes should be studied; criticising the role of equilibrium in neoclassical theory implies the need for analysis of disequilibrium behaviour. Neoclassical theorists look down from the commanding heights of their citadel and sniffily perceive the dangers of anarchy in the adoption of 'realistic', dynamic, disequilibrium analysis. In return for abandoning a theory of generality and scope they are offered alternatives of dubious potential as compensation for their sacrifice. The intellectual capital invested in neoclassical theory has not been easily swayed by such propositions. The position taken here is that each of the major objections to neoclassical theory (the ignoring of time, risk, uncertainty and expectations according to Bell and Kristol, eds (1981, p. ix), and, in similar vein, neglect of time, uncertainty, contracts, finance and market institutions according to Davidson (1978, p. 367) are all reducible to one basic issue; information problems. These are the root sauce of the fundamental weaknesses in neoclassical theory and the necessary starting point for any reformulation.

A real problem is that neoclassical theory still tends to define the parameters of discussion for both disciples and heretics. The fundamental question in neoclassical theory is that of optimal product-market price, whether from the point of view of the private decision-maker or society. This is the focus in neoclassical theory throughout the range of its analysis in areas as diverse as competition, monopoly, externalities, public goods and oligopoly, though in the latter case indeterminateness is a recurring problem.

The concept of optimal product-market price is in fact reducible into its four components – optimality as associated with constrained maximisation techniques, product as a building block for analysis, market as the sole mechanism for resource allocation, and price as the information handling input into decision making. It is interesting that modern developments have tended to concentrate on selective modification to these four props of neoclassical theory. For example, Austrian[2] and post-Keynesian[3] economists have criticised the concept of *optimality* while retaining products, markets and prices as basic to their framework. The recent 'uprising' (as interpreted by Baumol) in the literature occasioned by contestable markets theory in fact modifies the role of individual *products* as basic building blocks[4] while retaining optimality, markets and prices. Also, the earlier normative literature on transfer pricing moved away from analysis of external *markets*, but still retained optimal product price as their basic question.[5]

It is the last item – price – that represents a Pandora's box as far as theorising is concerned. Optimality, individual product base and markets can all be dropped independently without directly affecting the other items. However, if information problems interfere with price as a resource allocating device, then not only price, but also markets may be inadequate to describe resource allocation questions, while optimality may be unattainable.

Such a possibility can be demonstrated with a simple example. A trader on a street corner offers you a packet of Hootenannies for a given price. You would probably wish to know a great deal more about the characteristics of both Hootenanny and trader than just price, and in the absence of sufficient knowledge market trading would take place on an unsatisfactory basis, or not at all, while maximisation of utility would be an inappropriate concept in the presence of real uncertainty as to the properties and characteristics of this possible trade.

Not surprisingly, economists have tended to shy away from such issues. Williamson (1975) is one of the few economists to attend to questions of this nature and he is representative of an approach we shall find useful later. More usually in the neoclassical literature it has been traditional to presume that if some decision maker is at an informational disadvantage, optimality can be rescued through the intervention of some omniscient policy maker with privileged access to informational secrets.

In short, the limited and highly specific agenda of optimal product-market price has focused and directed economic analysis. Extensions *within* the paradigm of neoclassical theory, such as monopolistic and imperfect competition,[6] still adhere to the four component items of this question. Consequently developments *outside* the paradigm frequently appear highly radical by comparison, even if they adopt a perspective which drops one of the items on the optimal product-market price checklist. Thus, the emergence of managerial theories of the firm (e.g., Baumol, 1959, Marris, 1966, and Williamson, 1964) in fact only represent marginal departures from the neoclassical approach; constrained maximisation of objectives in a deterministic equilibrium framework is still pursued (see Kay, 1982). Yet truly radical critiques too often destroy without creating alternatives. As a consequence the mainstream debate has tended to revolve around the neoclassical–Keynesian syntheses fashioned by Hicks and Samuelson and the neoclassical–monetarist perspective symbolised by Milton Friedman. The neoclassist microeconomic tradition is still fundamental to conventional economic theory. Nor surprisingly, the study of economics combines fascination with frustration; the use of scarce resources and appropriation of valued commodities are basic human preoccupations and the events of the 1970s and early 1980s have only served to heighten the public interest and concern in this area. The chronic economic problems associated with stagflating economies have been paralleled by widespread criticism and condemnation of the inadequacy of conventional economic theory. So much has been publicly written of the 'crisis' in economic theory that an interested lay observer could be forgiven for believing that any self-respecting economist with a conscience would be indulging in an orgy of breast beating and mea culpas, while those economists of a religious persuasion might be expected to wear hairshirts as penance for their failures of analysis.

Such a picture would be totally inaccurate. Academic departments are, and should be, havens of calm and peace isolated from the hustle of the outside world, and in this respect economics departments are no exception. Such isolation facilitates the development and continuance of reasoned argument and discussion. Hairshirts and public displays of emotion are no more frequently observed now in economics departments than they were in the days predating current economic horrors.

However, while the maintenance of intellectual equilibrium is a commendable objective, what is a matter for reasonable concern is the extent to which academic economists continue to develop and refine .tools which evidence suggests are not up to the task for which they are designed. Textbooks still extol the virtue of traditional theory, its contribution, and rosy prospects. Professional seminars concentrate on the process and result of constrained maximisation models with little, if any, discussion of the reasonableness of the underlying assumptions. Seekers of analysis of the 'crisis' and alternative theories would find little evidence of either in the top ranking journals which exhibit a remarkable degree of continuity rooted in traditional theory.[7] At the same time, there has been widespread recognition of the failure of economic theory if a groundswell of conventional opinion is to be believed. Whole books express concern (*The Crisis in Economic Theory*[8]), ask why (*What Is Wrong with Economics?*[9]), and assign blame (*The Irrelevance of Conventional Economics*[10]). Katouzian audits the general concern;

> 'Economics is in crisis'; every economist, or almost every economist, knows and agrees with that statement, even though they may disagree on the precise diagnosis or an effective prescription for the crisis itself. Katouzian (1980, p. 4)

Some leading economists have expressed strong reservations as far as the usefulness of conventional theory is concerned. The stagflating seventies signalled obvious deficiencies in macroeconomic theory but its microeconomic foundations have not escaped scrutiny. Leontief (1971), Phelps Brown (1972) and Worswick (1972) all have criticised the refinement of abstract neoclassical theorising having little, if any, relevance to empirical problems. There has been a number of studies expressly concerned with the crisis.[11]

Defenders of neoclassical theory such as Hahn (1981) have argued that criticism of neoclassical theory is not sufficient to lead to its abandonment as long as a credible alternative does not exist. It is hoped to argue that a useful alternative can be developed, and in this respect we shall be building on such theorists as H.A. Simon, R.H. Coase, and O.E. Williamson. The aim is to demonstrate an empirically relevant theory of industrial organisation can be framed, consistent with, and developing from, *The Innovating Firm* and *The Evolving Firm*. The intention, as with these two previous works is to provide a theoretical framework that may contribute to empirical analysis. Only in this manner can a credible alternative be developed. In *The Innovating Firm* a non-aggregative systemic approach to corporate resource allocation for R & D was developed which provides one strand of analysis pursued in *The Evolving Firm* and here. In *The Evolving Firm* the corporation was analysed as a network of interrelated product-markets in which the major strategic decision consisted of the extent to which the economies from links should be traded against the increased survival potential of a highly varied corporate system. Some of the specific analysis of *The Evolving Firm* is developed further in this present work, especially in Chapters 6 and 7. The effect of product life cycles, and product-market links were analysed in *The Evolving Firm* using a transaction cost approach; *The Emergent Firm* develops this line of analysis and extends it into other areas.

Before we start our analysis proper, it may be useful to provide an overview of the book. The bulk of the analysis falls into three phases; Chapters 2–5, Chapters 6–7 and Chapters 8–10 respectively. The first phase is concerned with setting up a framework for analysis of resource allocation problems facing the modern corporation. In Chapter 2 it is argued that there are two major difficulties associated with conventional (neoclassical) economic theory; the technique of aggregation and the presumption that prices eliminate all information problems. The first difficulty results in significant interrelationship between product-markets being ignored, while it is argued here that the second means that non-trivial resource allocation problems cannot be analysed using neoclassical analysis. It is the existence of imperfections of knowledge that forms the basis of problems of industrial organisation and business strategy.

This last point is developed in Chapter 3 in which the relationship between information problems and the structure and content of the modern corporation is examined. Chapter 4 explores the implications of information problems in other areas of microeconomic activity and develops the analysis of the preceding chapter. Chapter 5 examines the nature of information problems further and the implications they may have for economic analysis. This chapter integrates the discussion of the earlier chapters and highlights the central role of self referential paradoxes in information problems. The catch-22 impasse of neoclassical theory is summarised and possible remedies prescribed.

Chapters 6 and 7 constitute the second part of the analysis and build on Chapters 2–5 to analyse substantive problems in industrial organisation (Chapter 6) and multinational enterprise (Chapter 7). In this context transaction cost analysis developed by Williamson (1975) is identified as an especially useful framework for incorporating the information problems identified in Chapter 5. As well as discussing the foundations of this approach in Chapter 6, it is extended to cover problems of product-market linkages and the effects of technological change. Chapter 7 concentrates on one particular application of this framework, the existence and behaviour of multinational corporations.

The third major phase of the work is developed in Chapters 8 to 10 inclusive. Chapter 8 analyses major representative texts in the area of public policy – *The New Industrial State* by Galbraith, *The American Challenge* by Servan-Shreiber and *Small is Beautiful* by Schumacher. In each case the main thesis reduces to an analysis of bounded rationality and information problems in one form or another. In Chapter 9 the respective approaches are integrated and contrasted with the neoclassical perspective of Friedman's *Free to Choose*. The final Chapter 10 suggests policy implications following from the arguments of the preceding chapters.

To summarise, the book builds on two perspectives that are radically different from traditional economics; firstly, the belief that 'aggregative economics' based on the assumption of decomposible systems distorts and misrepresents the actual nature of economic relationships prevailing at firm, industry and economy level, and secondly, the idea that virtually all interesting economic problems stem from imperfections of information. It is argued here that traditional economic theory is not an appropriate basis for explanation of economic behaviour because it uses aggregative techniques and ignores information problems or represents them in an inappropriate fashion. As the quote from Shackle at the start of this book suggests, aggregation and information problems have not deterred neoclassical theorists.

If there is a single starting point for the analysis, it is the concept of bounded rationality as developed by H.A. Simon. Simon's work is contained in a large body of books and articles, though Simon (1961) and (1969) are particularly recommended as examples of his work on bounded rationality. Conventional economics presumes that the price mechanism effectively eliminates information problems since it economises on limited decision-making capacity. It is the implication of Simon's claim that bounded rationality still represents a pervasive and significant determinant of resource allocation – even in the context of a market system – that sets the tone for the analysis to follow. O.E. Williamson's work in developing bounded rationality considerations within a transaction cost analysis is an invaluable contribution in this context.

Analysis of bounded rationality considerations in a transaction cost context is combined within a structuralist perspective in this analysis.[12] Such a framework emphasising the centrality of the concept of system linkages in economic analysis is especially evident in Chapters 6 and 7. These involve the issues of non-decomposability[13] and aggregation discussed earlier in this chapter.

The purpose of this work, as with the two preceding works, is to provide an explanatory basis for economic analysis. Some normative implications are considered but no predictive theorising is attempted. An analogy may be drawn with evolutionary theory in biology which may be regarded as providing a more or less satisfactory basis for explaining the selection and emergence of species, but which does not provide an obvious basis for predicting future evolutionary patterns. Long-term prediction is not regarded here as a viable role for economic theorising, whereas understanding of the logic by which species of economic organisation have evolved is regarded as a more reasonable ambition. Consequently the emergent firm selected through this evolutionary process is the object of study in this book.

2 The Problem

All these pretty polite techniques made for a well-panelled board room and a well regulated market are liable to collapse. At all times the vague panic fears and equally vague and unreasoned hopes are not really lulled but a little way below the surface.

J.M. Keynes (1937)

economics is a leading example of uncertain knowledge.

J.R. Hicks (1979)

As stated in Chapter 1, this book is based on two complementary ideas. In this chapter, I will state both as simply as possible. The remainder of the book is taken up with developing the points in more detail. Both arguments start by identifying a fundamental economic problem, and then the implications of the problems are examined in turn. The problem may be labelled those of information and aggregation respectively.

The information problem appears as a will o' the wisp in economics; now you see it, now you don't. The importance of information is frequently referred to in verbal discussion of economic issues; by the time the formal analysis is presented it has usually disappeared. Occasionally it reappears in summary and conclusions. This vanishing act attains its most polished version in standard treatises in which the information problem is rarely visible. Indeed the observer is frequently persuaded of the non-existence of such a problem since the price system has supposedly eliminated it.

Such erratic appearances on the part of 'information problems' can be explained in terms of the difficulty of reconciling such problems with formal theorising. As we shall see in later chapters, information is a peculiar commodity with disconcerting properties for economic theories that attempt to integrate it within their framework. The information problem has been tackled head on by a number of approaches in recent years; yet frequently such analysis tends to be characterised by a case or institutional base to the analysis, and each encounters severe difficulties when attempts are made to generalise beyond this level.[1]

There are reasons for this case by case approach and the difficulty involved in developing a formal theory that ventures beyond specific instances. Firstly, recognition of information problems typically involves consideration of the role of uncertainty in decision-making. For a science enamoured of curve drawing and equation construction, uncertainty serves only to fudge orderly and rigorous analysis, and as such, represents a complication to be avoided in general by formal theories. The formal theories that do deal with information problems impose tight restrictions on the form that information problems may take, as we shall see in Chapter 3. Secondly, recognition of information problems invites consideration of the stock of knowledge possessed by the decision-maker which in turn tends to point to the need to analyse the specific background, experience, and history of individuals and institutions. The uniqueness of individual experience and learning opportunities encourages a case by case approach and militates against generalisation. Also, human behaviour under conditions of imperfect knowledge raises questions of a psychological nature; how does learning take place, in what form are aspirations and objectives expressed, how is uncertainty handled, and so on. In this connection nobody should be deceived by economic's nominal position within the social sciences – traditionally the appearance of actual human beings in economic analysis has been fiercely resisted. Economists have tended to prefer models based on skeletal assumptions of rationality and perfect knowledge, trading off relevance for rigor. Whether we are pursuing Keynesianism, monetarism, or the economics of command economies it is impossible to take more than a couple of steps before running up against problems of bounded rationality, information and uncertainty. Uncertainty is fundamental to Keynes analysis as Shackle and Davidson have pointed out (see, for example, Davidson, 1978). We shall be developing Shackles views on uncertainty in more detail in Chapter 5). As far as monetarism is concerned, the concept of *money* itself is meaningless unless uncertainty is explicitly recognised; complete knowledge precludes the need for a device of this nature.[2] The concept of *planning* itself is similarly redundant if knowledge is complete in a command economy; planning and decision-making are activities associated with situations of partial ignorance, as Loasby has pointed out.[3] Yet economists of all persuasions have sought refuge in the security blanket of constrained maximisation models with depressing regularity, and based their analysis on inappropriate assumptions of perfect knowledge.

Thus, there are strong incentives for economists to suppress information problems in their analysis. Information problems typically involve messy, complex, and individualistic psychological relationships.[4] We shall argue later that information problems occupy a central position in important economic issues and consider the form that those information problems may take, as well as the type of analysis that may be legitimately applied to them.

Aggregation problems are the second main area we shall be concerned with here. The technique of aggregation provides economists with a simple tool giving their analysis tremendous potential power and range. Once individual behaviour has been explained, analysis at industry and economy level is child's play; summation of individual characteristics is all that is required using this device. Like a photographer's zoom lens, aggregation allows the economist to concentrate on any desired system level, and rapidly adjust the level of magnification if desired.

The purpose of aggregation is creditable. If economists allow micro levels to be divorced from macro level, then compartmentalism is encouraged and explanations have limited scope. Micro levels and macro levels are interdependent, aggregation provides a simple and obvious way of stating this interdependence. Economics is not the only social science in which the ability to switch smoothly from one level to another is recognised as important; the title of C. Wright Mills *The Sociological Imagination* refers to the need for sociologists to be capable of transferring their analysis quickly and easily from the micro level of the individual to the macro level of society as a whole, and back again.

However, aggregation presupposes that the elements being lumped together are *separable*. That which can be aggregated can also be disaggregated, aggregation presumes we may cleave our economy into little islands of decision making without fundamentally distorting the behaviour and characteristics of the system as a whole. In the case of economics, this has traditionally meant that analysis can focus on individual products and consumers without directly considering the possibility of interrelationships between units. Once relations between elements are recognised, aggregation is no longer adequate to describe higher levels; to use a simple example, the properties of water cannot be obtained by summing the properties of its constituent elements hydrogen and oxygen. The relation between elements in this case takes the form of an ionic bond which also contributes to the characteristics of the system. The result is a colourless liquid whose constituent elements are gases. Introducing the concept of relation between elements means aggregation cannot usefully describe the characteristics of higher level systems.[5]

Suspicion should be aroused by the fact that economics is virtually alone in the natural and social sciences in relying heavily on aggregation as its central analytical technique. When it is used elsewhere, such as in thermodynamics and demography, the nature of the problem is such as to ensure that separability of elements is a reasonable assumption for the purposes of the analysis. In economics, very little in the way of serious attempt has been made to test the reasonableness and generality of this assumption of separability. To do so is to threaten the basic fabric of economics. Simple convenience effectively buttresses the position of aggregation in economics.

When considered together, the reasons for economists traditional attitudes towards information and aggregation problems become plain. The assumed absence of information problems and relationships between elements permits the construction of a theory of elegance and scope. The assumption of perfect knowledge, when combined with that of rationality, provides the basis for a rigorous analytical framework amenable to mathematical development, while the technique of aggregation allows the theoretician to range quickly and easily through all the levels in the economy. No wonder the relevant assumptions are fiercely defended when attacked; economic theory built on these foundations has become a sensitive and powerful instrument.

However, while it is pleasant to possess a rigorous theory of considerable range, these attributes should not be pursued for their own sake. Usefulness is the prerequisite for a viable theory. A well-honed instrument may be a thing of beauty in its own right, but the primary purpose of a tool is to be functional. Under certain circumstances an electron microscope can be an extremely productive aid, but if the primary task is digging a garden, only desperation or dementia is likely to lead to its being enlisted in the production process. Yet, as we shall see there has been a strong tendency on the part of economic theoreticians in the past to be beguiled by appearances at the expense of results in developing elegant, decorative and useless models.

Before alternatives are sought we shall consider in more detail the nature of conventional economic theory and the context in which it operates. This is the step taken in the next section in which we consider economic analysis as a logical sequence of stages which are either explicit or implicit in any study.

THE STAGES OF ECONOMIC ANALYSIS

Many interpretations and definitions of what constitutes 'the economic problem' are available, but most make some reference to economics' concern with problems of resource allocation and income distribution. We shall be primarily concerned with the area of resource allocation in this analysis, with problems of explanation rather than prescription, and with microeconomic foundations rather than macroeconomic developments.[6] There are good reasons for narrowing the analysis in this fashion; firstly, focusing on resource allocation allows us to concentrate on product markets without bringing in the added complications associated with factor-markets in income distribution problems.[7] Secondly it is widely recognised that economics is in a state of disarray due simply to the apparent inapplicability of the theoretical instrument to the empirical job in hand. The inappropriateness of conventional theory has been widely commented on and analysed,[8] and there has been some dutiful contemplation of axiomatic navels by economists, though little evidence exists of such meditation on the part of mainstream neoclassical theorists. Given this unsatisfactory state of affairs, a return to basics is called for, and basics in the context means effective diagnosis before prescription, and microeconomic foundations before macroeconomic superstructures. Therefore, the primary objective of this study is a better understanding of how individual units in the economy cope with resource allocation problems.

Having established our objectives, we may now identify three conceptually distinctive stages in economic analysis. Each stage poses a specific question for participants and analysts as far as resource allocation is concerned. The stages are outlined in Figure 2.1.

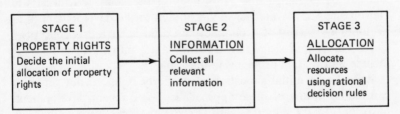

STAGE 1	STAGE 2	STAGE 3
PROPERTY RIGHTS	INFORMATION	ALLOCATION
Decide the initial allocation of property rights	Collect all relevant information	Allocate resources using rational decision rules

FIGURE 2.1   *Stages in the allocation process*

Stage 1 is concerned with the initial allocation of property rights; who owns what. Stage 2 is associated with the provision of information relevant to the decision making problem such as expected costs, revenues, etc. Stage 3 is the stage in which appropriate decision-making techniques are utilised to provide criteria for resource allocation. Thus the three stages mark questions of ownership, information and allocation, respectively.

This three-stage breakdown is particularly interesting because it provides a useful basis for discriminating between alternative economic theories. To start with, neoclassical theory concerns itself only with the third stage in this process. Property rights are not questioned since the status quo is taken for granted, while the price system is presumed to eliminate information problems. The only items permitted to appear on the neoclassical agenda relate to questions of constrained maximisation of specific objective functions and have resulted in the profit maximising theory of the firm and utility maximising consumer theory. The marginalist base of these theories provides a logical foundation for theories of choice when information problems are absent.

However a number of developments in recent years have attempted to extend analysis back into the second stage. For example, the Bayesian school have developed principles and theorems based on subjective probabilities; individuals assess probabilities of events occurring using available information and the derived estimates are used as basic data for appropriate decision making rules. Also, the Behavioural school, associated particularly with H.A. Simon, R.M. Cyert and J.G. March,[9] have developed theories of resource allocation based on the concept of bounded rationality. A third distinctive development has been the re-emergence of the Institutional school led by O.E. Williamson in which the behavioural concept of bounded rationality is paired with the implications of individual opportunism in analysis of exchange and co-ordination problems. Further, R.R. Nelson and S.G. Winter have contributed to the development of an evolutionary theory of economics based on behavioural concepts.[10] Each of these approaches moves us back a step into the second stage to include information problems in the analysis.

Stage 1, the initial allocation of property rights, is not generally considered in any of these approaches. Some recent developments have concerned themselves with the circumstances surrounding trading of property rights, but these do not question initial allocations of rights. Theories applied to stage 1 tend to have a highly political colouring as we would expect of an arena which is the stamping ground of Marxism. Indeed Marx was largely concerned with social, political and economic consequences following upon property rights in capital; basing his approach on the labour theory of value he analysed the implications of capitalist control of the accrual of labours product due to their ownership of the means of production.

Thus, the focus and scope of economic theories in this 3-stage process of economic analysis is highly varied. Of the approaches we have briefly referred to here, neoclassical theory is preoccupied with stage 3 problems, Marxism tends to emphasise the implications of stage 1 problems, with a motley body of theories attempting to integrate stage 2 and stage 3 problems. Some problems associated with theoretical investigating of the latter will become evident in later analysis. In this respect our main focus of attention to start with will be on the restricted scope of neoclassical theory and its limited applicability to economic problems.

However, before we begin to look more closely at neoclassical theory, it is necessary to pre-empt a possible defence that could be made by neoclassical theorists, that we are setting up a straw man in describing neoclassical theory as implying perfect knowledge and decomposable systems. It might be claimed that extensions of neoclassical theory in recent years have included behaviour under conditions of risk[11] and in contestable markets (in which non-decomposable economies of scope are shared between product-markets).[12] However adaptations of neoclassical theory to deal with problems of uncertainty have been characterised by desperate attempts to retain constrained maximisation techniques so that typically the decision-maker is expected to have perfect knowledge of all possible future outcomes and expected means and variances; only minor and highly restricted modification to the perfect knowledge assumption is permitted. As we shall consider further in Chapter 5, neoclassical extensions into risky analysis are such as to render them subject to the same criticisms of neoclassical theory made below. The theory of contestable markets is a very recent development and in fact tends to ignore information problems just like traditional neoclassical theory, and does not go far enough in developing the implications of non-decomposability.

THE ECONOMICS OF NIRVANA

Neoclassical theory is based on the principle of marginalism. From an allocative point of view, decision rules are grounded in the central principle that reallocation of consumption and production should take place until the marginal benefit from any switch just equals the marginal cost.[13] This principle is applied to efficiency of allocation of goods and resources and holds for consumers, resource owners and firms. The beauty of the marginalist principle lies in its simplicity; if equality of marginal benefit and marginal cost does not hold, then shifting existing allocations will improve matters. If marginal benefit exceeds marginal cost for a specific allocation then it will lead to an overall improvement in efficiency and should be undertaken; if marginal cost exceeds marginal benefit then cutting back on the allocation will improve efficiency. Marginalism lends itself to rigorous development and to formal mathematical theorems, yet this simple outline is the basis of subsequent development.

If all costs and benefits are incurred by the relevant decision makers then rules for optimal decision making are uncomplicated and involve straightforward application of the efficiency rules sketched above.[14] However some other possibilities require closer attention and we will examine these by reference to a simple example below.

Suppose we have a firm manufacturing aluminium skis (Alski Ltd). It is the only firm based around aluminium technology making sports goods in this region. Now, consider the possibility that a second firm decides to locate next door to the established firm and that the firm manufactures aluminium tennis rackets (Alten Ltd).[15] This may have a number of possible effects but we shall consider effects under two main categories, externalities and potential economies.

We shall look at the problem of externalities to start with. Externalities result from interdependency in consumption and production; a change in one party's consumption pattern or level of production has a direct effect on the costs or benefits occurring to another party. Therefore, the source of the externality does not directly bear all the costs and benefits associated with the appropriate consumption or production decision.

We may illustrate the concept by suggesting two examples in this case. The ski firm, Alski, could possess a smoky chimney which increasingly pollutes the neighbouring racket firm as more skis are produced, and requires remedial measures to protect the quality of the rackets. Secondly, the racket firm, Alten, may be expanding production to such an extent that auxiliary industry may be pulled into the area. Small sub-contractors may set up to provide small scale or specialised services for Alten in the area of aluminium technology. However, as the scale of racket production increases, Alski may also benefit from the availability of these aluminium selected services which have spun off from racket development.

The effect of the smoky chimney is to impose a cost on Alten as Alski expands production. The effect of the growth of auxiliary services is to provide a benefit to Alski as Alten expands production. Both are externalities insofar as they do not accrue to the party whose production decisions have caused them. Neoclassical theory presumes self-interest on the part of decision-makers and so these effects would be ignored by the decision-makers who are responsible for them, since their impact is felt elsewhere. Therefore, from the point of view of the whole system, it would appear relevant costs of ski production and relevant benefits of racket production will be ignored.

So we have a problem. The racket firm will tend to expand production until the private marginal cost and benefit of doing so is equated. However, this fails to take into account the benefit accruing to the ski firm and therefore the racket firm will tend to underproduce from the point of view of society as a whole. Likewise, the ski firm will tend to overproduce from the point of view of society as a whole. It fails to take into account the pollution costs of increased production of skis.[16] From the point of view of all involved parties, production should equate all marginal costs of increased production with all associated marginal benefits; self-interest of producers restricts their concern to their own costs and benefits and therefore we are liable to have a misallocation of resources and underproduction of rackets and over-production of skis.

Traditional economic analysis has indicated a number of methods by which externalities can be taken into account in deciding the optimal allocation of resources.[17] However, here we are less concerned with the range of techniques available than the range of types of economic organisation available. In this respect there are basically three alternative forms of economic organisation; state direction, firm co-ordination and market transaction. For example, the ski/racket system could be nationalised, merged into one firm, or the parties could continue to settle issues of mutual interest in the market place respectively. We shall consider all three solutions and concern ourselves first with the feasibility in principle of employing each form to deal with the question of externalities before turning to the problem of the suitability in practice of doing so.

Suppose we nationalise both firms under one state run organisation, National Aluminium Sports Goods Corporation (NASC). Could this organisation unilaterally take into account the effect of the externalities and contribute to an overall optimal allocation of resources? In principle yes, since the externality has now been internalised within the one organisation. If NASC pursues simple profit maximisation objectives, what were formerly external effects (the smoky chimney and the auxiliary services) will be taken into account as internal costs and benefits where appropriate since the decision-maker, NASC, now bears all relevant costs and benefits. Thus the pollution costs of extending ski production and the auxiliary service benefits of extending racket production will be recognised and accounted for in NASC's profit calculations.[18]

A similar argument holds for the merger of Alski and Alten into one firm, Alskiten Ltd. The internalisation of the former external effects means that the decision-maker, Alskiten takes all relevant costs and benefits into account in its resource allocation calculations. In this respect there is no difference in principle between state-owned NASC and the Alskiten company.

The third form of economic organisation is market transaction. While this is a less straightforward case than state direction and firm co-ordination this will also lead to an optimal allocation of resources if certain conditions hold. What has been termed 'the Coase Theorem' (from R.H. Coase's original statement in 1960) states that an efficient outcome will obtain if property rights are unambiguously defined and if there are no transaction costs.[19] We will discuss transaction costs in more detail later. What we are concerned with here is the meaning and relevance of property rights in this context.

Property rights may refer not only to the ownership of a resource, but also to the effects of that resource in use. For example, there may be defined property rights in the pollution effects of the smoky chimney which may be traded in the market place. If the property rights are possessed by Alski they possess the legal entitlement to pollute; if the property rights are possessed by Alten they possess the legal entitlement to be protected from pollution. The interesting thing about the Coase Theorem is that it demonstrates that it does not matter for efficiency purposes who possesses the property rights; all that matters is that they should be unambiguously allocated.

The clue as to why this should be is found in the solutions provided by NASC nationalisation and Alskiten incorporation. In both these cases internalisation of the externality encourages the decision-maker to choose the optimal levels of ski and racket output. This is also what is achieved by unambiguous allocation of property rights in the market transaction case. Suppose first of all, Alski possessed property rights in pollution. Under these circumstances Alten should be prepared to pay a financial inducement up to the cost of additional pollution imposed on it to persuade Alski to cut back production. If Alski chooses not to cut back production it sacrifices Alten's financial contribution as well as private costs of production – the pollution cost has been internalised in Alski's calculations. Suppose now Alten possesses property rights in pollution; in this case it would be rational for Alten to accept pollution if Alski provided financial compensation for the effects of the smoke which at least covered these pollution costs. Again, the pollution cost is internalised in Alski's calculation. Irrespective of *who* possesses the property rights, the specification of property rights in the externality leads to internalisation of the externality and efficient resource allocation in so far as marginal cost equals marginal benefit.[20]

So our naïve excursion into the realm of economic organisation has not so far provided us with any basis for discriminating between different forms of economic organisation. Each appears to offer potentially efficient solutions to the externality problem; effectively the same solution, arrived at by internalisation of the externality. Curiously, no preference for any of the three alternative forms of economic organisations has emerged from this analysis up this point.[21]

In fact, we should not be surprised by the stalemate because so far we have been playing the game according to neoclassical rules. Our decision-makers display the comforting properties of rationality and omniscience. While this removes the fun of criticising the efficiency of market, corporate or socialist organisation (depending on one's point of view) it has the advantage of providing an uncomplicated, if indecisive, role for economic organisation. It does not seem to matter whether we choose transactions, co-ordination or direction as our method of allocating resources.

This inconclusive result can be reinforced by briefly considering an alternative set of circumstances obtaining for Alten and Alski. Externalities refer to economies and diseconomies that result from the independent operation of the respective firms, but there may also be potential economies achievable which require prior agreement and synchronisation of the activities of both parties. For example, there may be economies in distribution to the extent retail outlets and trucks can be shared; economies in operation to the extent aluminium technology is shared; economies in investment to the extent specific R & D results can be applied across products; economies in management to the extent management skill is a scarce resource and both teams are in aluminium sports goods facilitating transferability of management experience. The list of possible economies is indefinite since the number of potential links between Alten and Alski could be enormous. Links may offer opportunities for specialisation and division of labour, exploitation of capital indivisibilities, and so on. We will be further concerned later in the analysis with the form and impact economies such as the above may have. For the moment our interest lies in how our alternative forms of economic organisation may deal with these questions and the four examples we have outlined above will serve as test cases.

The basic question is: where potential economies exist, can they be exploited by the respective forms of economic organisation? In the NASC and Alskiten case the answer is a simple yes, in principle. Both institutional forms exert direct control over the range covered by potential economies in this case, and exploitation of economies through direction and co-ordination of resource is achievable within the respective institutions.

The case of market transactions requires more detailed consideration. To simplify matters let us continue to assume that Alten is the progressive firm and has a distribution network, quality machinery, and R & D team and capable management already established, while Alski's corresponding resources in the respective areas are of inferior quality or non-existent. NASC or Alskiten solutions could exploit the potential economies in the appropriate areas, but is this possible using market transactions?

The answer again is yes, in principle. Alski could rent space in trucks, lease machinery, purchase R & D results or employ the Alten R & D team and management on a consultancy basis. The exploitation of each of these potential economies can be arranged through market transactions. Where a potential economy is not fully exploited it would be in the interest of both parties to arrange a mutually satisfactory trade involving use of resource for a fee. What we cannot know in advance is how the gains from these potential economies will be distributed between the parties, this depending on situational factors such as bargaining strength, attitudes of the respective parties, etc. However, the rationality and omniscience of the parties involved should naturally lead to mutual agreement to plunder all potential economies – which is all that we are concerned with. Market transactions should lead to efficient outcomes where potential economies exist providing both parties do not incur transactions costs.[22]

In fact, in a section of the economic literature concerned with aspects of institutional behaviour, there has been a growing awareness in recent years that unless information problems are explicitly brought into the analysis, the neoclassical assumptions of rationality and perfect knowledge inevitably result in *all* misallocation or under-utilisation of resources being corrected as Demsetz (1968) points out:

> A world in which negotiating costs are zero is a world in which no monopolistic inefficiencies will be present, simply because buyers and sellers both can profit from negotiations that result in a reduction and elimination of inefficiencies. In such a world it will be bargaining skills and not market structures that determine the distribution of wealth. . . . The co-existence of monopoly *power* and monopoly *structure* is possible only if the costs of negotiating are differentially positive, being lower for one set of sellers (or buyers) than it is for rival sellers (or buyers). If one set of sellers (or buyers) can organize those on the other side of the market more cheaply than can rivals, then price may be raised (or lowered) to the extent of the existing differential advantage in negotiating costs. (p. 61)

As Dahlman (1979, p. 142) points out in this spirit, both monopoly and public goods can be treated as sub-categories of externalities; misallocation of resources under monopoly occurs because market power on the part of the monopolist allows deviation from the optimal competitive solution. There is therefore an externality in consumption since the utility of the consumers is affected by the utility maximising behaviour of the monopolist. The same argument holds with respect to public goods; Calabresi (1968) argues, if there is rationality, and costless legally unimpeded bargaining, *all* resource misallocation may be cured. It follows that externalities, monopoly, public goods and economies may all be dealt with efficiently by market transactions in the absence of transaction costs. Dahlman (1979) points out these transaction costs reduce essentially to problems of search and direct information costs, bargaining and decision costs, policing and enforcement (p. 148).

It is necessary to take the definition of transaction costs by Coase a little further. A natural classification of transaction costs consistent with his definition can be obtained from the different phases of the exchange process itself. In order for an exchange between two parties to be set up it is necessary that the two search each other out, which is costly in terms of time and resources. If the search is successful and the parties make contact they must inform each other of the exchange opportunity that may be present, and the conveying of such information will again require resources. If there are several economic agents on either side of the potential bargain to be struck, some costs of decision making will be incurred before the terms of trade can be decided on. Often such agreeable terms can only be determined after costly bargaining between the parties involved. After the trade has been decided on, there will be costs of policing and monitoring the other party to see that his obligations are carried out as determined by the terms of the contract, and of enforcing the agreement reached. These, then, represent the first approximation to a workable concept of transaction costs: search and information costs, bargaining and decision costs, policing and enforcement costs. (Dahlman, 1979, pp 147–8)

Dahlman summarises these as being reducible to one type of transaction cost – resource losses incurred due to imperfect information (p. 148). As we shall see in the final section of this chapter, this leads to an implicit contradiction in neoclassical theory – if the consumers and entrepreneurs are rational and genuinely possess complete knowledge, resource misallocation due to externalities, monopoly, public goods, and unexploited economies will be automatically corrected.

At this point it is worthwhile reviewing how far we have got in our analysis. The first impression is, not very far. We have identified three basic forms of economic organisation; trading through market transactions, co-ordination by firm management, direction by state bureaucracy. We have looked briefly at externalities and potential economies and how they might be dealt with by the respective forms of economic organisation. Implicit in our discussion has been a marginalist neoclassical approach which has been unable to discriminate between the respective forms as effective alternative modes for dealing with externalities and potential economies. We are neutral between the market, the firm and the state as methods of dealing with economic problems.

However, the impression that we have not travelled very far is mistaken. In itself this is a very interesting conclusion with important implications. While conceding our argument has been naïve, it has indicated no *a priori* reason why each respective form could not cope adequately with the two major categories of economic problems discussed above. The market economy, the corporate economy and the socialist economy appear as equally virtuous systems. As in

Demsetz's (1969) analysis, we are dealing with the economics of Nirvana; each case apparently provides us with the means for effortless attainment of the ideal solution.

In fact, the apparently neutral interim conclusion we have reached is a direct result of playing the game according to neoclassical rules. We have ignored the problem of information and knowledge in our analysis up to this point. Implicit in our consideration of how respective types of economic organisation would deal with externalities and potential economies was the assumption that the decision-maker had complete knowledge of all relevant circumstances. The assumption of perfect knowledge effectively inhibits discrimination between the firm, the market, and the state as alternative economic institutions. This should not be regarded as altogether surprising since we shall see the economic (as opposed to political) basis for choice between these strategies is essentially informational. Economic choice between the types of economic organisation hinges on their information handling characteristics.

At this point some neoclassical theorists might comment that the price system not only gives the market tremendous power as an information handling system, but also in general reduces information problems to the extent that complete knowledge is a reasonable assumption.[23] As Blaug (1978) points out, 'the history of economic thought . . . is nothing but the history of our efforts to understand the workings of an economy based on market transactions' (p. 6). The price system in neoclassical theory *is* the market mechanism. State direction is automatically presumed to be more inefficient since it does not possess the attractive informational properties of the price system. The role of firm co-ordination is more ambiguous in neoclassical analysis since for many neoclassical theorists the firm is an empty box whose function is to follow the market's bidding. The price system signals, and the empty black box of the firm responds immediately in this view of the world where the firm is the entrepreneur responding to the invisible hand of the market-place. However, if we interpret the firm more realistically as the modern corporation in which management organises and co-ordinates *internally* problems of externalities and potential economies, then the same arguments held against state direction hold for firm co-ordination also in neoclassical analysis; the information handling properties of the price system are lost.[24]

In fact the information handling properties of the price system are limited and there are costs attached to its usage, as with the other two systems. Just as firm co-ordination involves management costs and state direction involves bureaucratic costs, so also market trading involves costs; transaction costs. We shall look at the nature of each of these costs in more detail in the next few chapters. For the moment, it is worth noting that analysts have already considered aspects of each of these forms, usually on a bilateral basis. For example, Williamson (1975) considers markets versus firms and the circumstances in which one or other form is liable to prevail, while Friedman (1980) reviews markets versus state direction and dogmatically evinces an unqualified preference for the former.

The problem facing the application of neoclassical theory in this context can be summarised as follows. To begin with, neoclassical theory is based on the presumption of complete knowledge on the part of decision-makers. However, the assumed absence of information problems means that we have no basis for distinguishing between the efficiency of the firm, the market and the state as alternative forms of economic organisation. For example market transactions, mergers, state regulation, joint ventures are alternative methods of exploiting externalities and economies, yet neoclassical theory is silent on the issues and criteria concerning selection of these alternative mechanisms. It is consequently neutral on the question of how economies should be organised.

We can round off our discussion of the sterility of neoclassical theory for policy purposes by considering the implications of neoclassical modelling in the next section. As usually represented, neoclassical models are based on simple limited assumptions. Unfortunately, as we shall see, when the neoclassical models are probed more deeply their elegant simplicity is seen to conceal a number of information based requirements. Explicit consideration of these issues offers a Pandora's Box that neoclassical theorists have chosen to ignore. The irony underlying their position is that standard neoclassical results only hold if a number of information imperfections are actually operational in the market-place, a consideration that runs counter to the explicit assumptions of perfect knowledge on the part of utility maximising consumers and profit maximising firms, and the supposed sufficiency of the price mechanism as an information handling mechanism. In the next section we shall consider this point by looking at a simple neoclassical model.

NEOCLASSICAL THEORY AND TRANSACTION COSTS[25]

We shall consider the example of an externality-creating monopolist. The standard assumptions for monopoly are as below.[26]

1. *Seller assumption.* A single seller exists in the market for this product.
2. *Product assumption.* The single seller produces a differentiated product for which there are no ready substitutes.
3. *Entry barrier assumption.* Substantial barriers to entry exist.

In those circumstances, the firm maximises profits at Q_0 below at a price of P_0. Demand or average revenue is D, average cost is AC, marginal cost and marginal revenue are MC and MR respectively. We further assume that our monopolist is a natural monopoly, that is there are continuing economies of scale over the range of industry demand relevant to our analysis. However, since we would also like to examine the issue of increasing costs, we assume managerial diseconomies eventually set in, and marginal and average costs increase.

The profit maximising behaviour of the monopolist follows from the general assumptions of rationality and perfect knowledge associated with the neoclassical paradigm. In addition, we add an externality in this example; the monopolist imposes a social cost on other participants in the economic process. This is represented in marginal terms by the vertical distance between SMC (social marginal cost) and MC in Figure 2.2.

The standard neoclassical interpretation of this case is that monopoly leads to a misallocation of resources; the monopolist ignores the externality since he does not directly incur the cost, while still tending to underproduce and overprice to the extent that his profit maximising price and output (where $MC = MR$ at price P_0 and output Q_0) leads to a situation in which the consumers valuation of the marginal unit (price at Q_0) is greater than the marginal cost of producing that extra unit. The optimal output from the point of view of society is at $P = SMC$ (P_1 and Q_1) where price is equal to social marginal cost.

In fact the apparently straightforward monopoly result necessitates a number of *additional* assumptions if it is to hold. These are summarised below; each of them involves some form of information problem on the part of some or all of the transactors.

4. *Demsetz type assumption* (after Demsetz, 1968); transaction costs prevent buyers from organising and negotiating with the monopolist. Therefore the monopolist imposes $MR = MC$ solution on a

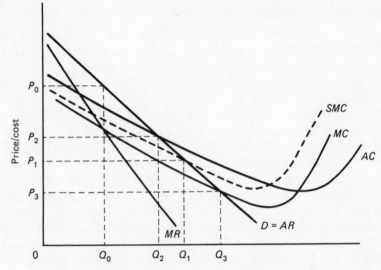

FIGURE 2.2   *Externality – creating natural monopolist*

passive, uninformed and/or disorganised set of buyers. If buyers could combine and offer a contract on a franchise basis to the seller who offers the lowest price then a competitive bidding system would tend to eliminate monopoly profit; as long as profit could be obtained from a given bid price, there is an incentive for a competitor to offer a lower price. Consequently bid price will lower until $P = AC$ at P_2, Q_2 (see Demsetz, 1968). Assuming, for simplicity, that we ignore externalities, a further contracting pattern might result in the efficient $P = MC$ solution being obtained. As long as price is greater than marginal cost, some buyers find it worthwhile to pay financial inducements for extra production up to the amount represented by the demand curve (which indicates their valuation of the marginal unit). This would be lower than market price – e.g., would be up to P_3 for the marginal unit at P_3. Such progressive price discrimination would lead to the optimal solution since it would always be in the mutual interests of buyers and sellers to strike a bargain. Whether such price discrimination takes place depends on institutional and behavioural factors ignored by neoclassical theory.

5. *Coase type assumption* (after Coase 1960); transaction costs prevent those being affected by the externality negotiating effectively with the monopolist. Therefore the externality is not internalised by the monopolist and is ignored in his profit calculations.

6. *Kaldor type assumption* (after Kaldor, 1934); diseconomies arising from bounds on managerial co-ordinating ability mean that the average cost curve will eventually increase. In the absence of such bounds, it is difficult to identify any factor which will demonstrate in the long run the requisite fixity of supply leading to increasing costs.[27]

This assumption is also transactional in nature. Kaldor's source of diseconomies would be eliminated if the absence of transaction costs permit atomistic ownership of property rights to resource usage. In such circumstances partial property rights to indivisible inputs could be allocated to other firms, or subcontracting of work could be arranged, if managerial diseconomies are likely to be encountered in single firm operation. Franchising or subcontracting would be undertaken before the managerial bottleneck is reached. The absence of transaction costs could ensure that a deal of mutual benefit to both parties could be arranged. Therefore managerial diseconomies of scale are also ultimately traceable to transaction costs, in so far as they may result from costs of market agreements impeding franchising and subcontracting options.

7. *Non-tradeable economies.* Neoclassical theory presumes a unique relationship between cost and output. Transaction costs may create the conditions for firm specific/product specific economies of scale consistent with the unique cost function identified in Figure 2.2.

The basic argument surrounding this assumption goes as follows: indivisibilities do not necessitate decreasing cost functions for a single firm, since anything the firm can do, in principle the market can also do. Suppose, for example, we have a three-stage technological process; the first stage produces an output of two intermediate products per machine, the second stage converts three intermediate products per machine and the final stage finishes five products per machine, all in a given time period. The minimum efficient scale of output is the lowest common denominator of 30 – this will fully utilise 15 first stage machines, 10 stage two machines, and 6 stage three machines.

The problem with indivisibilities is that in the absence of some information based assumption such as the one above, we have no basis for judging whether one firm or many will organise production in this industry. A single firm could exploit all economies. So could 15 stage one entrepreneurs, 10 stage two entrepreneurs, 6 stage three entrepreneurs, each with an appropriate machine tacked on to their firm, each transacting and trading in intermediate inputs.

However we could go further. As discussed earlier in this chapter, a *single* indivisibility (say a machine) may be exploited by bilateral or multilateral firm contracts (as in the Alten and Alski example). In principle the number and size of firms is indeterminate in the absence of information considerations. The possibilities are extended even further once it is recognised that different products may share resources and exploit indivisibilities (as for Alten/Alski). As Loasby (1976, p. 69) points out, even a single giant machine or power station could be used by very many operators if their property rights could be unambiguously determined. As far as the existence of economies of scale above is concerned, neoclassical theory cannot tell us whether this situation will be organised by one firm or a thousand. The organisation of the industry depends on information related trans-action costs and organisational costs.

To summarise the implications of the above assumptions required to patch up the neoclassical result discussed above; in the absence of information problems, the problem of monopoly and externality (of which monopoly is a sub-category) can be eliminated by market transactions as Demsetz, Dahlman and Calabresi have argued. The absence of information problems also removes the standard reason for diseconomies of scale and also removes the necessity for a single firm organising economies. In short, unless information problems exist in the situation above, resource misallocations due to monopoly and externality will be eliminated by market transactions, diseconomies of scale will not exist, and the number of firms is indeterminate. The neoclassical result above is crucially dependent on these information related considerations; unless they hold, the elegant structure of neoclassical theorising crumbles away. Differences in market structure and resource allocations are a *consequence* of information problems, whether these are implicit or explicit. As a final point, it is also worth noting that the barriers to entry that are generally invoked to justify the existence of monopoly tend to be questions of property rights (e.g., regulated utility, patents) or based on information imperfections (e.g., advertising,[28] technical know-how). Large-scale capital requirements, often identified as a source of barrier to entry, may in fact be decomposable in the fashion discussed in assumption 7.

In this respect the argument above suggests a revision of William-son's comment that 'a common definition of perfect competition is that transaction costs are everywhere zero' (1980, p. 7). If transaction costs are indeed zero everywhere, then the standard long run output for the firm at the base of the long run average cost curve is no longer a unique outcome. *Any* output level and associated size of firm below such an output is equally feasible since economies from indivisibilities may be exploited through costless segmentation of property rights. The standard bowl-shaped long run average cost curve is replaced by an indeterminate model characterised by a one to one correspondence of price and average cost up to the minimum point on the long run average cost curve.

We can go further and point out that since monopoly can itself be regarded as a reflection of transactional problems, then whatever the starting point in terms of market structure and resource ownership, 'the firm' is reduced to a single horizontal line representing average revenue, average cost, marginal revenue and marginal cost if uninhibited competitive bidding and transaction cost free conditions prevail.

This point is of fundamental importance and worthwhile considering further. Suppose we have a monopoly franchise in which a Demsetz-type competitive bidding system has resulted in a bid price of P_2 and an output of Q_2 in this industry. If there are no transaction costs, this output may be provided by one, few or many operators for a price of P_2 and the same average cost of P_2. In fact, since normal profits are obtainable individually and collectively whatever the market struc-ture, there is nothing to choose between alternative structures in terms of efficiency or profit incentives. From the point of view of individual firms the product may be sold for a price of P_2 and at a cost of P_2 whatever the level of firm output, as long as agreements between operators ensure that economies up to industry output Q_2 are exploited. Thus, in a transaction cost free system, size of firm is indeterminate, and all economies can be exploited from output of one unit from the point of view of individual firms.

Therefore information problems in a variety of forms are necessary to prop up the neoclassical structure. Yet they contradict the perfect knowledge assumptions that allow neoclassical theorists to identify prices as the sole information containing variable, and permit them to concentrate on the behaviour of *markets* to the exclusion of institu-tional and behavioural considerations. The internal contradictions of neoclassical theory are critical and pervasive, and should signal the need for fundamental modification or abandonment of the paradigm. However, depressingly for the prospects of paradigm shift, the history of conventional economic theory could have been written by the three wise monkeys; fifty-seven years ago Piero Sraffa (1926) demonstrated that the formal requirements of perfect competition were incompat-ible with static partial equilibrium analysis, yet his signal contribution is effectively ignored by present day theorists with a few significant exceptions such as Loasby (1976). There is little evidence from the historical development and maintenance of the neoclassical paradigm that theoretical economics will be shaken by such matters as internally inconsistent assumptions, let alone the problem of unrealistic and inappropriate assumptions. Ignoring information problems means that neoclassical theory can concentrate on the process of exchange rather than institutional and behavioural problems involved in the process of decision, and can also build optimising techniques on the presumption of solid informational foundations.

But neoclassical theorising inevitably involves assumptions based on information *imperfections* (such as assumptions 4–7 above) if it is not to collapse into the standard competitive solution with no resource misallocation and with an indeterminate number of firms in the industry. It is argued here that it is not legitimate to leave these conditions as hidden informational props. In Chapter 3 we shall begin to look directly at the informational foundations of the modern firm as well as moving away from the neoclassical position that price is the sufficient informational variable permitting consumer and firms to maximise their respective objective functions.

CONCLUSION

We identified three main stages in analysing resource allocation problems: (1) property rights identification; (2) information collection; and (3) the allocation or decision stage. Different theoretical approaches generally operate over one or two of these stages and none gives all three detailed consideration. To the extent that different stages are examined we would expect different problems to be identified, and this is indeed the case as is evidenced by neoclassical theory's concern with efficiency and Marxist preoccupation with social and historical perspectives. We have also considered briefly alternative forms of economic organisation: the firm, the market and the state. A simple analysis of how the respective firms would deal with externalities and potential economies reveals no essential differences between the three types. Each would tend to efficient resource allocation in the presence of an externality by internalising the respective effect. Each would tend to lead to full exploitation of potential economies either by internal organisation on the part of the appropriate institution or by market agreement for the pursuit of mutual self interest. The neutral conclusion which this simple analysis leads to is a direct result of the ignoring of informational questions. It was suggested that information based properties were the general economic criteria by which alternative forms should be evaluated. It is to a consideration of these properties that we now turn.

3 Entrepreneurial Salome

> A thing exists . . . if a world without it can't function normally.
> Robert Pirsig, *Zen and the Art of Motorcycle Maintenance*

In this chapter the existence of information problems relating specifically to firms are established. In doing so, the role of the firm as an information handling system will be emphasised and consideration given to the full implications of the perfect knowledge assumption in this context. The likely nature of information problems will be considered in more detail in later chapters; here we are content to identify their various origins. In doing so, Pirsig's comment above will help signpost the significance of empirical phenomena obscured by neoclassical theory.

Neoclassical theory grants a simple, modest role to the firm. The consumer and the producer are endowed with perfect knowledge over all relevant events; the consumer is in possession of complete information concerning the price and other relevant characteristics of all goods and services he could conceivably consume, while the producer (incarnated as the entrepreneur) possesses complete information concerning the prices, costs and other relevant characteristics of all goods and services that he could conceivably operate. Each consumer and producer being in possession of all relevant information, as well as being of sound mind, resource allocation proceeds by the maximisation of utility by each consumer and of profit by each producer. The firm consists of a black box within which the entrepreneur manipulates capital and labour in the pursuit of maximum profit according to the marginalist neoclassical rules.

There has been considerable controversy in the past over whether or not these assumptions are reasonable. Much wasted effort was devoted to the task of attacking the profit maximisation principle on theoretical grounds, given the question is ultimately an empirical one. Frederick Scherer (1980, p. 38) has summarised the present day neoclassical defence as basically Darwinian in nature:

When forced into the trenches on the question of whether firms maximise profits, economists resort to the ultimate weapon in their arsenal: a variant of Darwin's natural selection theory. Over the long pull, there is one simple criterion for the survival of a business enterprise. Profits must be non-negative. No matter how strongly managers prefer to pursue other objectives, and no matter how difficult it is to find profit-maximising strategies in a world of uncertainty and high information costs, failure to satisfy this criterion means ultimately that a firm will disappear from the economic scene. Profit maximisation is therefore promoted in two ways. First, firms departing too far from the optimum, either deliberately or by mistake, will disappear. Only those that do conform, knowingly or unknowingly, will survive. If the process of economic selection is allowed to continue long enough, the only survivors will be firms that did a tolerably good job of profit maximisation. The economic environment adopts the profit maximisers and discards the rest. Second, knowledge that only the fit will survive provides a potent incentive for all firms to adapt their behaviour in profit-maximising directions, learning whatever skills they need and emulating organisations that succeed in the survival game.

Unfortunately, neither of these two methods of promoting profit maximisation fairly reflect Darwin's natural selection theory. Firstly, departure from optimal behaviour does not necessarily lead to failure since neoclassical optimality may be unattainable in principle or not pursued in practice.[1] As Alchian (1950) pointed out 'Even in a world of stupid men there would still be profits' (p. 213) and for the selection mechanism to promote optimality requires the existence of at least one profit maximiser to prise out the less efficient.[2] Scherer's non-negative profits is not the same requirement as profit maximisation, and indeed he recognises this point (p. 38).

Secondly, neoclassical theory tends to draw selectively on the tenets of Darwin's theory emphasising repetition and similarity at the expense of variation and diversity. As Scherer remarks above, emulation tends to be a basic survival mechanism, and indeed Alchian saw imitation in economic behaviour as being the corporate parallel to heredity in biological behaviour. This is not surprising since Alchian viewed his work as a synthesis of Darwinian and Marshallian theory, and the emergence of competitive homogenous firms through an imitative mechanism produces an outcome consistent with Marshallian neoclassical theory.

However Darwin also emphasised the role of heterogeneity and diversification as a basic survival mechanism and strongly argued that divergence rather than convergence was fundamental to the natural selection process (1929 edition, pp. 82–100). We shall consider further how diversification may be incorporated as a survival mechanism in evolutionary economic theory in Chapter 6 but for the moment it is sufficient to note that the specialisation and homogeneity of Marshallian theory is not a true reflection of Darwin's paradigm; interestingly for economics, diversification was viewed by Darwin as a basically competitive strategy; 'the more diversified the descendants from any one species become in structure, constitution, and habits, by so much will they be better enabled to seize on many widely diversified places in the polity of nature, and so be enabled to seize on many widely diversified places in the polity of nature, and so be enabled to increase in numbers' (1929 edition, p. 83).[3]

Thus, neoclassical theorists, starting from a position of homogenous profit maximising firms resulting from competitive pressure have tried to invoke natural selection to justify this description of the economic world. However, survival of the fittest does not automatically imply maximisation or imitation, and consequently such defences are not strong ones. Neoclassical theory must be regarded as a thing apart from the theory of evolution and judged on its own merits.

To return, then, to the essence of the firm in neoclassical theory, the firm appears as an element in the market game played according to neoclassical rules, but a very simple element whose substance is embodied in the omniscient entrepreneur and his operational props, capital and labour. Bearing this view of the firm in mind, we will conduct a simple experiment in this chapter using an imaginary firm; however, the firm we conjure up will have the appearance and trappings of a 'real-world' firm, that is to say it will have managers, functions, an organisational structure, and so on. Our experiment will consist of identifying the consequences of assuming the absence of informational problems.

INFORMATION AND THE FIRM

We will start our experiment by considering below a functionally organised firm of moderate size operating four types of functions: marketing, R & D, finance and production.[4] The firm is hierarchically organised with a number of levels of managers up to general office. We also recognise that objectives other than profit may be pursued by corporate decision-makers; this is consistent with Baumol, Marris and

Williamson[5] who each argued that the evolution of the modern corporation led to the separation of ownership and control. The diffusion of ownership amongst numerous, poorly informed shareholders in combination with the increasing professionalism of managers could encourage pursuit of managerial objectives at the expense of profit.[6] The passing of the reins of control from owners to managers provides the latter with discretion over the allocation of resources, though this is usually hypothesised as being within constraints such as minimum profit required to preclude owner intervention. The form that managerial objectives take depends on circumstances; sales, growth, salary, staff numbers have all been identified as likely sources of managerial utility by one or more of the above analysts.[7] The position held by managers may also be significant; we might expect R & D managers to advocate technological change, finance managers to advocate financial considerations, sales managers and production managers to possibly advocate increasing sales levels.[8] Bargaining power, influence or status will dictate how the direction of the firm is influenced by these managerial objectives. A particularly strong manager or group of managers may be instrumental in influencing the corporate strategy according to his or her objectives.

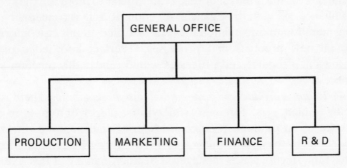

FIGURE 3.1   *A 'real-world' firm*

Therefore our firm is function-based, hierarchical and effectively directed by managers, not owners. Now let us assume there are no information problems of any kind and the actors in the economic process are endowed with the gift of perfect knowledge. How must the above picture be altered?

We will examine this question by identifying seven steps involved in modifying the 'real-world' firm in Figure 3.1 that follow from the assumption of no information problems. These are:

(1) *Remove marketing.* The marketing function is based on the existence of information imperfections on the part of the consumer.[9] If the consumer is poorly informed then sales promotions, whether of the persuasive type or the informative type, may succeed in changing his consumption pattern. If he has complete knowledge of the prices and characteristics of all relevant goods and services then persuasive ('Zazo is better') or informative ('Zazo is $1/kilo') advertising should not change his existing preferences.[10] In assuming the absence of information imperfections we also eliminate the justification for the existence of the marketing function in the first place. Therefore we remove marketing from Figure 3.1.

(2) *Remove finance.* The finance function is based on the provision of financial *information* to general office. Auditing and metering present performance as well as preparation of forecasts as to likely future performance is carried out at this level. Since information problems are absent in neoclassical theory, finance is a redundant function.

(3) *Remove R & D.* Marketing is concerned with sales information, finance with financial information and R & D with technological information. All three functions are information based, and the arguments for the removal of R & D are similar to those for marketing and finance. As with the financial function, R & D is concerned with the generation of information for general office, in this case information on new products and processes.[11] Perfect knowledge of all conceivable products and processes would render this function also unnecessary.[12]

(4) *Remove production, save capital and direct labour.* There is no need for managers, foremen, supervisors, clerks or typists in the absence of information problems. Metering, policing and directing production by these individuals are all activities derived from informational imperfections as is managerial decision-making at this level. If the general office is in possession of perfect knowledge, the need for these intermediaries disappears.

However, we leave capital and labour directly involved in the production process. Unlike the other information-based resources, capital and direct labour are concerned with the generation of physical product. The reason for their employment is therefore not directly affected by our perfect knowledge assumption.

(5) *Remove heterogeneity of labour.* The main distinguishing feature between types and grades of labour is *informational*.[13] Doctors, dentists, airline pilots, welders, machinists and labourers are dis-

tinguished by the level and type of skill they possess in their particular trade or profession. Remove informational barriers and the main distinguishing feature or type of labour disappears. Some motivational differences and necessary physical characteristics (e.g. good sight in pilots, physical strength in labourers) may remain to screen and separate individual employees, but these are minor qualifications. Thus, these are grounds for arguing that labour can reasonably be treated as homogenous if perfect knowledge exists.

(6) *Abolish internal organisation.* Hierarchy or internal organisation results directly from the bounded rationality considerations referred to in Chapter 2. The limited cognitive ability of individuals to assimilate and process information leads to the necessity to delegate and create a hierarchical structure of individuals having limited prescribed tasks within the overall structure. However if information problems do not exist, the necessity for hierarchy also disappears. Consequently our firm does not possess internal organisation.

(7) *Remove general office, re-establish entrepreneur.* General office, to the extent that is composed of subordinate managers, advisers, typists, clerks etc. is redundant. However, if we abandon general office entirely it seems we are in danger of leaving the firm goal-less and undirected. In fact, general office is a substitute for a role which information problems in the large modern corporation make literally unmanageable – the entrepreneur. General office attempts to perform the function of the entrepreneur in bringing together resources to generate goods and services, but being composed of human beings, it is of necessity an inferior mechanism compared to the omniscient entrepreneur. Now that the veil of information problems has been lifted, the entrepreneur can re-emerge in his original role in place of general office.

(8) *Eliminate non-profit maximising behaviour.* Non-profit maximising or managerial theories of the firm require weak and poorly informed ownership so that managerial discretion can operate effectively. However, if we have perfect knowledge, this condition no longer exists. Consequently, since profit is equivalent to the income of the owners and rational owners would seek to maximise income, deviation from profit maximising behaviour would not be tolerated.

However, since we have already eliminated all managers by steps (1), (2), (3), (4) and (7), and rejoined ownership and control, we have no managers left to seek managerial objectives. Thus non-profit maximising behaviour is dealt a double death.

What are we left with at the end of this experiment? An unstructured collection of profit-maximising entrepreneur, capital and labour, with heterogeneity being largely the property of capital, not labour. Our picture of the firm now looks something like Figure 3.2.

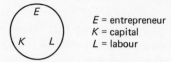

E = entrepreneur
K = capital
L = labour

FIGURE 3.2   *The firm in perfect knowledge conditions*

What is particularly interesting about this experiment is that by focusing on one aspect of corporate resource allocation – information problems – we have converted our 'real-world' firm into a passable imitation of a standard neoclassical firm having a profit-maximising omniscient entrepreneur controlling capital and homogenous labour (granted we have still some heterogeneity of capital remaining). By dropping the veils of information one by one we have uncovered our entrepreneur, a corporate Salome left with only his twin stage props of capital and labour once the eight veils are removed.

Now, this experiment would be a useful demonstration of the role of information even if this was as far as we intended to take it. We have shown the pervasiveness of information problems in creating the structure, content and behaviour of the modern firm; the various functions, managerial goals and internal organisation can all be reduced to information imperfections. It is a useful trick to demonstrate the influence of information problems on the modern firm.[14]

However we can take this analysis a stage further. What we have done is travel the reverse route from that which is usual in neoclassical analysis. Neoclassical analysis starts with the entrepreneur as in Figure 3.2, and the utility maximising consumer, and if it is intended to study empirical problems, then the analysis is extended from this base. We have travelled from the 'real-world' to the theoretical roots in the course of our experiment. What are the implications if we now retrace our steps; that is what can we say about the application of neoclassical analysis to the empirical problems in Figure 3.1?

We come up against real problems which our earlier experiment helps to illuminate. If we are to first apply our neoclassical analysis to the production function, then perhaps it could be applied without too many problems becoming apparent. However, once we move to other areas of application, contradictions and inconsistencies rapidly surface. We shall concentrate on only two for illustrative purposes, neo-classical analysis as applied to the marketing and R & D functions. We do so because of the large number of neoclassical studies in those areas.

EMPIRICAL APPLICATIONS OF NEOCLASSICAL THEORY

Let us consider first of all application of neoclassical analysis to one particular area, marketing. There has been much analysis at industry level of the relation between advertising intensity and measures of market structure characteristics such as concentration ratio and entry barriers.[15]

In principle there is a movement from theory to empirical analysis in these studies; for example, oligopoly is associated with high concentration ratios and high entry barriers, while (say) monopolistic competition is associated with low concentration ratios and low entry barriers. Therefore if advertising intensity is associated with high or low concentration, or high or low entry barriers, it seems a reasonable next step backwards towards the theoretical end to conclude that particular forms of market structure (monopoly, oligopoly, monopolistic competition, etc.) favour advertising intensity compared with others.

Not so. It is not legitimate to make such a step since neoclassical market structures based on perfect knowledge cannot deal with issues of marketing; this latter concept is dependent on knowledge imperfections, as was argued in the previous section. The assumptions which create such neoclassical market structures also serve to eliminate the need for advertising. In order to make a connection between neoclassical market structures and advertising/marketing phenomena the analyst must (1) assume perfect knowledge to identify the respective market structures in the first place, (2) assume knowledge imperfections to recognise the potential existence of the marketing function in the second place. Such perverse treatment of the knowledge conditions requires selective suspension of disbelief on the part of the analyst, and it is essential to have no sense of the absurd.

A similar treatment is accorded to analysis of technological change in the literature.[16] First of all the producer is typically analysed as a monopolist/oligopolist/competitive (etc.) firm with concomitant assumptions regarding knowledge conditions, and then the phenomenon of technological change is introduced with its implications for information generation. The market structures are the market structures of Nirvana, the phenomenon is that of the real world. We have theory and empirical reality operating on their respective, irreconcilable, bases.

The difficulties that neoclassical theorists involve themselves in this area are illustrated by the analysis of Nordhaus (1969). Nordhaus devotes his book to studying the optimality conditions for allocating resources to R & D, and comments that some of the work may also be interpretable as models for advertising. Yet he notes only in passing (pp. 55–6) that uncertainty may be a serious objection to the certainty assumption underlying his optimality analysis. He suggests that a complete discussion and resolution of the problem is outwith the scope of the book.[17]

Since information generating activities like R & D and advertising blatantly contradict the certainty assumption of optimising procedures (how can additional information be generated if information is complete already?), it is difficult to see how constrained maximisation techniques can be defended in this context. Yet the economic literature is swamped by such studies; Nordhaus is not the only one, and in a sense it is unfair to single him out. However it would be wasteful to recount all such studies.[18] It is sufficient to note that the end result of neoclassical modelling has been to detract from the sum total of economic knowledge in this field.

What are we to conclude from all this? We have seen how the picture of the 'real-world' firm in Figure 3.1 is eroded when we assume perfect knowledge until we arrive back at an approximation of the neoclassical view of the firm. Marketing, finance, R & D, management, heterogeneity of labour and internal organisation do not exist under a perfect knowledge regime. This experiment shows how this simple assumption reduces our firm to the familiar skeletal black box of neoclassical theory. However, rather than restrict their analysis to the limited territory for which it is appropriate, neoclassical theorists have attempted to introduce it to the various aspects of the 'real-world' firm, areas for which by definition it is unsuited.

Theory is by nature unrealistic; it abstracts from the empirical world and it is hoped that the abstraction captures the essence of a wide variety of behaviour – it is this which gives good theory its generality. What is wrong with neoclassical theory as applied in the context discussed here is not its lack of realism, which we encounter in theory building as a matter of course; the problem is that, rather than capture the essence of a phenomena, neoclassical theory blatantly *contradicts* its basic nature in the cases we have looked at here. Using a theory based on perfect knowledge to examine phenomena whose whole justification is based on the existence of imperfections of knowledge is like using the Ten Commandments to explain the behaviour of Piccadilly Circus or Hollywood and Vine after dusk; neoclassical theory, like Moses' tablets, is based on a utopian ideal with strong normative overtones. Expecting it to serve simultaneously as an explanatory approach is at best optimistic.

What is to be said regarding the various studies that have been conducted to examine possible links between concentration ratios, entry barriers and marketing and/or technological change? Simply that these retain validity as empirical studies, but that it is not legitimate to attempt to tie these into neoclassical theory. A positive relationship between entry barriers and advertising intensity should be simply left as an informative piece of number-crunching, or, more desirably, an alternative theoretical pigeon-hole to neoclassical theory should be found for it.

The standard ploy of neoclassical theorists is to start with the pure, unsullied black box picture of the firm and then *selectively* modify the assumption of perfect knowledge in looking at resource allocation problems. What is suggested here is that we should start at the other end and analyse the structure and behaviour of the firm regarded as a whole, rather than in the biased piecemeal fashion of most neoclassical analysis. When we do this, the neoclassical picture of the firm is seen as being potentially applicable to only narrow corners of the modern corporation; perhaps some of the capital and labour resources of the production function may be amenable to neoclassical analysis,[19] and possibly some ghostly vestiges of the neoclassical entrepreneur may be traced skulking in the corridors of general office.

Were neoclassical theorists to content themselves with this modest remit, there would be little quarrel with their approach in this chapter. The problem is that they do not. Neoclassical analysis still represents the dominant approach to resource allocation in the firm despite its entirely unsatisfactory theoretical base, as a cursory glance at the literature confirms. What is required is development of theoretical frameworks designed to cope with the true function of the firm as an information handling system.

In the next chapter we will review the existence of information problems in areas other than the firm, particularly state direction, before going on to consider the *nature* of information problems and appropriate theoretical methods for coping with these problems.

CONCLUSIONS

In this chapter we have analysed the importance of information in dictating the structure and resource content of the modern corporation. We conducted a simple exercise to demonstrate the pervasive informational base of most types of corporate functions and resource. Neoclassical theory, being built on the assumption of perfect knowledge is consequentially an inappropriate framework for all but an extremely limited range of corporate functions.

We have not yet identified either the types of information problems that resource allocation may involve, or possible theoretical approaches that may be suitable for dealing with such problems.

4 More Salome

Shall I tell you what knowledge is? It is to know both what one
knows and what one does not know.

Confucius

Confucius knew more than neoclassical theory. Neoclassical theory
not only knows solely 'what one knows', but is also based on the
premise that such knowledge is complete. To know what one does not
know means we must 'expect the unexpected' as Boulding (1968)
advocated, and we have already demonstrated the fatal consequences
of accepting the neoclassical assumption of perfect knowledge in
Chapter 3. In that chapter the role of information problems in
corporate resource allocation was examined. In this chapter we extend
the analysis to look at further areas in which information problems
may be encountered, particularly in the area of state direction. We
shall also look at types of activity which are likely to be based around
information problems and contrast them with activities that do not
involve information problems.

We shall continue to use the simple exercise used in Chapter 3 of
assuming no information problems exist – and seeing what happens. It
will be shown that this experiment will provide a decisive technique for
separating activities into two types, information based and physically
based, and that this dividing line cuts cleanly through industries,
departments, occupations, and firms in a manner not necessarily
intuitively obvious.

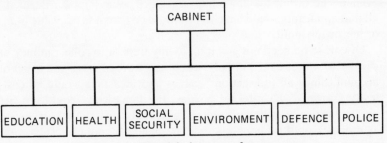

FIGURE 4.1 *Simplified system of government*

43

To continue the experiment, let us assume first of all that we have state direction run by a cabinet office with six ministries; Education, Health, Social Security, Environment, Defence and Police. This simplified government system is illustrated in Figure 4.1 above.

To return to the brave neoclassical assumption of the previous chapter, if we have no information problems, how must we alter the above picture?

Firstly, education disappears entirely. Having returned to Nirvana, information problems have been eliminated and education is redundant. Teachers, lecturers, professors are no longer required. Imperfect knowledge is a prerequisite for education.

Secondly, the Health minister finds a great deal of his responsibilities eroding. Administrators, matrons, clerks, typists also disappear for similar reasons to the disappearance of the counterparts in the firm – they require the prior existence of information problems to justify their own. What about doctors, dentists and nurses – should they be retained? Only in circumstances where medicine could not be self-administered. Since perfect knowledge exists each individual possesses complete medical and dental skills and can assess his treatment for himself. If doctors, dentists, nurses remain, they exist as roles, not as distinctive qualifications, and would serve only those who are unable or unwilling to physically treat themselves. Further, they may not necessarily be provided by the state, but could trade these services in the market-place or through incorporation within firms.

Thirdly, the Ministry (though not the function) of Social Security is effectively abolished. The ministry would be entirely composed of administrative type personnel who would no longer be required. Nor would checking or monitoring of applicants be necessary since, of course, this implies imperfect knowledge – the credentials, veracity and general credibility of all applications would be automatically available according to our assumption. Once policy has been decided,[1] all that applicants would have to do would be to assess the value of his or her own benefit.

Of course he need not go along to any bureau to collect money or checks. Money is a medium of exchange, a store of value and a unit of account. Since all transactions, values and measures would be costlessly known to all relevant parties, the beneficiary could not act opportunistically or default successfully, and artificial measures such as money would be unnecessary. The need for money results from human imperfections of knowledge, and the absence of imperfections of knowledge indicates the absence of the need for money. Individuals could not spend more than their worth.[2]

Fourthly, the ministry concerned with the environment would also disappear. While such works as the building of bridges, roads and lighthouses would still be necessary, the Ministry of the Environment would not be required as intermediaries between cabinet office level and the direct provision of these goods and services. What about payment for these services? This could be done through direct taxation or toll charges, depending on policy. Either way, there would be no likelihood of default since opportunism of this kind would be pre-empted by the perfect knowledge assumption. For example, users of roads could deposit the appropriate payment at a point on the road, and the convenient assumption of omniscience would prevent deceit, cheating or theft with respect to toll payments. In addition it is worth noting that many of these services could be provided by the private sector (market or firm) as an alternative.

Fifthly, the Ministry of Defence role would be retained, though of course the bureaucrats associated with it would be redundant. Conditions of perfect knowledge makes no difference to the need to maintain at least a threshold level of ability to withstand external aggressors, though it may make a difference to the level considered appropriate. In principle there is no reason why this role also could not be performed by the market or a firm. While conceding that it is of greater potential importance than, say, the building of road or bridges, in principle it is no different. The reason why such activities as roads, bridges and national defence are frequently cited as classic examples of legitimate state provision even by neoclassical theorists, is that the information problems and costs of metering usage, excluding potential defaulters and extracting payment may be prohibitive. Absent information problems, absent need for state provision. Defence could be provided by Universal Defence Inc., with perfect knowledge reassuring citizens that U.D. Inc. will indeed provide the guaranteed safeguard from external threat.

Sixthly, police levels would be purged down to a skeleton task force. Existing policing levels are a consequence of uncertainty as to where and when crime will occur. The absence of information problems and immediate identification of actual or intended crime and criminals means that all that is required is a token mobile police team to deter wrong-doers. Presumably if too large a group of criminals for the police team to handle could band together, then the task could be handed on to national defence.

Lastly, the job of cabinet office could be more effectively handled by a single Solomon (Prime Minister or President) than by a coalition of officials. The chosen Solomon could be selected for objectivity, fairness, reliability, ability, etc. – perfect knowledge on the part of the citizens would allow these assets to be assessed. The choice of Solomon could be entrusted to a third party recognised for objectivity, or could be done by voting. Whichever method is chosen, Solomon could then proceed to make all policy and operational decisions for the tasks remaining within the state sector.[3] Further, the omniscience of Solomon obviates the need for hierarchy, and so the bureaucratic structure of Figure 4.1 is abandoned.

What does our exercise lead to in this example? It is a slightly more complicated case than the example of the firm in the previous chapter. We have eliminated education, the bulk of the police force, bureaucrats, the hierarchy and the cabinet office. We are left with some health and social security services, the works of environment and defence ministries, a token police force and a Solomon. However, we have no basis for advocating that these residual functions should be more reasonably handled by market transaction, firm co-ordination or state direction. In this respect we have again turned full circle to the argument of Chapter 2 in which the implicit assumption of the absence of information problems led to the neutral conclusion of that chapter regarding the respective merits of firm, market and state organisation. The neoclassical assumption of perfect knowledge transforms the picture of state direction as it did for firm co-ordination, though in a rather different manner in this case.

However, up to this point we have looked at the implications of the absence of information problems in a rather abstract fashion related to broad tasks performed by firm, state and market. We can perhaps obtain a better taste of what effect the assumed absence of information problems would have if we consider specific activities in this light. The result will be some impression of a neoclassical view of the world.

Firstly, the media would be transformed. Huge gaps would have to be filled in television schedules because of the removal of news and current affairs programmes. Comedians would be pulled out of variety programmes because everyone would have heard their jokes, destroying the basic element of humour; surprise.[4] Magicians would lose their mystery and employment.

By way of contrast, singers, dancers and acrobats would be unaffected since the entertainment they provide is channelled through the medium of physical perception as opposed to provision of information. However, film, theatre and drama in general would play to empty houses; not only all the plots would be known, but all interpretations and versions of Hamlet would already have been anticipated prior to staging or screening.[5]

There would be no sport. Knowledge of who would win would forestall the incentive for games, gambling, sport and competition. There would be no fun in playing solitaire, crosswords or patience since the player would always get out.

There would be no newspapers, articles or books. I would not have to sit at this desk since there would no longer be any purpose in doing so. Instead I could be sampling the product of the local baker, butcher or brewer whose trades are not directly affected by the purging effect of omniscience.

In fact a world of perfect knowledge would be a strange world. It contains train drivers[6] but not ticket collectors, singers but not comedians; plumbers but not meter readers. It has no managers, bureaucrats, scientists, travel agents, AT & T, test pilots, research engineers, IBM, advertising executives, weathermen, or explorers. Universities, schools, banks, law firms and insurance companies would vanish. On the plus side, lies, deceit and opportunism would be eliminated. Also, however, much of the fun of living would disappear since uncertainty and incomplete knowledge are necessary for a great deal that is worthwhile concerning living – curiosity, humour, competition and mystery all derive from imperfections of knowledge. Omniscience must be a rather boring condition.

This exercise serves to pinpoint and emphasise central inherent contradictions in the neoclassical view of the world. The neoclassical view is fashioned for, and only applicable to, a state of Nirvana in which the possibility of knowledge imperfections is excluded.

In case this attribution of such supernormal claims to neoclassical theorists appears unfair or extreme, the reader is invited to consider the work of Milton Friedman whose latest statement may be found in Friedman and Friedman (1980). The work is a eulogy to the virtually unqualified advantages provided by market transactions and the price system compared to the virtually unqualified evils and inefficiencies associated with state direction. Market exchange based on the price system is held up as a paragon amongst information handling systems, with no serious criticism of its efficiency mode – except when state intervention distorts it. The neoclassical assumption of perfect knowledge rests comfortably in the niche composed of market prices provided by the Friedmans in this work. Interestingly, however, occasional reference is made to the obvious imperfections of knowledge in the world, involving uncertainty, entrepreneurial risk-taking and so on.[7]

This inconsistency lies at the core of most neoclassical analysis. When neoclassical theorists construct their formal analyses, determinate solutions based on the assumption of perfect knowledge are an integral part of the demonstration of the efficiency of the competitive process (subject to the usual qualifications concerning the intrusion of monopolistic influences).[8] The policy conclusions reached by analysts such as Friedman and Samuelson are distilled from formal analysis based on the assumption of perfect knowledge (see, for example, the basic analytical frameworks contained in Friedman (1962) and Samuelson (1961)). Thus their view of the world is constructed from the rigid formal framework of neoclassical theory.[9]

This has two important results. Firstly, when 'real-world' analysis and policy formulation is required, the obvious and simplest course for neoclassical theorists to adopt is to move their formal analysis and policy conclusions wholesale into the 'real-world' arena. If, as we have argued earlier, their abstract principles embodied basic rules and patterns operating generally in the real world, then there is grounds for optimism that we have the basis for good theory and sound policy. The problem is, as we have seen in this and the previous chapter, rather than capture the essence of 'real-world' problems, neoclassical theory patently *contradicts* the fundamental informational basis for the existence of most types of such phenomena. The result is, as in Friedman and Friedman, general policy recommendations cultivated from a narrow and inappropriate framework, accompanied by a sprinkling of comments signalling token recognition of real-world informational problems. However the qualification and notes regarding informational deficiencies are not allowed to significantly detract from or modify the pristine purity of policy solutions based on the implicit neoclassical ideal. Concentrating solely on markets and prices is theoretically highly convenient. As Galbraith (1972) points out, 'Much of the appeal of the market, to economists at least, has been from the way it seems to simplify life. Better orderly error than complex truth' (p. 77).

Secondly, neoclassical analysis creates peculiar problems when the respective merits of intervention versus free markets are discussed. Suppose we return to the example of the smoky chimney discussed in Chapter 2; some neoclassical theorists would recommend state intervention or regulation to correct the externality, while others would indicate that a market solution based on voluntary exchange would lead to an efficient solution. If property rights are unambiguously allocated, Samuelson is generally regarded as leaning towards state intervention and direction to deal with externalities, while Friedman would undoubtedly favour a market exchange solution. How would a debate between such protagonists be resolved?

The short answer is that it could not be, as long as they played the debate according to neoclassical rules. As we have seen in Chapter 2, the assumption of perfect knowledge does not allow us to discriminate between any of the three basic forms of economic organisation. A debate between neoclassical theorists *qua* neoclassical theorists as to the appropriate form of economic organisation would be an empty debate.

The conclusion, which we have already anticipated in Chapter 2, strains the credibility of neoclassical theory to the limit. We have seen that neoclassical theory's assumptions render it inapplicable to problems of bureaucracy, management, R & D, marketing, finance, internal organisation, education, sport, gambling, insurance and policing to name a selection of no-go areas. Further, it appears that it cannot help us discriminate between the firm, the market and the state as desirable methods of economic organisation. The vision of the neoclassical ideal appears to retreat further into the mists of Nirvana.

A neoclassical theorist might complain that we have taken the theoretical assumptions to extremes. Not so – we have merely taken them to their logical conclusion and helped to delineate the legitimate territorial boundaries of the theory in the process. There is, however, a further issue of relevance that must be considered here; is the assumption of perfect knowledge presumed *ex ante* the existence of market prices in neoclassical theory, or *ex post*. In other words, does perfect knowledge exist independently of the existence of market prices, or are market prices necessary for the assumption to carry conviction? This is an issue that is not usually explicit in neoclassical theory; those who would argue in favour of state intervention would tend to favour the *ex ante* assumption since this allows the introduction of *deus ex machina* – the state or a Solomon – to correct externalities and other efficiency problems. On the other hand free marketeers such as Friedman strongly emphasise the role of prices in their analysis of the market as an efficient information handling system (see, for example, Friedman and Friedman, 1980, pp. 14–18). In themselves, prices are not sufficient to provide complete knowledge of goods and services since they do not provide information such as content, function, quality or other general characteristics of goods and services. However we must consider what implications, if any, the respective assumptions have for our analysis.

The *ex ante* assumption makes no difference to our analysis – it is effectively the one which has been employed in testing out the implications of the neoclassical model up to this point. The *ex post* assumption requires more careful consideration. What this effectively says is that the existence of a price system allows us to treat the economic system as a whole as one in which the assumption of perfect knowledge is a reasonable approximation. There are two main comments to be made here. Firstly, we have pointed out that prices only signify a limited class of information; they do not contain information on the substance of the good or service offered, only on what the consumer would have to sacrifice to obtain it. Consequently there remains a large variety of information classes that the consumer has to fill in for each good and service in addition to price. Friedman and Friedman (1980) argue that the price system transmits only the *important* information (p. 15), but this is patently not the case. To use the Friedmans' example of a pencil, price may tell us something of the market value of a pencil, but it tells us nothing at all about its colour, quality, hardness or softness of the lead, length, durability, etc. – in fact, price alone tells us very little in terms of the important information involved in buying a pencil. The consumer still has a great deal of information gathering to do if the condition of perfect knowledge is to be even approximated. Secondly, how would the 'invisible hand' of the market operate to set a price on those activities (such as R & D, marketing, drama) which are by definition based on information provision? Setting a value on a pencil is easy meat by comparison – all we have to do is try out various types of pencil and place a value on each type after we have used it. Future purchases can then be based on past experience and we can select the most suitable type of pencil – or, to put it another way, the type that contributes toward maximising our utility. However, how can we perform such a task in the case of R & D, marketing, drama, etc.? An essential ingredient of each of these activities is the *novelty* of individual output in each case. There are no prizes for re-inventing the wheel, resurrecting old advertising campaigns, or rewriting Hamlet. The consumer can place a concrete value on a pencil (possibly even under conditions approximating perfect knowledge) because of the opportunity for repetitious experimentation in this case. Indeed repetition (in the form of consistency of product or guaranteed standards) is not only a method of price determination but is itself a valuable source of information and reassurance to the consumer. By way of contrast, repetition in information generating services such as those mentioned above would guarantee the rapid expulsion, redundancy or bankruptcy of any producer unfortunate enough to indulge in such ill-advised practice.

Of course, prices can be placed on even these services. R & D contracts, marketing campaigns and film scripts can all be bought in advance of the actual provision of the restrictive good or service. However, such transactions cannot take place in conditions approximating perfect knowledge as to the value of the good or service – such knowledge is generally available only *after* provision of the good or service, or *ex post*. This is why the consumer can build up a fairly accurate calculus of values in the case of consumption of pencils – and why it is only at best crudely possible in the case of information generating services; the forging of the contract must be carried out *ex ante* provision of good or services, and it is only when the good or service has been provided that the consumer is in a position to make an accurate assessment of its true value, *ex post*. Since individual output is novel, such *ex post* enlightenment is of limited value when entering into future contracts, and consequently pricing is an activity of high uncertainty.

Reducing microeconomics to price theory is rather like developing a stethoscope theory of medicine. In some restricted cases of economic and medical problems, prices and stethoscope soundings respectively may provide sufficient information. In other cases, neither source of information may be practical or required. Prices and chest tubes are useful and pervasive information tools for decision-makers in economics and medicine, but by their nature they are limited and narrow sources. Other sources must generally be sought.

Nevertheless it is interesting to conjecture what a stethoscope theory of medicine would look like. It could provide an elegant basis for categorisation – all ailments, major and minor, could be compared and categorised in terms of chest soundings. However, it is improbable that fine discrimination between types of illnesses could be achieved; groupings by respiratory characteristics are more likely. Similarly, price theory in economics recognises only a few distinct types – monopoly, oligopoly, normal and inferior goods, etc. It can explain *similarity* (competitive models) or *uniqueness* (monopoly), but it is singularly inept in accounting for *difference* in economic behaviour. The economic elements are typically homogenous or individualistic.

Yet biological, social and economic evolution is characterised by heterogeneity and diversity; the cloned firms of perfect competition and the environmentally insulated monopolist are instead characteristic of economic theory. As we saw in Chapter 3, economists have tended to draw selectively on the tenets of Darwinism to support this picture of the economic world.

Mercifully for medical science and patient health, doctors do not usually rely on stethoscopes as their sole source of information.

What is the implication of all this for the role of prices? Simply that, first of all, prices provide only limited information, and secondly that where they exist they may be built on shaky foundations of uncertain values and partial ignorance. Thus, the price system is not a guaranteed route to Nirvana; it provides limited information and may itself be a cloak for informational deficiencies in the areas to which it is applied. This is important in evaluating the claims made for market exchange by those like the Friedmans who imply that the price system automatically and effectively eliminates information problems. The price system cannot create a regime approximating to perfect knowledge; the conditions for Nirvana must already exist before its introduction. Thus, any claim of the *ex post* type, that prices and markets effectively lead to the neoclassical ideal, ignores both the information that prices omit, and the arbitrary and *ad hoc* manner in which prices may be fashioned in some instances. They cannot correct a world of intrinsically imperfect knowledge into one of perfect knowledge – or to put it more economically, they cannot make silk purses out of sows' ears. Conditions for perfect knowledge must exist independently of the price system and cannot be created by it. In this respect there is no essential difference between *ex ante* and *ex post* assumptions concerning the relationship between perfect knowledge and the price system. However, despite the obvious limitations and inconsistencies of neoclassical theory discussed here and in previous chapters, its basic precepts represent a fundamental cornerstone of the current Presidential Council of Economic Advisers' report; 'one critical advantage of a market economy is that it is "informationally efficient." That is, a market will function well even if each individual knows only his own preferences and opportunities' (Council of Economic Advisers, 1982, p. 41).

One might equally attribute 'informational efficiency' to stethoscopes. As long as other sources of information were excluded from the diagnostic calculus, *laissez-faire* medics could attribute disease and death to the natural order of things; in such perspectives there would be no grounds on which interventionist medicine could be based.

There are a couple of final issues relevant to the Friedmans' interpretation of the neoclassical system that merit comment. Firstly, it is interesting to compare the transformation wrought in the government system in Figure 4.1 after assuming perfect knowledge, with the Friedmans' view of what should be eliminated from state control. Bearing in mind how close our experiment in Chapter 3 took us to the neoclassical view of the firms composed of entrepreneur, capital and labour, it might be expected that our assumption of perfect knowledge in the case of state direction would be paralleled by a similar restructuring by the Friedmans.

In fact, the world the Friedmans describe is almost disappointingly 'realistic'. Bureaucrats and the bureaucracy or state internal organisation certainly get short shrift in the Friedmans' interpretation as in our experiment, and much activity is shifted into the private sector. However, while the hierarchical organisational bureaucracy of the state is a major target of their work, the actual content of Friedmans' world is extremely familiar – education, science, advertising, for example, all have a place. Basically what the Friedmans do is to castigate bureaucracy and recommend its effective abolition (with a limited government role based on Adam Smith's principles),[10] and switch the bulk of state directed activity into the private sector. Considering the rigorous demands of the theoretical foundations their analysis stems from, it seems strange to concentrate on eliminating *structure* while perversely neglecting to alter *content*. As we have argued in this chapter and Chapter 3, when firm organisation and state bureaucracy are exposed to the harsh glare of neoclassical theory there is extensive withering of both structure *and* content in the respective systems.

The second point is related to the first. Despite the fact that there are three alternative methods of economic organisation, the Friedmans virtually ignore the third – firm co-ordination. The closest that corporations come to examination is when they are compared to individuals and entrepreneurs as instruments for applying productive resources they control into income-generating work (pp. 20–1). Managers hardly figure in the Friedmans' analysis, as we would expect of a text that is devoted to propounding the *market* solution.

This prompts an obvious question; if the market is so clever, why do giant modern corporations exist?[11] Why have ICI, Du Pont, General Motors, Exxon evolved when the activities they operate could be

The Emergent Firm

carried out by market exchange? Where firms exist, why do they not look like the neoclassical ideal? Even economies of scale could be exploited by one man–one product neoclassical firms voluntarily trading the benefits, as was discussed in Chapter 2. The Friedmans' neglect of corporations appears curious when it is considered that firm co-ordination has strong similarities to state direction; for state bureaucrats read corporate managers, for bureaucracy read corporate hierarchy. Yet the Friedmans concentrate on the evils of bureaucracies and the virtues of market exchange with almost no reference to the private bureaucracies represented by modern corporations.

One reason for this neglect may be that corporations are regarded as instruments of the market by the Friedmans in much the same light as the neoclassical 'black box' firm. If this is so, then it is a simplistic and distorted view, as will be argued in later analysis and as we have already suggested with our 'real-world' firm outlined in Figure 3.1. An alternative, and perhaps unkinder reason is that state direction is an easier target for the neoclassical critique than is firm co-ordination. State bureaucracy, because of its obvious divorce from market pressure is easier to label inefficient, incompetent and out of touch with people's needs; it may well be all these things, but if it is not there is little in the way of objective tests or standards it can invoke to defend itself against the Friedmans' polemic. On the other hand, if the Friedmans raise their blunderbuss against any particular corporation, there is an immediate defence; corporations still operate in the market place, using market exchange and competing against other systems, some of which may be firms, and some of which may be mostly or entirely composed of market exchange. If market exchange is superior, why do actual or potential market exchange systems not supplant firm co-ordination? Using neoclassical theorys' own survival of the fittest argument, why does market exchange not drive out firm co-ordination?[12] It is easy to affirm relative inefficiency in state direction and attribute it to perfidy or possibly well-meaning incompetence. It is less easy to do the same for firm co-ordination.

That firms should exist in place of market transactions raises the suspicion that it may be because such institutions actually prove superior to market exchange in certain circumstances. If firms, why not state intervention? Discussion of these issues requires deeper analysis of the nature of information problems and how the respective forms of economic organisation may cope with them. Chapter 5 will consider both sets of issues.

CONCLUSION

In this chapter we have continued to conduct an experiment in viewing the world through a neoclassical perspective. The result has been a radical revision of what might be regarded as legitimate roles and activities under state direction. As with Chapter 3 in which we looked at the effect the perfect knowledge assumption has on the picture of the corporation, there are two main effects; firstly many functions and roles disappear when perfect knowledge is assumed, and secondly, we cannot discriminate between the firm, the market and the state as efficient methods of dealing with residual activities.

We have also briefly considered the Friedmans' argument that market exchange represents the superior form of economic organisation. We have suggested weaknesses in this argument on *a priori* grounds, but in the last resort the questions they raise are empirical questions which cannot be resolved by purely theoretical debate. We have, however, hopefully demonstrated the narrow territorial range of neoclassical theory, and how its perfect knowledge assumption can be used to cleanly divide activities into two camps; those that physically provide goods and services, and those that provide information based goods and services.

In Chapter 5, we shall turn to two problems which have been raised by the discussion so far; what is the general nature of information problems, and how do firms, the market and the state cope with them?

5 Risk, Uncertainty and Chance

Ros.: Heads [*he puts it in his bag. The process is repeated*]. Heads
[*again*] Heads [*again*] Heads.
Guil.: [*flipping a coin*] There is an art to the building up of suspense.
Ros.: Heads.
Guil.: [*flipping another*] Though it can be done by luck alone.
Ros.: Heads.

Tom Stoppard, *Rosencrantz and Guildenstern Are Dead*

Arthur looked up.
'Ford!' he said, 'there's an infinite number of monkeys outside who
want to talk to us about this script for Hamlet they've worked out.'

Douglas Adams, *The Hitchhikers Guide to the Galaxy*

My good friend Jacques Monod spoke often of the randomness of
the cosmos. He believed everything in existence occurred by pure
chance with the possible exception of his breakfast, which he felt
certain was made by his housekeeper.

Woody Allen, *My Speech to the Graduates*[1]

The dual purpose of this chapter is to identify the basic nature of
information problems and to suggest the types of information costs
associated with respective forms of economic organisation. So far we
have merely indicated the existence of possible cracks in the neoclassical construction of Nirvana. We continue the search here with a view to
more fully identifying the nature and source of structural defects in the
foundations of neoclassical theory, and the role of risk, uncertainty,
and chance in this ill-designed disaster area.

In doing so, economics is interpreted as a social science. Such
explicit perspective may appear unnecessary – after all the discipline
occupies a nominal position within the social sciences, economics
students are invariably enrolled in social science faculties. Why the
need to confirm economics status as such?

The need arises from the axiomatic–deductive tradition in economics which uses neoclassical assumptions to examine real-world issues. One problem we have seen with this approach is that the firm is regarded as a black box. No consideration is given to the manner in which inputs are converted into outputs other than to assume that allocation is made according to rational profit-maximising criteria. The entrepreneur is the mechanism by which the process is executed, but these same assumptions result in the treatment of the entrepreneur as an automaton with no discretion over resource allocation. The assumption of rationality and the existence of marginalist profit-maximising rules couched in the perfect knowledge assumption, ensures that the entrepreneur has no real discretion over questions of resource allocation. Again, this leads to a tension between the formal and informal analysis of neoclassical theorists such as the Friedmans, who emphasise the entrepreneurial role of risk-taking and his due reward for opportunistic decision-making in their informal theory. The picture of the brave buccaneering entrepreneur painted by such as the Friedmans in their informal discussions, is curiously at odds with the limited role afforded to the entrepreneur in formal neoclassical theory. In the latter, the entrepreneur has no discretion over which actions to take; the choice is made for him by the rules and conditions of the neoclassical game. The chosen outcome, or group of outcomes, will be calculated as providing the greatest level of net income to the entrepreneur. The twin assumptions of rationality and perfect knowledge, when combined with the certain knowledge that these outcomes do represent the most profitable set, completely determine entrepreneurial action. The buccaneer of the Friedman analysis is reduced to an ordinary seaman, with no decision-making capacity, no requirement for initiative, and no discretion over choice of future action. The elimination of ignorance, risk and uncertainty similarly eliminates the need for decision, choice and entrepreneurship as defined by the Friedmans. As Shackle (1969, p. 4) confirms, perfect foresight renders decision-making empty. Again, we find the informal discussion of neoclassical theorists at odds with their formal analysis.

The formal neoclassical theory of the entrepreneurial firm as a rational maximising unit operating under conditions of perfect knowledge is paralleled on the demand side by the idea of the utility maximising consumer. Both supply and demand sides in the neoclassical equation perform no more than clerical functions in the resource allocation process, using pre-ordained rules to attain pre-determined solutions. Imagination, endeavour, opportunism, initiative, deceit, and many other human characteristics, are screened out of neoclassical theory by the perfect knowledge assumption.

As a consequence, human beings *per se* have been disregarded by traditional formal theory; responsibility for their introduction has typically been left to qualifications, informal discussion and footnotes to the main analysis. In recent years, behavioural theory[2] has made a real contribution to analysing decision-making under conditions of uncertainty. It is a theory designed for conditions in which information problems are pervasive, though also one which is applicable only to a specific category of problems.[3] Strategic questions are neglected by this approach which concentrates on operational decisions in the corporation.

The introduction of the human factor into resource allocation questions is the natural consequence of recognition of information problems. We shall bear this point in mind when we consider the typical nature of information problems in the section below.

INFORMATION PROBLEMS

We have seen how neoclassical theory concentrates on the third stage of the resource allocation process and suggested that the neglect of the second stage – information problems – may effectively inhibit neo-classical theory from adequately dealing with allocation questions.

We may start our inquiry by first of all recalling the example of the pencil discussed in Chapter 4. The manufacture and consumption of pencils was used as an example by the Friedmans to illustrate the benevolent operation of the price system. We conceded that it was in fact an example in which the neoclassical assumptions might be reasonably argued to hold. What was it about this example that could justify excluding information problems?

It will be remembered that the crucial aspect of this example which permitted us to treat information problems as being of potentially little relevance was the existence of *repetition* and *replicability*. We concentrated on the consumer choice aspect and identified the opportunity afforded the consumer to build up a comprehensive store of knowledge regarding alternative possible purchases through trial and error. Given homogeneity of brand types, past purchases of specific types could be relied upon to give complete and accurate information concerning future purchases. It is the repetitious nature of consumer purchase in this example, together with the replicability associated with standardised units of production, that leads to the neoclassical interpretation being of possible relevance in this example.

We could have extended our discussion to cover the supply side of this example and found evidence to support the neoclassical perspective here also. The Friedmans concentrate only on the production side of this problem, ignoring such information-ridden areas as marketing, R & D, etc. However, within this limited remit, neoclassical theory may be potentially applicable to the supply side as well. Homogeneity of output, and consistency in terms of available technologies and resources, allows the entrepreneur to evaluate the physical characteristics of production using alternative methods. On price will depend choice of technology and level of output. Again, the qualities of repetition and replicability (in this case with respect to output, technology and resources) may permit the application of neoclassical theory to the areas suggested for it in the Friedmans' analysis.

Sameness may therefore be said to be an essential quality in providing the entrepreneur and the consumer with opportunities to learn relevant characteristics of marketed goods and services. Interestingly, other examples of this quality are emphasised by both Friedman and Machlup in different defences of the neoclassical approach.[4] Friedman and Machlup were concerned with demonstrating that lack of realism is not a fair criticism of the neoclassical approach (this much has already been conceded in the previous chapter). What is particularly interesting is the respective examples used to defend the reasonableness of neoclassical theory.

Firstly, Friedman uses the example of a billiards player in his defence. He argued that the shots of a very good player could be accurately represented using mathematical models of the angles and patterns of collision; however, says, Friedman, nobody seriously believes that good billiards players use such mathematical models in their play, or that such models would be of real use to them. In other words, says Friedman, real behaviour can be accurately described in certain circumstances by highly abstract 'unrealistic' models.

Secondly, Machlup employs the example of a car driver overtaking a truck to defend the neoclassical approach. As with the snooker example, it is possible to construct a mathematical representation of this physical action. We could develop a theory of 'optimal overtaking' based on relative velocities, gear changes, etc. However, Machlup argues that we do not need to assume that such mathematical representations of reality are utilised by the driver, only that he behaves *as if* he is using such a model. Consequently Machlup justifies using neoclassical theory even when there is evidence that the decision-makers do not explicitly employ marginalist rules. The 'as if' justification serves to defend neoclassical theory against criticisms of lack of realism in this context.

In both cases the examples are such that the decision-maker can take full advantage of repetition and replicability to learn optimal (or approximately optimal) action. The two examples use experienced decision-makers in situations which are highly similar to ones which they have encountered numerous times before. Even if the billiards player has never encountered precisely this angle before, or the car driver has never overtaken another vehicle travelling at precisely this speed, the wide range of experience of previous pots and passes encountered by the respective decision-makers should enable them to use extrapolation and averaging in their present situations.

Thus, the examples of the pencil, the billiards player and the car driver all have strong similarities in terms of the context and opportunities of their learning experience. The fact that characteristics of repetition and replicability figure so largely in each example is not a coincidence, but is instead a reflection of the need for such conditions to exist before information problems can be ignored and the neoclassical framework safely utilised. These examples, carefully selected by the respective analysts, help to illustrate the limits of neoclassical application.

What then are we to make of neoclassical theory's treatment of risk and uncertainty? These two concepts are frequently alluded to by neoclassical theorists, especially in the context of entrepreneurial activity, though we have seen that such concepts are not able to be accommodated within the formal theory. Such concepts are integral to decision-making; indeed it has been widely commented that selection of actions by firms and consumer in neoclassical theory does not involve true decision-making since the rules and assumptions eliminate discretion over price, output, choice of technology, etc. Perfect knowledge and rationality predetermine action.

However, risk and uncertainty are associated features of information problems, and consequently it is important to explore the nature and implications of both concepts. The definitive interpretation of the distinction between the respective concepts stems from Knight (1921). *Risk* was interpreted as future variability which could be predicted from the laws of chance, and is in principle insurable since objective probability distributions of expected likelihood of occurrence can be constructed. On the other hand, pure *uncertainty* is associated with unique events whose likelihood (and possible nature) cannot be objectively determined, and for which a probability distribution is not available. In principle the divide between the two concepts is clear-cut, in practice it is often difficult to determine.

A good example of a risky situation is playing a roulette wheel. Suppose the wheel has thirty numbers and two zeros. The payoff for a $1 bet is thirty to one or $30 if the number comes up, so there is a one in thirty-two chance of winning $30 for a single bet. These estimates are based on the assumptions that there is no bias in the wheel, and that each number has an equal probability of occurrence compared with all other numbers. The estimates may be obtained by *a priori* calculation as here, or by a process of experimental observation of actual frequencies of occurrence for individual bets. The laws of chance should ensure that both methods of calculation will result in the same set of estimates if a sufficiently large number of experimental observations are carried out.

Risk situations may in fact be incorporated in neoclassical type analysis with minimal modification of the framework. While risk situations involve information problems, they are problems of a precise and limited nature. Repetition and replicability are central and definitive features of risk situations as well as the standard neoclassical situations discussed earlier. For example, in the roulette wheel example there is nothing to distinguish between alternative holes in terms of size, shape and consequent likelihood of occurrence of a particular number. Each number may be regarded as a homogenous outcome in the set of 32 possible outcomes making up the roulette wheel. What is not known is which outcome will occur, but the highly structured nature of the decision problem already provides a great deal of information that permits calculation of objective probabilities. Imperfections of knowledge are therefore recognised, but repetition and replicability of events ensure that objective assessment of the implications of each choice is possible.

The same principle holds in the example of insurance. Suppose we have an individual who wishes to take out life insurance. The insurance company will produce an actuarial table based on the estimated probability of death for a person of this age, state of health, etc. Thus, again, the risk estimate is based on homogeneity and repetition, in this case the outcome being the distribution of lifespans for people of a similar type. Considered *ex ante*, old soldiers never die, they just become less probable.

The dramatic and comic content of the start of *Rosencrantz and Guildenstern Are Dead*, which introduced this chapter, is a direct consequence of the highly improbable sequence of events described. Indeed the improbability can be statistically calculated. By page 11 Guildenstern had tossed 92 successive heads; the probability of tossing a succession of 92 heads *or* tails is $2 \times (1024)^9$. Logic and experience dictate the element of the absurd in such an unlikely series of events. Presuming Guildenstern is not cheating and that the coin is unbiased, the assumption of equiprobability of heads and tails follows from the effective homogeneity of both sides of the coin; there is nothing to choose between respective sides in terms of the physical possibility of landing face down or up, just as for a well balanced dice. Again, repetition and replicability ensure objective measurement as in the standard neoclassical examples of the pencil, the billiards player and the car driver in the previous section. The roulette wheel, the coin and the dice are risk counterparts of these examples. As Shackle argues, probability of the dice kind 'requires as a *sine qua non* of its existence, some underlying stability and invariance of the system being described. Knowledge and constancy are so intimately related in all science, that we can say that science is merely the recognition and description of constancy' (1972, p. 18).

However, when we consider the characteristics of true uncertainty, there is no longer any element of repetition or replicability to provide guiding standards for measurement. True uncertainty exists where we have novel outcomes whose probability of occurrence cannot be objectively assessed, or indeed whose precise nature it may not be possible to anticipate in advance. In those circumstances, outcomes defy general categorisation, and tend to be extremely heterogeneous. To the extent similarities exist between outcomes, they are not strong or dominant enough to allow standardisation of outcomes for analytical purposes as in the roulette coin and dice examples. Thus, the information problems tend to be poorly defined in conditions of uncertainty and have no precise structure unlike risk situations.

There is a fourth concept applicable to knowledge conditions which is of relevance here; ignorance. Marshak (1968) represents the typical decision theory interpretation of uncertainty as negation of information; but it is not. As Loasby (1967, p. 305) points out, uncertainty is not simply ignorance but involves knowledge of possible future events. *Some* knowledge is required to create a state of uncertainty, and a great deal of knowledge may be necessary to adequately interpret a situation as risky. The opposite of perfect knowledge is ignorance, not uncertainty.

It may be possible to identify a spectrum of knowledge conditions running from ignorance (complete absence of information) through risk and uncertainty to perfect knowledge as in Figure 5.1.

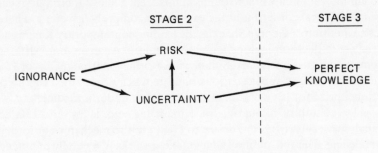

FIGURE 5.1   *Spectrum of types of knowledge states*

The transformation of a state of ignorance into risk and/or uncertainty and then a state of perfect knowledge is accomplished by the provision of information. As indicated by the direction of arrows a state of uncertainty may be converted into a state of risk; for example a naïve roulette player may possess all relevant information except the number of zeros on the wheel. A state of uncertainty becomes one of risk when he learns there are two zeros.

The spectrum indicates how the knowledge states relate to the allocation process outlined in Figure 2.1. Perfect knowledge is of course associated with the neoclassical stage 3, while the other stages are associated with the second or information stage. As we have seen, risk is a step back into stage 2 information problems, but a modest one; it does not depart from the principles of repetition and replicability that permit objective measurement.

In the next section we shall be concerned with the process by which these conditions are translated into axioms fit for economic consumption.

ECONOMIC ANALYSIS AND UNCERTAINTY

A recent major survey (Hirshleifer and Riley (1979)) of the contemporary economic approach to problems of uncertainty and information conveys an impression of consistency and unanimity in economic analyses of this area. In fact it is fairly typical of many conventional economic interpretations in basing its approach on certain limited and rigorous assumptions; we discuss these further below. However, it should first be noted, that Hirshleifer and Riley, in common with many other studies in this area, achieve their tight focus and analytical consensus at the expense of comprehensiveness. There is no mention of George Shackle, the leading contemporary Keynesian analyst of decision-making under uncertainty. An even more striking omission is that of Herbert Simon whose exclusion from the list of 150 references might appear curious since he was awarded the economics Nobel prize for his work on decision making under uncertainty.

The voluntary blinkering of Hirshleifer and Riley and related analyses results from the desire to facilitate the mechanics of formal modelling. The role of uncertainty in these works is generally presented in the form of three basic assumptions (see Hirshleifer and Riley (1979) and also Hey (1979)).

(1) All possible future states of the world can be identified by the decision-maker.
(2) The possible future states of the world may be assigned a cardinal probability of occurrence by the decision-maker.
(3) These probabilities of occurrence sum to one.

Future states of the world are treated as being acts of God or nature, and for the purposes of analysis of decision the assumptions above imply all states of the world relevant to a specific decision are identifiable and the likelihood of their occurrence measurable in probabilistic terms by the decision-maker. As is typical in such approaches, Knight's distinction between risk and uncertainty is rejected by Hirshleifer and Riley since a *subjective* probability measure is suggested as a means of turning objectively unmeasurable 'true' uncertainty in the Knight sense into a tractable area for model building. It should be especially noted that when Hirshleifer and Riley talk of the substitution of subjective probability for true uncertainty as having been 'fruitful' (p. 1378), they do *not* conduct an inventory of the empirical harvest produced by such implements, but instead turn to the proliferation and variety of sophisticated models that such assumptions have produced. Unfortunately, empirical produce has been conspicuous by its absence.

Decision theorists in economics adopt the basic assumptions above as a matter of faith. If such stylised decision-making did not exist it would have to be invented. It is necessary to legitimate the decision theory approach. What decision theory conceals is the substantial body of *knowledge* that decision-makers must possess before these analytical frameworks can be applied. Decision-makers must know and be able to identify all relevant future states of the world. They must be able to measure and compare probabilities of occurrence – e.g. a specific state may be identified as half as likely or three times as likely to occur as another. For rationality and consistency's sake these probabilities must sum to one. As we have seen in the previous section, such assumptions implicitly assume a considerable body of knowledge on the part of the decision-maker. What is also significant is that if any one of the assumptions do not hold we have a situation of 'true' uncertainty in the Knight sense.

The last assumption is not too troublesome in this respect. If probabilities sum to more or less than one, consistency could be achieved by weighting probabilities with an appropriate scale factor – providing assumption (1) holds and the relative likelihood of occurrence of possible states of the world is unchanged by scale adjustments.

It is the first two assumptions that are liable to be serious problems in empirical analysis of decision making under uncertainty. A comprehensive listing of possible states of the world and probabilistic estimation of their likelihood of occurrence may require prodigious information gathering and processing abilities on the part of the decision-maker. If pressed, he may indeed provide a listing of possible future states of the world and associated probability estimates. Such quantitative information may indeed have the aura and appearance of precision and 'hardness' that the decision theory machine needs to crank into action. However, in practice, surface hardness may conceal a soft underbelly. This does not pose a philosophical problem for decision theory in economics, since like its parent neoclassical theory, its development has more generally reflected a preoccupation with the trappings, mechanics and appearance of scientific precision than a concern for whether or not the initial assumptions are indeed reasonable. In-house criticism, discussion, and modification of decision analysis in economics tends to revolve around development and extension of the model assumptions and rarely touches down to empirical level.

Theory *must* be eventually judged on empirical grounds and not on its merits as a test of intellectual virtuosity. The fruitfulness – or otherwise – of the present dominant approach to the economics of uncertainty and information may be better evaluated when surveys of the field identify their contribution to the empirical analysis of resource allocation. The general shyness of theorists in this respect is not encouraging as far as their claims to relevance and legitimacy is concerned.

Which of these factors – risk, uncertainty, ignorance – are most applicable to information problems? We can look at this in two respects, firstly *a priori* examination of factors underlying information problems, and secondly consideration of actual behaviour at an empirical level. We hope to show that the general conclusions are mutually supporting in both cases, and will consider the theoretical aspects first before going on to look at more applied problems in later chapters.

When the neoclassical assumptions are satisfied and complete knowledge exists, not only are information problems eliminated, but an associated advantage arises that is central to the development of rational, objective criteria for resource allocation; provision of information and physical provision of the good or service can be treated as *separable*. We can simply demonstrate this in Figure 5.2.

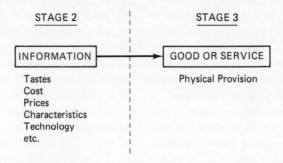

FIGURE 5.2   *Provision of good or service in neoclassical theory*

It is assumed in neoclassical theory that the information stage has been completed and that allocation can be decided according to the neoclassical rules. Provision of information and physical provision of the good or service can be treated as distinctive, separable problems in which information gathering precedes physical allocation. This separation allows stage 3 problems of allocation to be considered independently of information problems.

Suppose, however, that information itself is the good or service to be provided? We have seen that this is not a trivial or exceptional case; in the case of the firm all resources apart from capital and direct labour in production are concerned with this problem, while many functions and activities performed by the market and the state are also based on the production of information. In such circumstances the information stage in Figure 5.2 itself becomes the good or service to be provided, and we move a step further back into stage 2. Just as in Figure 5.2, information on the good or service is required if rational criteria for resource allocation are to be developed, and this is indicated in Figure 5.3 for a consumer and a firm.

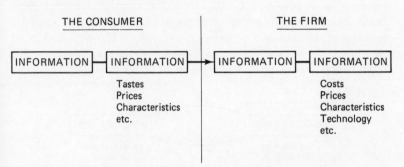

FIGURE 5.3   *Information as a good or service*

For both tasks, the consumer and the firm, information is both the guide to allocation and the good or service itself. The problem is: what type and context of information is required if we are to develop objective criteria for allocation?

We can provide a simple example to help answer this question. Suppose we select technological information for the firm in Figure 5.3 as being our object, and consider an R & D project designed to generate such information. What information is required to value the R & D project as a provider of an informational good or service?

The answer is straightforward. We need information on the resource usage of the project characteristics of the R & D output and net-revenue generating value of the output. This is the type of information required to evaluate physical provision of a good or service in neoclassical theory. The trouble is, this is also the type of information that is only fully made available after the project is finished. For example, we need precise technical specifications of the R & D output as information to evaluate the R & D project; but such technical specifications are precisely the purpose of the project in the first place – if we had such blueprints, we would not need to conduct the R & D project.

It was this type of problem which led Kenneth Arrow (1962) to identify some conceptual difficulties in valuing information; 'there is a fundamental paradox in the determination of demand for information; its value for the purchaser is not known until he has the information, but then he has in effect acquired it without cost' (p. 615).

We have a circular problem in the case of information as a good or service. To assess the value and characteristics of the informational good or service we require specific information. However this specific information is provided by the actual informational output itself. While information and provision of good or service could be treated as separate in the standard neoclassical example in Figure 5.2, they are compacted together when we examine informational problems. The relationship here is of the form described below in Figure 5.4

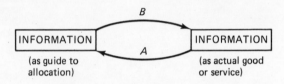

FIGURE 5.4   *The separation problem*

The closed loop in Figure 5.4 illustrates the circular nature of the problem; the arrow *A* indicates that we require information before we can make a rational decision concerning allocation of resources, but arrow *B* indicates that the information required will only be provided by the actual application of resources to the project. The two stages are non-separable and consequently it is not possible to discriminate between the information and provision stages in such cases.

The description of the separation problems in Figure 5.4 is in fact at a fairly high level of abstraction. In practice, complex decisions may well involve a package comprising numerous loops of the type described above. For example, a specific R & D project may simultaneously or sequentially search out multiple pieces of information. As the project proceeds, individual loops may be chipped away until successful completion. If the project is aborted, numerous loops may be left unreconciled.

The interesting thing about such closed loops is their pervasiveness in economic problems. The information a gasoline retailer may need before reducing price may include competitor reaction; but that may not be revealed until price has been reduced. An advertising executive may require to know how consumers will react to a specific campaign;

but such information may only be revealed by actually undertaking the campaign. The only way a designer might establish whether his idea might be opportunistically appropriated may be actual disclosure. Institutional arrangements may modify some loops, eliminate them, or make their effects more palatable; cartelisation, test marketing and patenting are examples. However, as with progressive revelation of information in the R & D project example above, these techniques may only chip away some of the loops in the information package required by the decision-maker rather than eliminate them altogether.

Not only are such separation problems common in economics, they constitute fundamental issues in many other disciplines, arts, and sciences. Hofstadter (1979) describes them as 'strange loops', and Figure 5.4 represents a simple example of such systems. The drawings of Escher are frequently interpretable as visual illustrations of strange loops; the lithographs of endlessly ascending stairs (Ascending and Descending, 1960) and of two artist's hands apparently drawing each other (Drawing Hands, 1948) are only two of many visual strange loops constructed by Escher. Hofstadter interprets some of the work of Bach, Mozart and Magritte as also incorporating strange loops in which progress from one stage to another unexpectedly returns the observer back to his initial state – as in Figure 5.4.

There is one final element which will allow us to tie together Hofstadter's strange loops, Arrows information paradox, and the economics of George Shackle and Joseph Schumpeter; the element of *surprise*. A surprising event may be regarded as one whose occurrence was not anticipated, or which had been allocated such a low probability that the possibility of its occurrence was effectively discounted.[5] By way of contrast, the possibility of the unexpected is excluded from mechanistic neoclassical and decision theory in which all possible future states of the world are identified. For example, Hey (1981) points out, in the Bayesian approach to price theory, the searcher must list all possible price and price distributions and characterise them within a family of distributions. Hey notes the Bayesian approach rules out the possibility of surprise, or rather what the decision-maker would do if he was surprised. As Shackle points out, novelty is 'wholly alien to the rational timeless static system', yet in real games the greatest secret of victory is surprise (1972, p. 92). He points out the irony that in Game Theory in the Von Neuman-Morgenstern sense there is no surprise but only calculation.

It is the role of novelty and innovation that is emphasised by Schumpeter; 'the fundamental impulse that sets and keeps the capitalist engine in motion comes from the new consumer goods, the new methods of production or transportation, the new markets, the new forms of industrial organisation' (1954, p. 83). Such novelty is interpretable as new knowledge (Shackle, 1972, p. 72) and is typically associated with tremors, shocks and surprises (Shackle, 1972).

We can summarise; Schumpeter argues that innovation is *the* fundamental phenomenon underlying economic development and we know that innovation is interpretable as new knowledge. Following the route of Arrow's paradox warns us of the strange loops underlying knowledge economics, while following Shackle's argument reveals the integral role of surprise in innovation and new knowledge.

In fact 'surprise' is an integral feature of strange loops. As Hofstadter points out, 'The surprise element is important, it is the reason I call Strange Loops "strange". A single tangle, like feedback, doesn't involve violations of presumed level distinctions. An example is when you're in the shower and you wash your left arm with your right, and then vice versa. There is no strangeness to the image. Escher didn't choose to draw hands drawing hands for nothing!' (1979, p. 691).

With innovation, separation problems, strange loops and surprise are fundamental and potentially catastrophic. Harold Geneen, while Chief Executive of ITT, tersely summarised his strategic philosophy as 'no surprises'. Minor innovation may involve minor problems – there may be little 'strangeness' or 'surprise' associated with an automobile manufacturer's new model. Major or 'genuine' innovation, however, will display a formidable bundle of information problems. What will happen? Who will develop it? What does it look like? How does it work? If answers to these questions concerning *future* innovation were known, there would be no surprise, no strange loops, no separation problems – and paradoxically no future innovation; if its various parameters are known in the present, its future specification would be repetition, not innovation.

In Kay (1982) patterns of diversification were examined and analysed in terms of potential vulnerability to environmental 'surprise'. While corporate decision-makers did not have the ability to anticipate the precise form of future threat, they could rank environments in terms of threat or 'mugging' potential. Strategies could be designed around the potential of the environment to throw up competing innovations – literally 'surprises'.

While this interpretation was not used in the 1982 work, such analysis may be regarded as one way of dealing with strange loops. We look at some implications and extensions of the 1982 analysis in the next chapter. Another method by which strange loops might be treated is suggested by the analysis in Kay (1979). Bounded rationality problems may be severe at individual product or project level but at higher levels patterns and relationships may emerge. Thus, individual projects may be shot through with strange loops but the R & D function as a whole may exhibit a stable and consistent relationship with other functions in the firm. However, this approach is obviously only of use if we wish to conduct analysis at a level above the strange loops. It is also a perspective alien to neoclassical theory, firstly because higher levels are simply the aggregate of lower levels in neo-classical theory, and secondly because the perfect knowledge assumption assumes away the existence of informational strange loops.

A further solution pursued in this present work is representing and analysing information problems by explicitly recognising the role of strange loops. Such an approach entails abandoning the comfortable solidity of neoclassical and decision theory for the uncertainty associated with the separation problem. The situation facing the decision maker in Figure 5.4 is one of true uncertainty once strange loops are explicitly recognised. As a consequence, we shall turn to bounded rationality and uncertainty problems ignored by neoclassical theory later in this chapter. We shall suggest that transaction cost analysis may represent an appropriate framework for dealing with information problems.

There is a further point of interest also revealed by Hofstadter's analysis. Hofstadter points out (pp. 698–9) that Western science has been traditionally subject to the criticism of dualism – separating subject from object or observer and observed. Progressively, however, Western science has been concerned with mixing subject and object as in artificial intelligence and quantum mechanics. The tangling of observer and observed is one consequence of the evolution of strange loops in those areas. David Bohm, Professor of Theoretical Physics at Birkbeck College, confirms this interpretation, 'approaching the question in different ways, relativity and quantum theory agree, in that they both imply the need to look on the world as an *undivided whole*, in which all parts of the universe, including the observer and his instruments, merge and unite in one totality. In this totality, the atomistic form of insight is a simplification and an abstraction, valid only in some limited context', (Bohm, 1980, p. 11). Such a perspective emphasises both strange loops and non-decomposability as characteristics of natural systems.

By way of contrast the *detachment* of observer from phenomenon is a feature of neoclassical and decision theory. Such a perspective, characteristic of 19th century physics and chemistry, is simply illustrated by unicausal relationships as in Figure 5.2. While such detachment may well have appeared properly 'scientific' in the early days of the marginalist revolution, it does appear curiously dated in the light of 20th century scientific developments.

Hofstadter identifies other strange loops in areas as diverse as language, government, and molecular biology. He goes as far as to suggest that cognitive processes or 'psychological software' – ideas, hopes, images, analogies, even consciousness and free will, are explicable in terms of strange loops. Such an interpretation provides an interesting parallel to Arrow's information paradox; we have argued that information problems are *the* economic problem, while Arrow makes explicit the strange loopiness typically inherent in such problems for decision-makers. Hofstadter, from an entirely different starting point, affirms the pervasiveness of strange loops in cognitive processes.

Even if we wanted to, it would appear impossible to avoid the embarrassment of strange loops in economic decision-making. Information problems are fundamental to economic decision, and strange loops are a standard form in which such information problems are encountered if we accept Arrow's paradox. Having established how the process can be represented, our next problem is how to interpret it.

In this respect neoclassical theory provides a clear answer: ignore strange loops and separation problems and represent the decision making problem as in Figure 5.2. Decision theory would presume that decision-makers at stage 2 in Figure 5.2 have complete information on the possible events in stage 3 together with their associated probabilities of occurrence. Strange loops in, for example, the set of possible future states, are excluded in decision theory.

Both neoclassical and decision theory allow formal, quantitative deterministic analysis to be imposed on the information problem. However information problems look like Figure 5.4 – not Figure 5.2. These frameworks do not fit the problem, they distort and misrepresent it. Where information problems are severe, such theories of economic decision making are as appropriate as our stethoscope theory of medicine.

How do risk situations fit into this type of analysis? Suppose we extend our example of the pencil to include the possibility that one in a hundred pencils are of inferior quality such that the lead breaks frequently and inconveniently – we may assume quality control testing and public knowledge communicates this information to the entrepreneur and the consumer respectively. How does this square with the separation problems described in Figure 5.4?

In special cases such as this, there is in principle still a separation problem – the consumer does not know *ex ante* whether he will purchase a dud or not, only *ex post*. This is similar to the problem faced by the decision-maker in the R & D example above. However the information that is still missing is a specific type in the pencil example. The decision problem is extremely structured with all other relevant characteristics being known to the entrepreneurs and consumer. The risk specification means that only one piece is missing from the information jigsaw, and that piece conforms to certain rigid and precise rules. Replicability and repetition here means that testing and observation leads to a perceived 1/100 chance of a dud; the consumer could have complete knowledge of every other relevant piece of information except for the unspecified possibility of a dud pencil, in which case we would be concerned with a situation of risk rather than uncertainty. Consequently a risk situation is typically a highly informed and limited one containing a great deal of contextual information. We have emphasised that the antithesis of knowledge is ignorance, not risk or uncertainty; as far as the relationship to the first two concepts is concerned, risk tends to fall much closer to perfect knowledge than it does to ignorance. The inherent homogeneity of risk situations allows the separation problem to be controlled and objective measurement to be carried out. Shackle wryly touches on this by pointing out 'Frank Knight had contrasted risk (which is not risky) with uncertainty (which is)' (1972, p. 364).

This is not the case in conditions of true uncertainty. In these circumstances the separation problem prevents objective measurement and assessment of the situation. Some circumstances will contain more information than others and consequently may be less uncertain. However, judgment, guesswork, inspiration, hunch, intuition, confidence, belief, are all human factors which begin to be relevant considerations in conditions of uncertainty, though they have no place in the highly structured perfect knowledge and risk situations.

Consequently it is important to establish whether the information problems we have described in Chapters 3 and 4 tend to be of the type associated with risk or with uncertainty. While it may appear a rather daunting prospect attempting to discriminate between respective knowledge states as in Figure 5.1 on *a priori* grounds, in fact our analysis above suggests a simple basis for such a task. Firstly, *perfect knowledge* conditions obviously obtain in the absence of information problems and when separability of information and provision stages is achieved. Secondly, *risk* conditions may obtain where relevant knowledge is complete except for selected information defining which of a series of alternative, homogenous events may occur. Thirdly, a condition of *uncertainty* may exist where the compactedness of the information and provision stages creates a separation problem in which the required information does not merely define a series of identical events as in the risk case. Fourthly, a state of *ignorance* indicates the absence of all knowledge; not only is there no information as to the likelihood of certain states obtaining, there is no information as to the actual context of such possible future states. Indeed, in the extreme, ignorance may be interpreted to mean that the possibility of any future states in this context is not recognised.

Thus, there are distinctive qualitative differences between the respective knowledge states. Two of the states – risk and perfect knowledge – may be said to represent 'pure' knowledge states in the sense that homogeneity and replicability impose rigour and structure on the situation; the only difference between alternative risk situations is the probability of occurrence. On the other hand, states of ignorance and uncertainty are typically messy and unstructured and range right across the knowledge spectrum from high to low; they are also applicable to the same state since partial ignorance represents a degree of uncertainty.[6] However, the distinction between, for example, perfect knowledge, risk and uncertainty is in principle straightforward, perfect knowledge involves homogeneity and no separation problems, risk involves homogeneity and a limited separation problem and uncertainty is characterised by heterogeneity and separation problems. It is interesting that we can relate knowledge states to the intrinsic structure and features of specific situations, and it is this which should permit us to make *a priori* assessment as to which knowledge states are likely to obtain.

Using these criteria, we can use the example of the corporate structure and functions examined in Chapter 3 to examine the applicability of concepts of risk and uncertainty. We have seen that perfect knowledge is restricted in potential application to the combination of capital and direct labour in production.[7] The existence of information problems elsewhere indicates that decision-making under conditions of risk and uncertainty will define such situations. We also know that homogeneity or heterogeneity characteristics will allow us to discriminate between states of risk and uncertainty.

A casual examination of the types of problem discussed in Chapter 3 is sufficient to provide convincing support for the argument that information problems in the firm are typically characterised by uncertainty and not risk. Some restricted categories of problems, possibly in finance, may be interpretable as risk. For example, the price of an agricultural input may be dependent on the risk of crop failure due to bad weather. The laws of chance permit the application of statistical techniques to calculate the risk here according to past experience. Similarly, if a specific advertising campaign developed by marketing is tested in selected regions, or a new product developed by R & D is used in limited areas to start with, then extension of future applications in the respective cases may face new information problems to the extent that there are similarities in marketing regions and new product areas. Repetition and replicability may control or effectively eliminate the influence of true uncertainty in such cases.

However, these risk situations represent a minor aspect in the context of the overall task of the firm for two reasons. Firstly, as we have seen, the context of the risk situation requires a great deal of structure and content before it can be treated as such. The testing of new advertising campaigns and technological innovations in the examples here is liable to be the end of a long trail of creative and deductive generation of information in the respective cases. Though this is dependent on actual circumstances, campaign and product development is typically a complex lengthy process in which final testing of the form described above is liable to be only the tip of the iceberg. There are far greater information requirements in designing, developing and marketing a sophisticated roulette wheel than in playing it. Secondly, not only do risk situations require a relatively small amount of information to be transformed into complete knowledge, the decision implications of risk situations are trivial compared to those of uncertainty. Suppose we have a firm, Casino Inc., which is entirely composed of a large series of roulette wheels in which it was known with certainty how many would play each wheel over a given time period, and there are no other information problems such as the honesty of the croupiers. What would this firm look like?

As we might expect, it would appear not dissimilar to our standard neoclassical firm. The laws of chance would provide expected profit for each wheel and for Casino Inc. as a whole, together with appropriate expected deviations from expected outcomes – and this is effectively the bounds of the information problem facing the firm. The information requirements of Casino Inc. are simple and minimal, and the running of it is mechanical and programmed. Just as the neoclassical marginalist rules were described as limiting the role of the entrepreneur to effectively a clerical function, so the laws of chance eliminate the need for any greater level of mental activity on the part of those running Casino Inc. Once policy regarding the effect of risk on resource allocation is decided, no other decisions require to be taken. There is no need for other managerial intervention – and consequently no need for managers. There is no need for internal organisation; if it were believed that unscrupulous or incompetent croupiers could cheat Casino Inc. there may be a need for middle level supervisors. In the absence of these problems derived from imperfect information, each croupier and roulette wheel becomes a single, occasional bit of information on the desk of those responsible for the running of Casino Inc. As in the example of the neoclassical firm, we are left with the equivalent of entrepreneur, capital and direct labour – in this case, those running the casino, the roulette wheels and the croupiers. Further, non-profit-maximising behaviour on the part of those running the casino would be easy to identify and control even if the owners operate at a distance for the simple reason that the laws of chance are universally known; as long as they are in possession of knowledge of number of games played, the owners of the casino can easily check and control deviant behaviour on the part of management.

For similar reasons the marketing, R & D, and finance functions are effectively eliminated or reduced to a programmable unit if only risk analysis is recognised in the respective functions. To continue the Casino Inc. example, one group of roulette wheels could be designated 'Finance', one group 'Marketing' and one group 'R & D'. There is no real difference as far as the top is concerned in terms of the restricted range and complexity of informational demands compared with the first form in which the example above was expressed. Where risk does exist, it is a lower level programmable decision problem. The justification for the existence of management lies not in the existence of risk, but in areas requiring judgement, discretion, experience, etc. – the areas of uncertainty.

Neither conditions of perfect knowledge nor risk can account for the existence of any of sundry veils of Salome discussed in Chapter 3. Perfect knowledge and risk both imply predictability and programmability; the structure and functions of the firm are built on the need to deal with heterogenous, non-programmeable decisions, or those involving true uncertainty. In fact the firm can frequently dispense with the risk content of its decisions altogether, for example it may trade the risk of crop failure in the case of the agricultural input above by using forward markets or insurance. True risk provides a statistically reliable basis on which market transactions can be based.

The need for management, hierarchy, labour heterogeneity, the R & D, finance and marketing functions all derive from the *non-repetitious*, complex and heterogenous situations that require true decision-making and judgment and involve genuine uncertainty. With respect to the problem of state direction, similar conclusions obtain – bureaucrats above clerical level and the bureaucracy depend on uncertainty to justify their existence, while there is also strong and obvious tendency for the selected examples of information problems discussed in the same chapter to be heterogeneous, non-repeatable services, in which uncertainty would be an integral part by definition; education, drama, comedy, the media are all examples of such types of service, just as marketing and R & D are obvious cases in the example of corporate functions. In fact there are strong grounds for arguing that non-replicability is the norm and that replicability is an unusual case; for example, Wiles (1977, p. 102) points out each act of ploughing is a unique task creating problems in costing, supervision and institutional arrangements. Since farming is frequently cited by neoclassical theorists as a special case in which the model of perfect competition may be applicable, the message of task heterogeneity and differentation is a specially worrying one. If homogeneity may not be a feature of even this classic area, it augers badly for it in other arenas.

A corollary is that if information problems faced by corporations could be genuinely characterised as risky, then the in house activities of the firm could be reduced to mechanical or clerical level guaranteeing wholesale redundancy and elimination of virtually all human resources not directly involved in physical production of goods and services.

The condition of uncertainty is the central feature of information problems in general, with a few special cases being analysable in terms of risk. Consequently, in the next chapter we will consider the implications of the effect of uncertainty on the appropriate form of economic organisation as well as alternative theoretical frameworks for dealing with such uncertainty. First, however, we shall consider the effect of uncertainty on the transaction costs of market exchange and how these costs may encourage the substitution of alternative forms of economic organisation.

BOUNDED RATIONALITY, TRANSACTION, AND ORGANISATION COSTS

The existence of bounded rationality creates a need for decision making under conditions of uncertainty. As we have seen in the preceding chapters, neoclassical theory's presumption that bounded rationality problems are absent means that no effective distinction can be made between alternative forms of economic organisation and excludes the bulk of significant resource allocation questions from sensible analysis. The recognition of bounded rationality issues represents the necessary starting point for investigation of these problems. The role of uncertainty as an integral part of this approach follows the discussion of this chapter.

Problems arising from bounded rationality generally involve the associated issue of coping with uncertainty as Simon's and Williamson's work makes clear. However these problems and issues are generally stated as an unfortunate fact of economic life without deeper consideration of why and how they arise. In many cases, problems of uncertainty can be traced to the existence of strange loops in the decision-making system. Consequently, strange loops may provide theoretical explanation for the form and severity of conditions of uncertainty in specific situations.

Bounded rationality is regarded here as contributing two major economic problems, transaction costs and organisation costs, and providing the characteristics by which these basic forms of economic organisation should be judged and compared. We shall look at each of these issues in turn, starting with transaction costs.

The role of transaction costs in seeking a justification for the existence of the firms was first highlighted by Coase (1937) and was extended by Williamson (1975).[8] The considerable gap between the initial work and Williamson's subsequent analysis in part reflected the incompatibility of Coase's original insights with the existing (neoclassical) paradigm. It was not until H.A. Simon's work on bounded rationality provided an alternative theoretical framework that Coase's analysis was significantly developed by Williamson and married with the issue of bounded rationality.

Coase argued in his 1937 article that firms exist because of transaction costs of market exchange. These costs are highest in conditions of rapid change and are attributable to two main sources. Firstly, the need to find out relevant price of inputs and exchanges is time consuming and expensive in rapidly changing circumstances. Secondly, market contracts are expensive; the contracting process may involve a costly process of evaluation and negotiation before a deal is made. These contractual costs are liable to be recurring since pervasive uncertainty encourages short term contracts. Parties will tend to avoid the creation of hostages to fortune associated with long term contracts in the face of significant uncertainty arising from informational strange loops.

These related costs mean that the frictionless ideal associated with neoclassical theory is liable to heavy qualification in practice. Williamson (1975) adds further interpretation to the sources of transaction costs by adding the concept of opportunism to transaction cost analysis. Though Williamson does not introduce the concept as such, it represents a natural extension of Adam Smith's principle of the rule of self interest in the market-place. However, Smith was concerned with demonstrating that the pursuit of self interest led the individual to promote his own interest and those of society by encouraging the direction of resources to their most efficient usage. The 'invisible hand' of the market-place converts self interest into social interest. Williamson's argument reverses Smith's conclusion. Opportunism is self interest seeking combined with deceitful intent; as long as parties are well informed deceit is impossible and opportunism not an issue. It is the introduction of bounded rationality and associated problems of *information impactedness* (one or more parties having access to information that cannot be costlessly displayed to other parties) that provide the conditions facilitating opportunism. Opportunism, or potential opportunism, may inhibit or distort the transactional process. As such it represents a major additional transaction cost beyond those identified by Coase.

An interesting feature of transaction cost analysis not considered by Williamson is that Coase-type transaction costs, Williamson-type transaction costs, and exchange uncertainty, may be substitutable one for the other. Bounded rationality creates exchange conditions surrounded by pervasive uncertainty concerning such matters as future costs, demand, innovation, competitor reaction, etc. Attempts to reduce such uncertainty creates the Coase-type contractual costs illustrated above. In addition, such exchanges may still be attended by costs of opportunism identified by Williamson.

Thus, in any exchange, bounded rationality may create three transactional problems – exchange uncertainty, direct contractual costs and opportunism. Coase-type contractual costs and Williamson type opportunism may be substituted for each other; for example a rigorously researched and tightly specified contract may reduce or eliminate potential opportunism, while a loosely drawn contract may provide a great deal of scope for opportunistic behaviour. Similarly, extensive search and contracting activity may eliminate much exchange uncertainty. However, due to strange loops there will frequently remain residual uncertainty that is either outwith the control of the contracting firms or too expensive to reduce. Unexpected competitor innovation is an example of the former source of exchange uncertainty.

Therefore, in exchange processes in which bounded rationality is an important consideration, problems in the exchange uncertainty and opportunism basket may be traded off against contractual costs of the Coase-type. Unfortunately for neoclassical theory, controlling, reducing or eliminating one of these elements is liable to be reflected in costs elsewhere in the transactional system. Pressing down on exchange uncertainty means contractual costs pop up. Sitting on top of contractual costs means exchange uncertainty and/or potential opportunism raise their ugly heads even higher. Squashing opportunism pushes up contractual costs.[9] Uncertainty, contractual costs and opportunism all represent transactional problems which may be at least partially interchangeable but which cannot be collectively eliminated. Attempting to impose the conditions appropriate to neoclassical optimising behaviour in such circumstances is like trying to flatten a particularly robust balloon. Unfortunately for neoclassical theory, there are many such balloons. The usual neoclassical response involves tightly closed eyes, crossed fingers, wishing and hoping.[10]

However, even though economists have been slow to recognise the bounded rationality implications of market transaction, historically they have been conscientious in their consideration of the bounded rationality problems associated with socialised or bureaucratic alternatives. Transaction costs have received close scrutiny only recently, but the inefficiencies associated with organisations insulated from the pressures of the price mechanism have evolved as an article of faith in economic thought. Von Mises (1951) argued that central planning was too bureaucratic and administratively inflexible since price is essential to rational economic calculations. Hayek (1945) argued that a socialist system would be unresponsive to changing supply and demand.[11]

Williamson (1975) provides a systematic comparison of market and organisational alternatives and associated costs. Unlike Von Mises and Hayek, Williamson is concerned with the market versus the firm, not the market versus the state. However, while his analysis of hierarchical costs is directed towards corporate organisation, it may generalise to state direction to the extent that both types of organisation involve bureaucracies. Organisation implies hierarchy, and the pattern of hierarchy is directly by bounded rationality considerations. Bounded rationality on the part of decision-makers requires delegation of tasks once the information burden reaches certain limits. Progressive decentralisation and delegation of tasks creates a hierarchical structure. Thus, the alternative to market organisation is hierarchy, as recognised in the title of Williamson's text.[12]

Just as bounded rationality creates transaction costs, so it also leads to organisational costs. The earlier analysis of Von Mises and Hayek has been overlain with work by organisation theorists in recent years. Williamson discusses cost of organisation associated with hierarchical substitution of market transaction. As discussed in Chapter 8 these may be summarised as the costs of decay, delay and distortion. Within hierarchies, serial reproduction of information leads to loss of information, lags in information transmission and warps in the quality of information, respectively.

As will be discussed further in Chapter 8, Williamson argues different organisational forms may be appropriate depending on the extent and severity of information problems. However, alternative organisational forms can at best reduce these information problems, not eliminate them. Decay, delay and distortion are informational costs basic to the organisational process.

There is a further cost of organisation identified by Williamson and that is the possibility that decision-makers may pursue their own objectives rather than those of their owners. Goals as well as information may be distorted in the organisational process. In this context, Adam Smith may be given credit as the first managerial theorist.

> The directors of . . . (joint-stock) companies, however, being the managers rather of other peoples' money than of their own, it cannot be expected, that they should watch over it with the same anxious vigilance with which the partners in a private copartnery frequently watch over their own. Like the stewards of a rich man, they are apt to consider attention to small matters as not for their masters honour, and very easily give themselves a dispensation from having it. Negligence and profusion, therefore, most always prevail, more or less, in the management of the affairs of such a company.
>
> Adam Smith (1776)[13]

Thus, organisations may incur substantial costs in resource allocations just as market exchange may be associated with transaction costs. It should be mentioned that even the last noted organisation cost, distortion of goals, is ultimately an information problem since it results from an information impactedness condition; owners are at an informational disadvantage compared to managers leading to a separation of ownership and control as we observed in Chapter 3. In modern managerial theories of the firm bounded rationality and information impactedness on the part of the owners means that management may be given discretion to maximise their utility, subject to constraints. Managerial theories may therefore be regarded as a special case of transaction cost problems in which difficulties in writing and enforcing employment contracts for managers leads to non-profit maximising behaviour.

Consequently, market and hierarchical alternatives have differing associated costs. The market exchange system incurs transaction costs while corporate decision making incurs organisation costs. Market exchange through the price system avoids the growth and elaboration of organisation and associated costs, while hierarchy replaces contractual costs with organisational costs.

Less obvious is the role of hierarchy in managing opportunism in any market exchange system substituted by organisation. Potential opportunism may be eliminated or reduced by screening, direct monitoring and penalising of individuals in the organisation. The improved access to information and direct control afforded by hierarchy facilitates such management. The duplicated search and evaluative processes associated with market exchange systems may also be substituted by one search/evaluative process. Such duplication is a contractual cost resulting from attempts to reduce opportunism; were both contracting parties in a market exchange system to trust each other, duplicated effort could be substituted by one search/evaluative process jointly paid for.

Thus, hierarchy and market exchange are alternative systems of economic organisation. We observed earlier, in the absence of information problems, there is nothing to choose between market and hierarchical alternatives on efficiency grounds as systems of resource allocation. Each leads to the same result. Costs of organisation on the one hand and transaction costs on the other, provide criteria by which such systems can be judged on efficiency grounds. These information-based problems are *the* discriminating feature of economic organisation.

CONCLUSION

In this chapter we have examined the nature of information problems more closely and demonstrated the close affinity between perfect knowledge and risk in terms of homogeneity and replicability of associated events. Consideration of the implications of these factors for decision-making led to the conclusion that risk situations are relatively trivial as far as the informational requirements and rules are concerned. It was also suggested that, in general, the areas we have already looked at under the heading of information problems are characterised by uncertainty rather than risk.

True uncertainty and information costs represent the dominant consideration in areas of firm, market and state organisation. It remains to be seen how they may influence the choice of economic organisation, and we shall discuss this question in later chapters.

6 Industrial Organisation and Bounded Rationality

> During the incessant struggle of all species to increase in numbers, the more diversified the descendents become, the better will be their chance of success in the battle for life.
>
> Charles Darwin, *The Origin of Species*

In this chapter we turn from investigating the general features of firm, market and state organisation to consideration of the implications of bounded rationality for one major field of economics; industrial organisation. We shall suggest that the interesting, non-trivial problems in this area derive directly from bounded rationality influences and we shall conclude that theoretical approaches in industrial organisation must build directly on this concept if they are to have any hope of empirical relevance. While concern here is limited to the field of industrial organisation, it would be extremely surprising if similar argument could not be developed against neoclassical theory in consumer theory also.

In this chapter also we give more attention to the problem of non-decomposability. Our aim was stated at the start to be the investigation of the effect of bounded rationality and non-decomposability in economic organisation, and so far we have concentrated more on bounded rationality problems. We attempt to rectify such bias in this chapter. Put at its simplest, if the world cannot be divided into independent individualist elements then aggregation will generate a distorted picture. Bohm (1980) clearly summarises the problems; 'a fragmentary self-world view . . . in scientific research tends very strongly to reinforce the general fragmentary approach because it gives men a picture of the whole world as constituted of nothing but an aggregate of separately existent "atomic building blocks" and provides experimental evidence from which is drawn the conclusion that this view is necessary and inevitable. In this way people are led to feel that fragmentation is nothing but an expression of the way everything really is and that anything else is impossible. So there is

84

very little disposition to look for evidence to the contrary. Indeed . . . even when such evidence does arise, as in modern physics, the general tendency is to minimise its significance or even to ignore it altogether' (p. 15).

While Bohm is mostly concerned with natural science, his conclusions apply with equal force to neoclassical theory in economics. The presumption that the economy is decomposable down to the level of individual product-market and households facilitates the development of models based on aggregation. However, if significant inter-relationships exist between parts of a system at any one point in time, then decomposability is not a reasonable assumption. This was a major argument in Kay (1979) and Kay (1982) and is also a theme developed in this chapter.

To start with however, we can utilise the results of the corporate striptease in Chapter 3 to identify the effect of bounded rationality on different facets of industrial behaviour in Table 6.1.

Each of the items on the right of the table results from bounded rationality on the part of the individual or group on the left hand side. By 'labour' we mean direct labour in the production process. We shall consider each aspect of bounded rationality in turn.

In the absence of information problems, there is no effective distinction between categories of labour. The difference between a carpenter, a welder and a bricklayer effectively reduces to an informational basis. Bounded rationality determines the specialisation, division and heterogeneity of labour.

Bounded rationality amongst owners facilitates managerial discretion. This can take two main forms in current theories of the firm. If bounded rationality can be regarded as primarily an afflication affecting owners, then managerial theories of the firm may be applicable. A managerial utility function may be maximised, usually subject some minimum profit constraint. If owners are at an informational disadvantage *vis-à-vis* managers, then managers may opportunistically pursue objectives other than profit; for example, sales, growth, perks, income, staff are all possible sources of managerial utility in so far as they contribute variously to prestige, status, or other components of managerial well being. However, if bounded rationality affects the decision-making capabilities of owners *and* managers, then it may be more appropriate to apply a satisficing model in which decision-makers do not maximise but instead aspire to a specific level of performance.

As Table 6.1 indicates, managers are themselves a consequence of

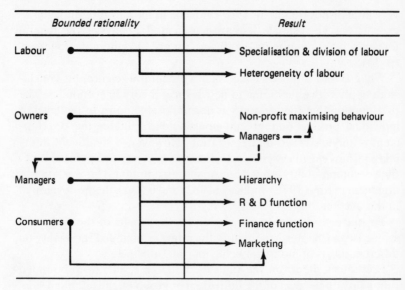

Bounded rationality	Result

- Labour ● → Specialisation & division of labour
- → Heterogeneity of labour
- Owners ● → Non-profit maximising behaviour
- → Managers - - -
- Managers ● → Hierarchy
- → R & D function
- Consumers ● → Finance function
- → Marketing

TABLE 6.1 *Selected effects of bounded rationality*

owner bounded rationality. The existence of bounded rationality on the part of the controlling managerial coalition creates functions based on supply of information, such as R & D and finance, and creates an internal organisation or hierarchy. The logic of function specialisation may parallel that for heterogeneity of labour. Finally, bounded rationality on the part of consumers and managers leads to a role being created for advertising and the marketing function in the firm.

These effects of bounded rationality follow naturally from our analysis of 'entrepreneurial Salome' in Chapter 3. If bounded rationality does not directly affect the information handling abilities of the relevant parties in any particular case then the 'result' disappears. For example, if owners have access to all relevant information, managerial effects (such as functional specialisation, hierarchy and non-profit maximising behaviour) dissolve if owners employ rational profit-maximising rules.

However, while these results of bounded rationality are of relevance in analysis of industrial organisation, there are further problems that also require consideration; how do issues of vertical integration, diversification, merger, takeover, regulation and antitrust policy fit into this analysis?

Ironically, the proper basis for analysis of vertical integration, diversification, merger and takeover has been available in published form for over four decades, yet has been studiously ignored by neoclassical theorists; R.H. Coase (1937) argued that the boundaries of the firm are determined by costs of using the price mechanism. These costs are information related costs of forming contracts in the market-place. Although Coase does not use the phrase bounded rationality, the term accurately describes the source of these costs of market transactions. Bounded rationality, when combined with potential opportunism on the part of transactors, results in high costs of forging detailed contracts at any point in time; further, inherent uncertainty means that market contracts will be short run and that costs of contracting will therefore be regular and recurring. The advantage of firm co-ordination is that potentially expensive control costs of this nature are substituted by entrepreneurial direction. While intra-firm co-ordination itself involves costs, in certain circumstances these may be less than the alternative costs involved in market trading. For example, strange loops based on potential opportunism on the part of trading partners may be eliminated by conducting the activity in-house.

However, until recently the standard approach to the vertical integration problem has been to identify cost savings that may be achieved by vertical integration, either backwards towards suppliers or forward towards the retailing end; for example, securing control over quality, rationalising physical location to reduce production costs, reducing variability in supply of inputs, etc. The problem is that there are no cost savings that could not in principle be obtained by market solutions, e.g. by establishing contracts, futures markets, etc. Our analysis in Chapter 2 indicates that as long as the neoclassical presumption of omniscience in market transactions lurks in the background, there is nothing that can be unequivocally stated in favour of vertical integration.[1] Not surprisingly, analysis of vertical integration in this context has led to generally inconclusive results.[2]

In retrospect, with the benefit of Coase's early articles and Williamson's recent work, the answer appears obvious. The market and the firm are alternative forms of economic organisation, both of which are liable to involve species-specific costs. While a particular vertical relation may be expressed alternatively in vertical integration or market exchange terms, superiority or inferiority of these alternatives must be judged according to their relative effectiveness in coping with the particular problems of bounded rationality in each case. In crudest terms, it boils down to comparing transaction costs with organisation costs for any particular economic activity. Coase's analysis indicated the role of transaction costs in determining boundaries, and it is this question of where the boundaries between firm and market should be set that underlies such varied issues as diversification, divestment, merger, takeover and multinational expansion.

Williamson (1975) represents a systematic attempt to lay the foundations for such a comparative analysis of economic organisation in terms of markets versus hierarchies (or firms). In doing so he interprets his system as contributing to an organisational failures framework. 'Organisational failure' is interpreted symmetrically as applying to both market failure and internal organisation failure (1975, p. 20). In one sense the term is unfortunate since it may be taken to imply a breakdown or potentially remedial defect; in this respect it is only a short step from suggesting an ideal state of the world to which policy should be directed, and the emptiness of Nirvanian economies. Williamson recognises the danger that 'failure' may be judged with respect to a frictionless ideal but argues that his concern is with comparative institutional choices, not with ideal states of the world (1975, p. 20). In this context, his use of the term 'organisational failures' is asymmetric since his work could easily be labelled as contributing to an 'organisational successes' framework. Once bounded rationality enters directly into analytical perspectives, choice of form of economic organisation boils down to relative success (or failure) in dealing with its consequences. Organisational success/failure are the two sides of the comparative institutional coin.

Williamson (1975) develops an explanation of vertical integration in terms of transaction costs of market trading involved in vertically related but disintegrated sectors. Vertical integration may harmonise interests, reduce potential opportunism and impose information exchanges to encourage co-operative behaviour (p. 104–5). These benefits must be set against costs of internal organisation; for example, as Williamson argues in Chapter 6, markets may evolve sanctions on opportunistic behaviour without requiring the extension of organisational boundaries, while enlarging the organisation may create a cumbersome bureaucracy with attendant management costs. Vertical integration may provide net benefits compared to a market solution – or it may not. Comparative analysis is required to decide relative effectiveness of alternative economic organisational forms.

As far as the problem of diversification is concerned, again neoclassical theory does not provide a useful framework.[3] As Marris (1971) argues, traditional theory of the firm is based on analysis of individual product-markets, with the corporation being treated as an aggregate of these product-markets. The presumed separability of product-markets implies the concept of a corporation whose boundaries are essentially arbitrary, since the portfolio of product-markets held by the corporation do not provide any benefits from joint effects; all costs and benefits are presumed decomposable to product-market level.

Marris points out that the typical corporation does not disaggregate in this fashion. These are usually common elements running through product-markets incorporated within organisational boundaries. Casual observation is sufficient to confirm this point. Shell in petroleum, ICI in chemicals, Ford in automobiles, Texas Instruments in electronics, all exploit strong commonalities in terms of market and/or technological links between product-markets. Synergistic bonds between corporate subsystems imply non-decomposability. Just as decomposition of water into constituent hydrogen and oxygen atoms would change the character of the system, so decomposition of ICI or Du Pont into individual product-markets would radically alter the nature of the corporation being described. Product-market bonding impairs decomposability just as chemical bonding requires a systemic approach to the analysis of chemical molecules.

This was one of the arguments used as a basis for a previous work (Kay, 1982) in a transaction cost analysis of the large diversified corporation. Where links exist between product-markets they may give rise to economies, as we saw in the case of Alten and Alski in Chapter 2. However, as we saw in Chapter 2 such gains may be exploited by market trading between Alten and Alski without the need for combination within our firm. Why then should corporate diversification take place at all if market exchange systems provide effective alternatives? The simple answer is, that in certain circumstances, corporate management may prove superior to market trading because exploitation of potential gains involves potentially higher transaction costs than management costs.

We shall argue in the next section below that this answer is in fact too simple; there are a rich variety of diversification strategies varying from modest differentiation of specific product-markets to full-blown conglomerate diversification. However we shall suggest that two specific forms of bounded rationality help contribute to explanation of corporate diversification strategy. Patterns of diversification only become potentially explicable if bounded rationality enters explicitly into the analysis.

To the extent that transaction cost analysis based on the concept of bounded rationality contributes to explanation of vertical integration and diversification, so also it provides a framework for analysing merger and take-over activity.[4] This will be an associated topic discussed in the next section.[5] However at this juncture we can summarise these issues of corporate behaviour and their market alternatives in Table 6.2 adding the topics of corporation and multinationals to complete coverage of major issues in industrial organisation.

The oval shapes in the central column illustrate the corporate boundaries for each particular topic. The market alternative in the right hand column substitutes a trade for corporate management in each example. In return for provision of a service (an input in the case of vertical integration, an idea in the case of innovation, technology or market links in the case of diversification merger and takeover, and technology transfer in the case of multinationals) the second party to the trade pays compensation to the originator of the service. Thus, a market exchange alternative to intra-firm exploitation of the potential efficiency gain always exists to the topics listed in the left hand column. Each corporate boundary may be broken up into a series of market transactions and if bounded rationality problems are absent there is every reason why they should be, since the price system encounters no informational hindrances to its smooth operation. Again, as in the case of entrepreneurial Salome, the entrepreneur can be resurrected once information problems are ignored and in this case eliminates the need for such industrial organisation solutions as vertical integration, diversification, corporate innovation, mergers, take-overs and multi-nationals.

Finally, there is no basis on which realistic guidelines for regulation and anti-trust policy can be developed in the absence of consideration of bounded rationality.[6] Here, the benefits and costs of state direction of industry must be set against and combined with the costs and benefits of firm and market organisation. We shall not give detailed consideration to this point here, but will illustrate it by reference to a simple example.

Suppose we have a classic problem for competition policy in which exploitation of economies of scale appears to be associated with monopoly power. For example let us assume the existence of a marvellous machine called a Hootenanny has been invented that is capable of producing the entire world demand for bagpipes.[7] The trouble is that the Hootenanny comes in one indivisible lump, which

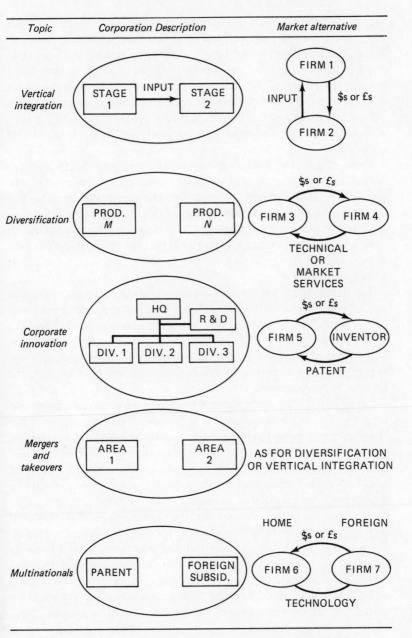

TABLE 6.2 *Industrial organisation, firms and markets*

means operating at levels less than 100 per cent of market share results in spare capacity and higher average costs for any individual firm. The Scottish government is faced with a problem; leaving the market to itself is liable to grant a monopoly position to the first firm quick enough to whip its Hootenanny into sufficiently high levels of operation as to be able to drive out smaller high cost producers. In an uncontrolled market situation there is liable to be a trade-off between economies of scale and monopoly profits from the point of view of society.

Presuming that we can ignore complications of potential technical or X-inefficiency and potential dynamic inefficiency,[8] the government problem reduces to one of potential allocative efficiency in this market: monopoly restriction of output through profit maximisation leads to a misallocation of resources by separating price from marginal cost. The usual recommended solution is that government intervention should impose marginal cost pricing in the absence of second best considerations.[9]

The details of the solution are well worked out in the literature and will not concern us further here. What is of interest is that our three basic forms of economic organisation – the firm, the market and the state – can all be involved in one form or another in any regulatory or anti-trust scheme. Choice of form of economic organisation, or the appropriate mix of forms, should be made in the light of bounded rationality consideration.

For example, state direction may be chosen as the solely appropriate form of economic organisation, as in the case of nationalisation of the Hootenanny. Alternatively, a private Hootenanny monopoly could be regulated by government ordinance to produce the desired solution, providing a mix of state and firm economic organisation. However, we could go even further and create a franchise system in which the government (or a regulated monopoly) leases limited property rights in the operation of the Hootenanny; for example each producer could own operating rights in the Hootenanny for a specific day in the month. He would establish labour, material and additional capital requirements for that day, and spend the rest of the month distributing and marketing that single day's output. Other producers would be granted rights for other days. Since the Hootenanny could in principle be worked to full capacity, economies of scale would be fully realised, while we have also created an atomistic market of thirty or so competing firms. This solution obviously involves state direction and firm management; where potential links exist between firms, say in marketing and distribution, market exchange can exploit further economies. Thus, all three forms of economic organisation may be involved in obtaining an ideal solution – or only one or two.

This is entirely consistent with the argument of Chapter 2. Until and unless information problems are explicitly incorporated in the analysis, all manner of weird, wonderful and impracticable solutions may be regarded as legitimate contenders. In practice, each form would involve associated information based costs; nationalisation would involve costs of bureaucracy and bureaucratic regulation, while franchise allocation would involve costs of this nature plus those associated with market exchange; in this case one obvious set of costs are those of recontracting labour, material and capital for each production period. Heterogeneity and lack of consistency in the administration of the Hootenanny and its associated labour force are also liable to lead to auditing and metering problems for the production process. Separability of production for each firm may also be a problem.

Each of these problems reduce to information problem and bounded rationality sources and lead to a potential set of criteria for discriminating between potential solutions. Discussion of alternative solutions is meaningless in the absence of such considerations.

As we would expect from the discussion in Chapter 2, analysis of non-trivial problems in industrial organisation not only requires recognition of the existence of bounded rationality, but in fact must revolve around the concept as a central focus. However, the effect of bounded rationality depends on individual circumstances and therefore we must probe deeper to incorporate the concept in specific theoretical frameworks. The fact that information problems underpin transaction and organisation costs suggests that such problems will tend to be characterised by strange loops and, indeed, this is the case. Strategic shifts of corporate boundaries are usually non-repeatable unique events in which critical knowledge may only be obtainable after the event as a consequence of undertaking the strategic move itself. For example, the merger literature illustrates the difficulties involved in measuring and judging the effects of specific proposed mergers. Unexpected problems, disappointing results and surprise difficulties are recurrent themes in this area. See Scherer (1980, pp. 127–41) for a review of recent merger studies in this spirit.

We shall concentrate on two particular topics, diversification and internal organisation in the next section to consider further the role of bounded rationality in industrial organisation. Parallel discussion of both of these topics has been pursued in the managerial literature under the banners of corporate strategy and structure respectively. We shall discuss both in turn.

CORPORATE STRATEGY AND BOUNDED RATIONALITY

In Kay (1982) a transaction cost based analysis was developed to analyse patterns of development for the large modern corporation. Corporate strategy and structure were central topics and we shall outline here and develop further some of the major points that were argued in this work. We shall start by looking at diversification strategy in this section.[10]

Suppose we return to the basic example of Alten and Alski discussed in Chapter 2, and introduce the further possibility that Alski believes that it could improve the quality of its ski design by drawing on the expertise of an aerodynamics engineer employed by a small local firm constructing helicopters, Rotor Ltd. For simplicity, we assume all three firms are of similar size. There are now two sets of potential links that may provide economies, between Alski and Alten, and between Alski and Rotor. We can illustrate suggested potential links in Figure 6.1 below.

As was argued in Chapter 2, we may identify numerous common elements between Alski and Alten that may give rise to potential

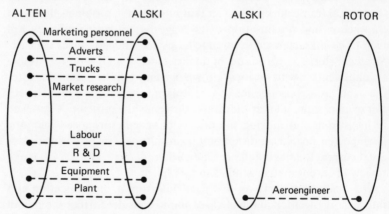

FIGURE 6.1　*Potential links between product-markets*

economies. Without attempting to exhaustively discuss all those identified in Figure 6.1, wherever a potential link exists it may give rise to a potential economy; for example by facilitating specialisation and division of labour, or by improved exploitation of an indivisible resource. To take some examples, increased specialisation and consequent productivity of marketing personnel may be permitted by having two aluminium sports goods to sell; research and development costs may be spread over two products and duplication avoided; the increased range of application and output for common tools and equipment may permit better utilisation of indivisible resources and reduction in spare capacity.

However, in the case of Alski and Rotor there is only the potential common element of the aerodynamic component of design as illustrated in Figure 6.1. If we exclude the possibility of state direction for simplicity of analysis, we have a choice between firm and market organisation if we wish to exploit these potential benefits involving Alski.

The relative ease with which managerial direction is likely to coordinate and administer product-markets combined within one firm is likely to be directly related to the number of links between product-markets. The more links, the greater management familiarity and the easier assimilation of product-markets within corporate boundaries as in the case of Alski and Alten. In the event, where there is perfect or complete links between product-markets, we have identical product-markets and no qualitative difference in managerial problems for firm combinations only potential differences in scale. By way of contrast, the information problems involved in exploiting links between product-markets by market transaction will be directly related to the number of links. Each link will generally imply precise and detailed contracts; the costs of market-trading increase with the number of links to be contracted.

In crudest terms, firm coordination of economies is potentially cheap and easy when there are a larger number of links, market exchange of gains from economies is potentially highly expensive. The reverse applies; in the case of Alski and Rotor, firm combination is liable to mix two extremely differentiated systems each with their own specific managerial problems. Attempts to transfer managerial skills across these boundaries may be counterproductive. On the other hand, exploitation of the single potential economy can be simply obtained by the market device of purchasing consulting services of the aerodynamics engineer.

In short, increasing potential links eases the bounded rationality problems involved in firm co-ordination and increases bounded rationality problems involved in market organisation. The conclusion appears obvious; systems that are potentially richly linked should exploit economies by firm co-ordination, systems that are poorly linked should exploit links by market trading. In circumstances where the gains from potential economies are exceeded by the costs involved in economic organisation neither option should be adopted.

Therefore bounded rationality considerations involved in transaction costs of exploiting economies implies that firms will be composed of richly-linked product-markets. Some are – some are not. This aspect of bounded rationality explains specialisation by firms; it does not explain diversification around loose or non-existent links as, for example, in the conglomerate case.

In order to cope with different patterns of diversification, a second stage analysis is required in which an alternative effect of bounded rationality shapes the form diversification takes. The existence of links between product-markets may provide potential economies, but there may be an associated danger; where links exist they may create mutual or common vulnerability on the part of linked product-markets.

We can illustrate this with reference to Figure 6.1. Suppose both sets of links are exploited by firm co-ordination. Because of the rich links between Alten and Alski, the whole business may enter into decline if one link suffers external attack. For example, suppose a novel sport developed as a substitute to both skiing and tennis – the market links here would result in simultaneous decline of both markets. Suppose a competitor developed a superior aluminium alloy that improved the quality of skis and rackets, then this development would attack both products together through their material link. Suppose a competitor employed a skilled designer specialising in aluminium sports goods, both products could be attacked through their labour link if a competitor develops a superior design team or finds a specially talented individual – and so on. On the other hand, the differentiated nature of product markets involved in an Alski/Rotor merger virtually ensure that external attacks will be localised and affect only individual product-markets – unless, for example, a competitor develops superior aerodynamic qualities in both product-markets by access to superior designer skills.

Potential vulnerability to surprise external attack is directly related to the extent of linking between product-markets. Alski/Alten is highly vulnerable due to its rich interconnections. Alski/Rotor is only partially vulnerable to external attack since the effect of any specific threat to product-markets is localised to that product-market, with a single potential exception in the design link.

The environment is a crucial factor in determining the potential danger in firms exploiting links. Suppose we have a stable environment with long product life cycles and slow changing technology – such as the Swiss watch industry before the development of electronic watches. In those circumstances firms may exploit product market linkages with low expectation of external threats to these connections. However if we have an environment characterised by short product life cycles and rapidly changing technology, such linkages may prove potentially fatal. The effect of a single innovation may be relayed along a specific link, attacking all the firms product-markets simultaneously – as in the case of the impact of electronic technology on the Swiss watch industry.

If firms could anticipate the form specific threats will take, product-markets that are expected to obsolesce could be phased out and new opportunities adopted, to pre-empt the catastrophic effect that simultaneous decline in linked product-markets would have. However innovation, like mugging, tends to be both surprising and swift. All that can be reasonably expected of the decision-maker is that he or she can rank environments in terms of danger of mugging – or innovation. Strange loops in the assessment of potential future threats pre-empt systematic and precise anticipation of future events.

In environments where innovation potential is high, we would expect decision-makers to evolve strategies that will localise the effect of external threats. One method by which such localisation of potential impact may be achieved is by adopting a conglomerate strategy, based on product-markets having minimal or no linkages between product-markets.[11] However, there is another strategy that can achieve this, the related–linked strategy. This strategy localises the impact of technological change by creating a 'chaining' effect around short-range links. The chain effect may indirectly link all products to each other – but the effective link changes between groupings of product markets.

Therefore mergers may intentionally *avoid* linkages as well as be intended to pursue and exploit them in other cases. In the former circumstances, merger would be expected to contribute to survival potential not profitability. Consequently the absence of profits as a consequence of merger need not signal the failure of the merger, contrary to the interpretation of some industry analysts. It may well be that the objective of merger was not profit in the first place.

It is important to note the difference between this explanation of diversification and the portfolio theory of diversification which interprets corporate diversification as a risk spreading activity. This latter approach requires specification of (a) possible future profitability states (b) expected mean profitability (c) variance in profitability. The portfolio theory is subject to the same objections raised in Chapter 5 against loose and inappropriate interpretation of uncertain situations as risky. Loopy situations in which the firm faces the possibility of surprise attack from external innovation cannot be twisted into the rigid structure of portfolio theory. The decision-maker faces a truly uncertain environment in which there is an asymmetric emphasis on the possibility of life cycle decline rather than life cycle growth. In such circumstances to express the decision in risky terms is to misrepresent it; all we assume the decision-maker is able to do is to order the environment in terms of surprise potential. This much weaker requirement is sufficient to allow us to examine and explain patterns of diversification.

The strategies illustrated below are a series of 'ideal type' descriptions. It should be borne in mind that actual strategies are liable to be more complex in practice. For example, firms may exploit rich links in some sectors, hedge their bets by avoiding links in others; also the product-markets operated by the firm may differ in their vulnerability to technological change. For simplicity we assume internal consistency in the corporate strategy in terms of patterns of links, and also consistency in the gradient of technological change associated with the corporate environment. From our arguments we would expect corporate strategy to evolve away from tightly linked strategies to strategies exploiting only short-range local links as environmental technological change increases.

Figure 6.2 is intended to be suggestive of trends rather than indicative of precise forms strategy will take. The rapidity of technological change increases and product life cycles shorten as we move from left to right in Figure 6.2. In conditions of relatively stable technologies and slow changing product life cycles, firms will tend to pack links tightly as a corporate strategy, whereas in conditions of rapidly changing technology and short product life cycles, product-markets will tend to be loosely linked, if at all. This trend is illustrated by a shift from single/dominant product/richly linked strategies at the left of the diagram to related–linked (*A* and *B*) and conglomerate (*C* and *D*) strategies at the right of Figure 6.2. Strategies switch from richly linked to poorly linked as we move from left to right in order to

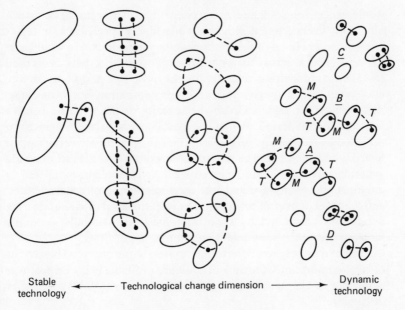

Stable
technology ◄——— Technological change dimension ———► Dynamic
technology

FIGURE 6.2   *Corporate strategies*

localise the effect of external changes. The related–linked strategy involves a series of different links connecting product-markets in A and B. Individual market (M) and technological (T) links extend over a short-range in the strategy; although a chain effect may ultimately connect each product-market to each other through intermediaries, the local nature of individual links means specific external threats would inflict limited damage. Similarly the links in the conglomerate cluster at local level; between clusters there is minimal links so external threats are localised here also.

Size of firm is liable to be an important consideration in practice. The smaller the firm, the less liable it is to have the luxury of freely designing its own strategy – there is likely to be a trade-off between exploiting multiple economies by concentrating on a single product-market or closely related product-markets versus achieving a sufficient spread of activities consistent with the technological threat potential of the environment.

If these patterns hold in practice, they would facilitate exploitation of product diversification, merger, takeover and overall concentration trends in industrial organisation. In Kay (1982), it was argued that evidence was consistent with these expectations; for example we would expect conglomerate and related–linked strategies to be associated with science based industry while highly specialised strategies would tend to clump in the low technology industries. We would also expect a general across-the-board rise in inventive activity as accrued for US manufacturing industry in the post-war period up to the mid-sixties to lead to a general shift in corporate strategies towards less richly linked strategies. Given the rapidity of the rise in inventive activity over this period, we would expect conversion of strategies to be achieved by merger and take-over rather than by the slower option of internal development. The extent of corporate diversification would generally increase, the rise in inventive activity would be paralleled by a merger/take-over wave and increased importance of conglomerates, and the level of overall concentration (e.g. the level of manufacturing net output controlled by the 100 largest firms) would generally increase due to the subsequent creation of larger firms.

Each of these expectations found support in the observed behaviour of large corporations, the bulk of evidence available being on post-war behaviour of US manufacturing industry. See Kay (1982) for further discussion.

We can now summarise the effect of bounded rationality on corporate strategy. Bounded rationality in market exchange and associated transaction costs creates an incentive for managers to build their corporate strategies around highly specialised and richly linked systems. Bounded rationality and strange loops in the face of the mugging effect of external technological change leads to an incentive for managers to diversify into loosely related or unrelated areas to localise the effect of external attacks. The first form of bounded rationality will be dominant in stable conditions, the second form will be dominant in rapidly changing environments. When we recognise the possibility of a spectrum of environments ranked in order of technological change, the managerial problem becomes one of designing an appropriate strategy in which exploitation of economies is traded-off against vulnerability to mugging. The appropriate strategy will be determined by the level of environmental technological change. Thus, the environment is the ultimate designer of corporate strategy.

STRATEGY AND STRUCTURE

Writers such as Loasby have suggested that it is paradoxical that in the theory of the firm, the firm does not exist. We have shown in Chapter 2 how this state of affairs came about. The field of industrial organisation is the applied branch of the theory of the firm; also paradoxically, organisation itself is excluded from analysis in traditional industrial organisation. The concept of the firm and internal organisation both require explicit recognition of bounded rationality issues. In this section we consider how the structure of the firm can be analysed in this respect.

The environment fashions strategy which in turn fashions structure. The second step in this argument has been well analysed by Chandler (1966) and Williamson (1975), and developed in the context of transaction cost analysis in Kay (1982).[12] Hierarchy itself is necessarily explicable in bounded rationality terms; as Williamson (1975) argues, if the scale and/or complexity of a given managerial task increases beyond certain limits, so managerial bounded rationality is liable to create problems of monitoring, control and decision-making, leading to progressive delegation and specialisation of tasks. As scale/complexity of decision-making increases, bounded rationality leads to delegated tasks being broken up into further delegated segments and specialised tasks being separated into even more specialised components; hierarchy results.

In Kay (1982) analysis of the relationship between strategy and structure was based on the effect of links in the corporate strategy. We can briefly discuss the relationship with the help of the diagrams below. The examples below are similar to those in Kay (1982). We start from the premise that bounded rationality requires decentralisation; the next task is to decide *how* to decentralise.

We assume that bounded rationality considerations requires each of the four firms in the above diagram to separate out into three or four major decision-making units. However the firms differ in their corporate strategies. The aluminium sports goods firm is richly linked, the engineering firm has strong technological links, the confectionery firm has strong market links, while the conglomerate exploits no significant links between its product-markets.

The problem reduces to one of deciding the boundaries of the delegated units. The principle used is one of creating 'natural decision-units' (Williamson). In Kay (1982) it was argued that interfunctional relations for a given product-market would be generally weaker than intrafunctional links between product-markets where technological or market links exist. To give examples: for the engineering firm above exploiting strong technological links, R & D personnel in different product-markets are liable to spend more time

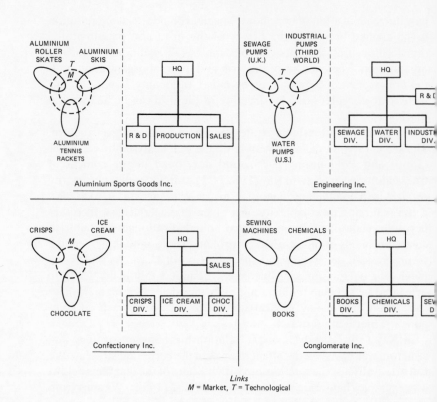

Links
M = Market, *T* = Technological

FIGURE 6.3   *Strategy and structure*

talking to each other and transferring technological know how
between product-markets than they are to spend time talking to
marketing personnel in their home products markets; marketing
personnel in the confectionery firm are more liable to spend time
co-ordinating and exchanging sales and market information between
product-markets than they are to spend time talking to production
personnel in the same product-market.

The boundaries around natural decision-units should be drawn to
minimise necessary exchanges of information. In the case of the
aluminium sports goods firm, the strong markets and technological
links are liable to swamp the weaker inter-functional links, encouraging a functional or U-form structure (Williamson, 1975) as indicated in
Figure 6.3. In the case of the conglomerate, the absence of significant
links means that the weak inter-functional links become the dominant

consideration, leading to the creation of a multidivisional or *M*-form organisation.

The other two cases, of the engineering and confectionery firm, are less clear cut and in practice would require careful consideration of actual circumstances. However, the two suggested associated structures may be reasonable if our simple assumption of weak/strong relationships hold; weak interfunctional relationship may encourage divisionalisation in both cases, with the technological link in the case of the engineering firm, and the market link in the case of the confectionery firm, leading to R & D and marketing respectively being taken out of divisions as special functions. These solutions are illustrated in Figure 6.3.[13]

Strategy thus determines structure; the extent and content of links dictates the appropriate form of internal organisation. It should be borne in mind that although the principles should generalise to more complex organisational strategies, the solutions may not suggest themselves as clearly as in the above examples – for example the related–linked has a series of links which in themselves constitute pressure towards functional or U-form organisation, yet since the links in this strategy are only of restricted scope covering a limited range of product-markets a functional organisation would create ill-sorted 'unnatural' decision units. Full scale divisionalisation would cut across technological and market links making co-ordination of economies more difficult. If the partial linking was consistent in the sense that where links existed they ran through all the product markets such as for the engineering and confectionery firm, then partial divisionalisation with auxiliary functions as in these cases might be appropriate. The difficulty with messier strategies like the related–linked is that although they may be based on a sound logic in strategic terms they may present real problems in structural terms since they lack the consistency in internal relationships that facilitated analysis of strategy and structure above.

We can demonstrate the potential complexities of strategy/structure relationships and their possible resolution, by using the example of Garden, Aluminium and Plastics Inc. (GAP Inc.) in Figure 6.4.

GAP conducts a related–linked strategy based around three main links; plastics technology in radio casings, rainwear, cutlery and garden gnomes; the gardening market in the case of garden gnomes, manure, seeds, and garden tools; and aluminium technology in the case of garden tools, beer cans and aerosols.[14] Although the links which define its respective businesses may provide potential economies and points

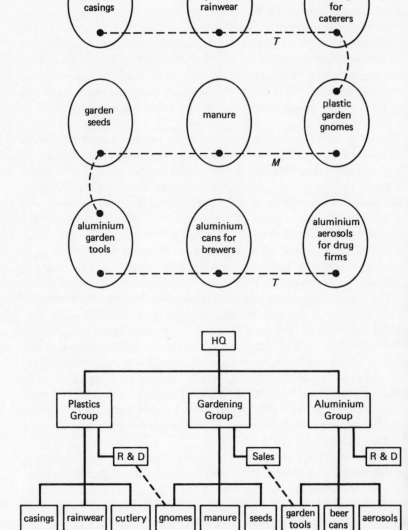

FIGURE 6.4   *Strategy and possible structure for GAP*

of vulnerability, their local nature helps to buffer the firm against any specific external attack. We assume that each of the businesses are of comparable size say, in terms of value added, and therefore map them as roughly equal areas on Figure 6.3.

GAP's pattern of diversification may have attractive properties in strategic terms; while economies can be exploited through the market and technological links, each link is restricted in terms of the number of product-markets it covers. Profitability *and* survival in high technology environment may be facilitated by such a strategy. However in structural terms it provides real problems; a pure functional organisation would lump together diverse and unrelated fields, while full divisionalisation would cut across and separate synergistic links between product-markets.

We can approach the problem in two stages. Firstly, if we take each business – plastics, garden and aluminium – in turn, then we might suggest a divisional basis for each business with the local links being drawn out as special functions; for example R & D in plastics and aluminium, marketing in gardening. The logic is essentially the same as for the engineering and confectionery cases above. The appropriate base for garden gnomes and garden tools is not clear-cut since they are both product-markets around which two links pivot; to obtain a balance between divisions in order that groups are of comparable importance, we allocate garden tools to aluminium and make plastics our gnome home. Hopefully, we have created 'natural decision' units as far as possible. Each business constitutes a group based around a common link; the link is exploited by an appropriate special function while the weaker inter-functional relations are exploited within product-market decisions. Full-scale divisionalisation would cut across the definitive business link while complete functional specialisation would add little in terms of information advantages outside the definitive link while inhibiting inter-functional co-ordination for a specific product-market. The mixed organisational form offers a method of settling decision-making boundaries around cognate resources as well as providing qualified profit-centre advantages. These are illustrated in Figure 6.4.

Secondly, the remaining control, coordination and minor strategic problems can be dealt with at group headquarters where group management can overview the business segment as a whole. At a higher level, general office can oversee each of the groups in terms of their relation to the corporate strategy as a whole. Further, profit centre status can also be accorded to each of the groups, adding a second layer of divisionalisation in the corporation. The resulting corporate structure is one which attempts to minimise frictional costs of information exchanges and task coordination across decision-making units.

The pivotal product-markets, gnomes and garden tools, are connected by dotted lines to plastics R & D and garden marketing respectively. The appropriate relationship may depend in practice as much on inter-group politics as on any intrinsically logical relationship. However co-ordination across these decision-making units is liable to be desirable in this case and we indicate·this in Figure 6.4.

Though it may appear complex, the internal organisation in Figure 6.4 is based on simple principles. The resulting structure accommodates a strategy which may be attractive in terms of profitability and survival objectives but which cannot be easily fitted to the simple organisation forms of Figure 6.3 without creating information handling and co-ordination problems. Therefore we have designed a structure which intentionally economises on bounded rationality by reducing information flows and co-ordination problems *across* decision-making units as far as possible, consistent with the principle of creating 'natural decision units'.

We illustrate a related aspect of the relationship between strategy and structure in Figure 6.5 using the example of Consumer Goods Inc. Consumer Goods Inc. is split into five levels, each having two decision-making centres; we concentrate on the path in the organisational tree leading to the leather sports goods sections. We have concocted the example to illustrate the basic principle that links between centres tend to diminish at higher levels in the system, and vice versa. For example, there is only a single link (say departmental store retail outlets) between the two major divisions, leisure and kitchenware. Sports goods, camping and travel have an additional marketing link, say in advertising through recreational journals. Within sports goods, market research costs can be spread across both types of sports goods indicating a further link, while at the lowest (product-market) level, a whole range of technological links may be available as in the Alten/Alski example. Designing hierarchy to minimise information flows across decision-making centres leads naturally to an arrangement whereby the most richly linked decision-making centres are combined at the base of the organisational pyramid. The more loosely linked any particular groups of activities are, the higher level in the organisational pyramid before they are combined within one decision-making centre. This is a corollary of the

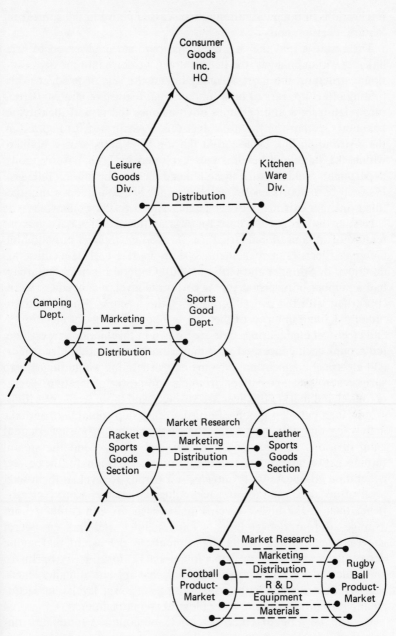

FIGURE 6.5 *Synergy and partial structure for consumer goods*

implications of bounded rationality discussed above in the context of 'natural decision units'.

The result is that the organisational pyramid is observed to *nest* linkages within linkages; the deeper down we delve into the organisational structure, the more strongly linked the sets of product. This nesting effect appears to be a fundamental feature of strategy/structure relationships and becomes obvious once the task of identifying common elements between product sets is performed. In Figure 6.5 the distribution link exploited at the top level nests or is contained within the fuller market linkages exploited by both leisure goods departments, while in turn these linkages nest in the market linkages between both sports goods sections, which are contained within the fuller linkages existing between leather sports goods sections.

Nesting of linkages as a basis for organisational design is a common feature of organisational structure. A good example is provided by General Electrics management system in the early seventies as described by Springer and Hofer (1980). General Electrics hierarchy had a number of levels; at top or corporate level, management were concerned with the overall strategy of the business which could be broadly defined in terms of the slim technological link of electronics and electrical engineering. One step down in this hierarchy were the ten groups each concerned with major businesses within electronics and electrical engineering, in some cases spanning whole industries, such as aerospace, consumer products and power generation. Technological and market linkages are stronger and more frequent within groups than between groups. In turn, each group contained approximately five divisions, such as the home entertainment, housework and lamp divisions for the consumers products groups and the steam turbine, gas turbine and nuclear energy product divisions for the power generation group. As for group *vis-à-vis* corporate level, at the lower level of divisions, market and technological linkages were typically richer than at the higher level. Finally, each division contained an average of four departments. Commonalities and linkages were generally very strong within departments to the extent that some departments were organised on a functional (U-form) basis (Springer and Hofer, p. 454). In each case the link that appears at higher levels is generally contained within relationships at lower levels, the latter adding further market and technological commonalities.[15]

We can now tie together the effect of bounded rationality on corporate strategy. Bounded rationality in the face of complex problems leads to the need to create hierarchy. Bounded rationality in terms of the information handling problems of co-ordinating decision-making units leads to creation of natural 'natural decision units' to keep information exchanges 'in-house' as far as possible. Thus, bounded rationality both creates the need for hierarchy and determines the form it takes.

CONCLUSION

This chapter represents a natural extension of the arguments first introduced in Chapter 2. Bounded rationality lies at the heart of major issues in the theory of the firm and industrial organisation, and to ignore it is to omit the central influence in the behaviour of firms.

In Chapters 1 and 2 it was argued that the major issues in economics revolved around information problems and problems of non-decomposability. In this chapter we have examined industrial organisation questions from this point of view and discussed how information problems are pervasive and fundamental. These information problems are liable to take the form of strong loops and true uncertainty as discussed in Chapter 5, and we have looked at how the transaction cost literature may help to analyse such problems.

To look at major resource allocation questions without considering the role of bounded rationality is rather like trying to understand how a car works while ignoring the engine. However this is how mainstream neoclassical theory operates. The major areas examined in this chapter, including the strategy and structure of firms, cannot be properly assimilated within the neoclassical calculus because of congenital design defects in the framework. Yet all too often such warnings have been ignored in economics. Caves (1980) a leading industrial organisation theorist, epitomises the prevailing attitude of many economists in a review article of the corporate strategy and structure literature in the *Journal of Economic Literature*, economics major review journal:

> I shall not let professional modesty blur an important conclusion: well-trained professional economists could have carried out many of the research projects cited in this paper more proficiently than did their authors, who were less effectively equipped by their own disciplines. If one accepts the weak postulate that the firm is a purposive organization maximizing some objective function, it

follows that its strategic and structural choice represents a constrained optimization problem. My reading is the students of
business organization with disciplinary bases outside of economics
would accept that proposition but have lacked the tools to follow its
blueprint. Constrained-maximization problems are mother's milk to
the well-trained economist. (p. 88)

Mother's milk has curdled somewhat in recent years. The statement
in fact tells us more about the state of economics than the state of the
business policy and organisational behaviour being surveyed by Caves.
I would only add that my experience conflicts with Caves in that I
have not found students of business organisation deprived of an
economics background optimistically awaiting the arrival of economics
doctors with their optimising balms and salves.

As far as non-decomposability is concerned, this issue is fundamental to the analysis above. Linkages and commonalities between
product-markets means that disaggregation to the level of individual
product-market description distorts the innate non-decomposability of
such systems. Instead of pretending that such linkages do not exist,
theory should incorporate them as fundamental aspects and features of
economic systems where appropriate.

Chapter 7 represents a logical extension of this chapter in looking at
one further issue in industrial organisation, the existence and form of
multinationals. We have argued that transaction cost analysis is useful
in examining the behaviour of corporations by providing guidelines as
to where the boundaries between firm and market should lie, and since
multinationalism is the extension of corporate boundaries on an
international scale we should expect to find transaction cost analysis
applicable in this context as well. As we shall see, this approach does
facilitate analysis in this area also. Multinationalism is characterised by
distinctive patterns of behaviour, but useful insights may be generated
using the same techniques and perspectives adopted in this chapter.

7　Multinational Enterprise[1]

you gotta have a Yen,
to make your Mark,
if you want to make money
10 c.c.

The growth of multinational enterprise (corporations conducting a significant promotion of their operations in foreign countries) has become a major issue in recent years. Though the first multinationals evolved in the 19th century, it is during the post-war period that they have become major economic and political issues. They have been variously seen as threats to national policy, exporters of capital and jobs, autonomous sovereign empires, symbols of a new imperialism, and symptoms of a healthy capitalist development.[2]

Our concern in this chapter is with a more fundamental issue; why do multinationals exist? We hope to show that the growth of multinational enterprises is neither as natural or obvious as might appear from superficial observation, and that our analysis may contribute in this area also.

In Chapter 6, we have suggested that corporate strategy is determined by trading off the gains from specialisation against the gains from diversification. The ultimate choice among strategic alternatives is determined by the level of environmental technological change, and the resulting 'mugging' effect on links. The heart of the analysis is the identification of non-decomposable links at more microanalytic levels than that associated with the traditional product level analysis of neoclassical theory, combined with bounded rationality considerations. In this chapter we consider the possibility of analysing multinational strategy using this transaction analysis approach. As well as contributing to the analysis of multinational enterprise, it is hoped that this exercise will demonstrate the usefulness of our framework when applied to one specific area in industrial organisation. Non-decomposability in the form of market, technological and country linkages will also be examined as major features of the multinational phenomenon.

111

A central point for our analysis so far is that market and technological links may be double-edged in terms of their ability to create potential economies and common vulnerabilities to external threat. Consequently, consistent with this perspective, we argue that multinational enterprise should exploit gains from either hedging (avoidance of links) or synergy (exploitation of economies from links). We shall argue that pursuit of economies rather than hedging is a more likely motive for multinational expansion, though the latter also may contribute to the formulation of multinational strategy.

Our basic framework developed earlier requires extension in the chapter. Analysis of domestic corporate strategy involves consideration of the existence or absence of specific market and technological linkages; when multinational strategy is involved, a further set of linkages become important, country specific linkages.

We can demonstrate this in Figure 7.1 with an example of a US manufacturer of personal computers. It makes two major lines, Nero and Zero, and is now considering two strategic alternatives: domestic diversification or multinational expansion. We presume Nero, Zero, and any possible diversification involve similar markets and technologies within the US national boundaries, while multinational expansion would involve building overseas plants to sell Nero and Zero in overseas markets. Figure 7.1 illustrates the present strategy of the firm.

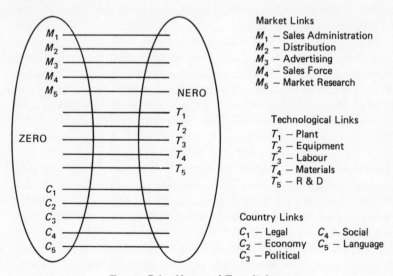

FIGURE 7.1 *Nero and Zero linkages*

Nero and Zero are so closely related in markets (M-links) and technologies (T-links) that they represent a near case of economies of scale. Shared resources in sales administration, distribution, advertising, sales force and market research permit economies to be drawn on the market side, while a shared technological base facilitates economies in plant, equipment, labour, materials and R & D.

There is a further set of links identified in Figure 7.1 that was not part of our analysis in Chapter 6. These are country-specific linkages (C-links) that permit resource economies due to common characteristics associated with single country operations. Nero and Zero can exploit a number of advantages in this respect. A shared language and legal framework, common social and economic characteristics, and political context may provide economies, particularly informational economies. As with shared markets and technologies, country type economies may be partially transferable between countries – for example, US experience and knowledge in some of these areas may extend fairly easily to Canadian operations, but is less likely to be applicable to Japanese subsidiaries. Further, country type linkages, like market and technological linkages, may be vulnerable to mugging; concentration in one country may generate associated economies, but individual links may also make the firm vulnerable to, say, changes in tax policy, union legislation, political coups, etc. Thus, country level linkages may provide a double-edged sword like market and technological linkages in terms of economies and environmental threat. Country links may facilitate internal economies in information based resources, but also may make the firm vulnerable to country-specific 'surprises'. The major difference is that country specific threats are not liable to take the form of technological innovation.

This provides a basis for analysis of multinational strategy. As with other forms of corporate strategy, multinational enterprise must provide economies or hedging potential to be justified, and linkages still represent the basic currency around which our analysis must develop.

An interesting feature of our argument below is that, contrary to popular interpretation in general, multinational expansion is neither obvious nor inexorable. Instead, the existence of alternative strategies and various disadvantages of multinational expansion usually require a peculiar combination of circumstances before it is undertaken. We can illustrate this below by considering the synergy and hedging motives in turn.

Firstly, for a multinational enterprise, economies are likely to be particularly elusive. Locating a subsidiary abroad typically requires separate plant and equipment, with a separate labour force, selling in separate, distinctive markets. Even if there are similar market and technological developments between parent and foreign subsidiary, spatial separation and distinctive markets will generally inhibit exploitation of economies across national borders. For example, in the case of our personal computer manufacturer above, let us suppose it is considering opening up multinational operations in the UK. We may consider what economies from links, or 'synergy' in Ansoffs (1965) analysis, are potentially achievable.

On the market side, (M-links) economies will be very difficult, if not impossible, to realise. The separate distribution system, retail outlets, sales force, and advertising channels mean that marketing and sales efforts must be paralleled and duplicated on both continents. In this respect multinational enterprises will not provide exploited synergies from increased specialisation and division of labour and improved utilisation of physical indivisibilities. Further, distinctive buying behaviour of consumers in different countries is also likely due to the bundles of country-specific information that must be assimilated by the firm to produce and market in a foreign country. Thus, the expansion of multinational enterprise is facilitated by firm-specific information, such as R & D, and inhibited by country-specific information, such as marketing and legal know-how. It follows that multinational enterprise typically represents a potentially expensive strategic alternative in terms of synergy sacrifices. To the extent that there are limits on the firm's access to capital, multinational enterprise fails to exploit non-informational market and technological synergies that may generally be expected from alternative options of domestic expansion or diversification. In addition, it may create significant diseconomies of country level information to set against the specific economies of information that multinational operations can exploit. The dilemma for firms contemplating expansion is that multinational enterprise involves additional dangers that the analysis in the preceding section may help to illustrate. In terms of Figure 7.1, multinational expansion by our personal computer manufacturer would sacrifice the M-links, the C-links and all T-links except R & D.

Further, while product-market links between parent and foreign subsidiary do not provide sources of synergy except in the case of economies of firm-specific R & D information, such links still represent areas of common vulnerability to external technological change. For example, similar market characteristics between UK and

US operations mean that both operations are vulnerable to specific product innovations in the personal computer field, while shared technological elements mean that both operations may be mutually vulnerable to individual process innovations. In short, multinational operations exposes the firm to the hazards of technological mugging associated with specialisation strategies without the corresponding gains from market and technological synergy (with the single exception of informational economies). Links may exist and create strong vulnerability to external environmental mugging, but they are typically dry in terms of potential synergy. In contrast, domestic diversification allows the firm to balance the benefits of a richer, varied mix of physical, human, and informational economies against the hazards of the common links between respective product-markets. For example, our personal computer manufacturer may introduce a new personal computer, Hero bearing a family relationship to Nero and Zero in technological terms. Hero may exploit the whole gamut of M-, T-, and C-links effectively neglected by multinational expansion; even the R & D link exploited by multinational operations may be exploited by Hero to a significant degree, while to the extent that Hero does involve differentiated markets and technology, external technological threats may be localised. Set against Neros advantages are the possible mugging dangers associated with country specialisation by the personal computer manufacturer. However, for a relatively stable, developed economy like the US, domestic country-specific threats to corporate survival are unlikely to be a serious consideration as far as the overall design of corporate strategy is concerned. Economic recession might offer an obvious exception, but recession frequently tends to be global rather than country-specific.

We can summarise these arguments in Figure 7.2; for simplicity we assume the firm has to choose between diversifying from its domestic base of Nero and Zero into Hero, or going multinational by producing Nero in the UK. We assume capital scarcity means it can only start up either Nero production in the UK or Hero production in the US in the foreseeable future. The dotted lines between Nero UK and Nero US represent 'dry' links providing mutual vulnerability between divisions but no synergy.

Hero may exploit rich veins of synergy in conjunction with Nero and Zero as illustrated in Figure 7.2 below from market, technological and country linkage while Nero UK only provides informational economies for the benefit of the firm. As far as the obverse benefits of avoiding linkages is concerned, the multinational option only offers

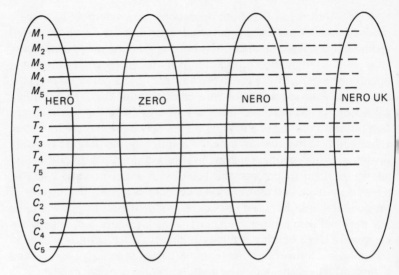

FIGURE 7.2   *Domestic diversification versus multinationalism*

the dubious advantages of avoiding country specific linkages, while Nero might still offer some gains here to the extent that external attacks are specific to product-market characteristics of Nero and/or Zero. The multinational option in this context appears as poor cousin to domestic diversification.

It appears, therefore, that the justification for multinational operations must rely heavily on informational economies, particularly economies of R & D information.[3] As we have seen, however, multinational operations are not the only way that information economies can be exploited. Domestic strategies based on technological or market links may also exploit common technological and market knowledge respectively – indeed the transferability of market research knowledge may be greater for domestic market related products than for the same product on an international scale, while specific R & D findings may be embodied in a variety of technically related products. Thus, in a world of scarce capital, multinational diversification can mean an additional opportunity cost in that the informational economies they provide could have been at least partially obtained through domestic expansion or diversification strategies that are foregone to support multinational enterprise.

Thus, as mentioned earlier, contrary to the opinion given by some authors, the logic of multinational enterprise is neither natural nor inevitable. Indeed, seen in the perspective of synergy and transaction cost analysis, the potential dangers and sacrifices a multinational may encounter for apparently limited gains, suggests that only a limited class of corporations are suited for multinational efforts. Our preceding arguments suggest that this class of corporations has two characteristic: first, they would have a relatively high level of expenditure on firm-specific informational resources, especially in the area of research and development.[4] The greater the firm-specific information resources content, the higher the potential for information economies.[5] Second, information must be product-specific; in the absence of the second characteristics, domestic diversification strategies could exploit informational economies without the barriers and potential problems facing the multinational enterprise. Evidence that R & D costs tend to rapidly escalate as projects move toward product or brand level specific development end of the R & D spectrum for a wide range of technologies suggests that this second condition may be applicable to a number of cases (Kay, 1979, pp. 26–7). This indicates that a significant proportion of R & D expenditure is liable to be product-specific.

Recent work by Buckley and Casson (1976), Hymer (1976) and Rugman (1980a, 1980b), supports the argument that the existence of multinationals is a consequence of transaction costs.[6] A general conclusion emerging from these studies is that imperfections in international trade and market exchange systems may lead to a decision to locate production abroad, and that within this option multinational enterprise is preferred to licensing technology in circumstances where the transaction costs of licensing technology are high. These conditions exist where the licence agreement is difficult to establish and police, and where the licensee may opportunistically appropriate gains from the technical knowledge without compensating the licensing firm. The multinational enterprise can thus be viewed as a result of its desire to internalise firm-specific informational advantages. We can extend this argument by analysing the extent to which technical information is also product-specific.

MULTINATIONAL STRATEGY OPTIONS

The importance of considering the degree of product-specificity of technical information can be demonstrated by considering the three basic strategic options open to firms considering selling overseas:

exporting, multinational diversification and licensing technology. Although the following arguments are restricted to technology transfer, they could be extended, in principle, to the transfer of market knowledge when appropriate.

If there are no barriers to free trade, exporting would be preferred to foreign investment. This can be simply demonstrated in Figure 7.1. Neither option is likely to exploit market links M_1 to M_5, but exporting would allow the consolidation of production activities and the exploitation of links T_1 to T_5. Locating production abroad, however, can only exploit the R & D (T_5) link. Simply stated, given free international trade, exporting strategies can achieve greater technological economies over foreign production, whether in the form of licensing or multinational operation.

Impediments to free international trade, such as taxes, tariffs, quotas or transportation costs, may encourage foreign location by creating barriers to exporting. The foreign location option includes both multinational enterprise and technology licensing, and the role of transaction cost analysis is critical in understanding which option is to be preferred.

From our previous analysis, two necessary conditions for multinational enterprise were suggested. First, a high level of firm-specific advantages in information must exist to provide the critical level of informational economies required to overcome the fundamental barriers to multinational enterprise. Second, these economies must be product-specific or otherwise a firm would exploit synergy by domestic level diversification. However, within the foreign location option, the degree to which these information economies are product-specific will determine whether licensing or multinational operation strategies are appropriate.[7]

If the R & D information necessary to transfer technology abroad is entirely product-specific then there is minimal transaction costs associated with the licensing option. This is true to the extent that patent and copyright protection safeguards the property rights of the technology licensing firm. The R & D information can be bundled up as patent Y or brand X, and leased to foreign firms. Although the potential for opportunism still exists, increasing the product specific content of R & D information will minimise its effect. In addition, the local licensees are likely to possess the country specific market and technological information that would otherwise present a barrier to the multinational option.

As the R & D information becomes less product-specific, transaction costs for the licensing option rapidly increase. Property rights for non product-specific information are difficult, if not impossible, to define.[8] Technology transfer from the firm to a licensee involves a discrete bundle of knowledge, in which some elements are product-specific and others are applicable to other products not covered by the licensing agreement. To the extent that this package of information is non product-specific, the licensing option becomes an imperfect mechanism for appropriating desired profits for the licensing firm.

For example, instant cameras are a high technology product in which R & D represents a significant proportion of costs. Suppose Country *A* imposes a tariff barrier on photographic equipment and an instant camera manufacturer, rejecting exporting as a viable option, decides to adopt a foreign direct investment strategy to penetrate Country *A*'s market. If the firm's R & D is strictly product-specific and cannot be transferred to other products outside the product line offered by the instant camera producer, then the terms of the licensing agreement should be straightforward, and, in essence, merge the country-specific knowledge of the licensee and the product-specific technical knowledge of the original developer.

In practice, however, instant cameras are based upon extensible technological links that may transfer into other product technologies, such as miniature batteries, electronic components, chemicals, sensing and measurement devices, and precision machine tooling. A foreign licensee would be in the position to build on the technical knowledge provided, and enjoy gains from diversification that could not be anticipated before the licensing agreement was established.[9] In such circumstances, there is increased incentive for a multinational option to be followed in order for the parent firm to gain the additional benefits from non product-specific technology knowledge that is difficult to articulate within a formal license agreement.[10]

Consequently an R & D intensive firm may face potential opportunism if it adopts the licensing option and therefore the in-house alternative of multinational expansion may be adopted for transaction cost reasons. In fact potential opportunism by foreign interests may strongly influence the strategy of multinational enterprise; a number of studies have suggested that expatriate control of foreign subsidiaries by home nationals facilitates control of technical knowledge and knowhow,[11] while centralisation of R & D in the home country has also been interpreted as a device for limiting possibilities of foreign access to firms technical knowledge.[12]

While we have discussed the market alternatives in the limited context of technological licensing, more complex and involved market transactions, such as joint ventures, may be interpreted in similar fashion. For example, an innovative US corporation that makes a deal with an established third world firm to market its product in that firms country may use joint venture to organise linkages – the market and country links in the joint venture being provided by the third world firm and the technological links by the US investor. Licensing, joint ventures and multinational enterprise may be isomorphic in terms of patterns of exploitable linkages, differing only in the respective institutional managements and associated costs of organisations or transaction. In fact, we can use our technique for mapping synergy to illustrate the problems facing an innovator considering joint venture or licensing arrangements with a foreign firm. The firm in Figure 7.3 is at the moment located only in the home country and it is considering multinational expansion and a market agreement with a firm located in the potential host country as alternative options. M, T and C represent the appropriate bundles of market, technology and country specific resources represented for both home and host location. As discussed before, the firm may directly exploit the R & D informational economies if it was to adopt the multinational option; other than that, the only advantages the multinational option would provide would be to the extent that similarities (dotted links) in markets and technologies facilitate start up in the foreign location. In particular, differences in market and country specific requirements between home and host countries are liable to create start up difficulties.

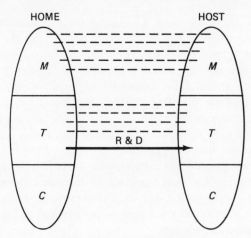

FIGURE 7.3   *Foreign operation*

By way of contrast, a licence or joint venture with a host country firm could provide all relevant market and country specific skills and expertise; the complementarity of home country firms technology with host country firms market and country knowledge would appear an obvious solution for many cases of this type. In fact, such cosy deals may be vulnerable to opportunism of the type discussed above. Consequently the living together of joint ventures and licensing may be abandoned for more stable marriage arrangements, whether through taking over a native firm or by starting up from scratch.[13]

To summarise the story so far; as the degree of non product-specificity of R & D information increases, there will be an increased propensity to adopt the multinational option rather than the licensing option. However, as the degree of non product-specificity increases, there will be an increased tendency to move out of the foreign location option in favour of domestic diversification for the purposes of exploiting informational economies. Since the justification for a foreign location strategy is exploited by domestic diversification there is no need to pursue multinational expansion, losing non-informational economies and incurring country-specific informational costs. This point is made by Wolf (1977) who identifies domestic diversification as an alternative to multinationals in this respect.

The product-specific aspect of R & D necessitates foreign direct investment to exploit informational economies which cannot be exploited through domestic diversification, while a high degree of product specificity would mean that a licensing option is feasible. Multinational enterprise is therefore seen to be restricted to an intermediate case in which R & D information is partially product-specific. The required technological information on a new product or process will typically involve a bundle of product-specific and non-product-specific characteristics. The product-specific aspect encourages the foreign expansion option as opposed to domestic diversification, while the non-product-specific aspect encourages the adoption of the multinational option (versus licensing) within the foreign location decision. Such influences are illustrated in Figure 7.4 in which the likely preferred strategic options for exploiting R & D economies moves from foreign licensing through foreign direct investment in multinational operation, to domestic diversification as the level of R & D product-specificity diminishes.

A related point worth noting is that as the nature of the technology moves toward the basic research end of the research and development spectrum the informational content becomes less product-specific and

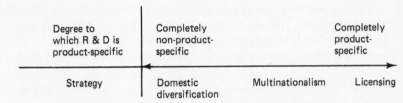

FIGURE 7.4   *Alternative strategies and R & D specificity*

more easily transferable to other products and processes. As this occurs the task of policing the use of the informational content of the technology across international borders becomes extremely complicated. Transaction costs, in the form of potential opportunism by a licensee, is thus related to the location of the transferred technology on the research and development spectrum. (See Kay, 1979, for analyses of the characteristics of the R & D spectrum.)

A further point is that domestic diversification and multinational enterprise have thus far been presented as substitutable corporate strategies. This is consistent with our argument that both strategies exploit informational economies, and also with Wolf (1977) who identifies domestic diversification as an alternative to multinational enterprise for similar reasons. However, while consideration of informational economies suggests that the corporation might regard domestic diversification and multinational enterprise as substitute strategies, empirical evidence suggests that the multinational corporation is also highly diversified (Vernon, 1971).[14] Rather than simply substituting diversification with multinational expansion, it appears that the typical multinational corporation tends to operate both strategies jointly. A tentative explanation for this phenomenon already is provided on the basis of the types of informational economies each strategy exploits; multinational expansion directly exploits the product-specific informational economies, while domestic diversification may also exploit the non-product-specific informational economies neglected by multinational expansion. Thus, the two strategies may exploit different aspects of a given bundle of technological knowledge. However, while this indicates one reason why multinationals may also be diversified, this does not go far towards explaining why there appears to be such a distinct association between multinationalism and diversification.

A stronger argument for the observed association follows directly from our analysis. From our earlier discussion we would expect firms in technologically dynamic industries to be more diversified than firms in technologically stable industries as a defence against the threat of technological 'mugging'. In addition, we also expect firms in technologically dynamic industries to be loaded with a high level of potential economies in R & D, exploitable through multinational expansion. Thus, multinationalism and diversification may be associated through technological change in the case of diversification, and the scale of R & D activity in the case of multinational expansion. By way of contrast, firms in low technology industries would be expected to be more specialised and less multinational because of the lower level of external technological threat, and internal R & D activity, respectively, in those industries. Thus, diversification and multinationalism will tend to be concentrated in the high technology industries, though for slightly different reasons. High levels of *internal* R & D encourage multinationalism to exploit informational economies, while high levels of *external* R & D encourage diversification to pre-empt the potentially disastrous effect of competitors' 'surprises'.

AN EXTENSION; MULTINATIONAL HEDGING AND VERTICAL INTEGRATION

The role of multinational enterprise as a vehicle for technology transfer has been discussed in the previous sections. However, there are two types of multinational enterprise that pursue objectives other than technology transfer and we shall briefly consider both in turn.

Firstly, hedging may be a stimulus to multinational operation in certain circumstances. If a specific country is susceptible to mugging then country diversification may be pursued by individual corporations to localise threats along *C*-type linkages such as in Figure 7.1. For example, Lonrho, the large UK conglomerate, based its corporate strategy around businesses in emergent African nations in the sixties. Businessmen in the respective countries feared political threats of nationalisation and expropriation of assets without compensation. Lonrho was able to buy up businesses in the various countries cheaply and spread the political threats of country specific nationalisation. In similar spirit, US multinationals in south east Asia have used multiple locations in various countries to localise the country specific threats of economic changes and unionisation on their labour-cost sensitive assembly operations.

Both of these examples of possible country-specific 'mugging' have implications for corporate strategy similar to technological mugging – fear of technological mugging encourages strategic limitation and localisation of market and technological links through product-market diversification, while fear of country-specific mugging encourages country diversification. Further, such impetus to country diversification is not simply analysable in terms of portfolio theory,[15] any more than is product-market diversification; the relevant environmental threat here is not in the form of quantifiable, risky variance around a stable mean performance level, but instead involves the possibility of decline (or disappearance) of expected profit due to unquantifiable environmental 'surprises'. As with technological mugging, country type mugging involves the possibility of decline in fortunes; portfolio theory emphasises symmetric variation around mean profit levels, with equiprobable positive and negative deviation. Figure 7.5 illustrates the use of a multinational company which has pursued country level diversification to mitigate the possible threat of country-specific catastrophes. Unrelated product-markets are operated in three countries, Fasia, Gasia and Hasia, politically unstable third world countries. In this case, Gasia has developed a policy of nationalisation which means that this firm's Gasia-specific business has been mugged; thanks

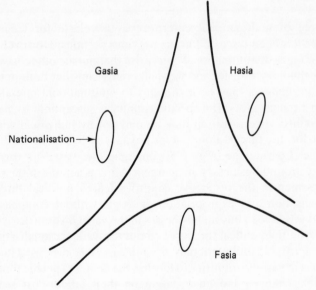

FIGURE 7.5　*Country diversification*

to this firm's country diversification the adverse effects are localised around the limited country-specific links in this case. If similar circumstances held in the case illustrated in Figure 7.2, it would lend increased weight to the multinational option represented there, versus the domestic diversification option.

Secondly, another form of multinational enterprise involves vertical integration across national boundaries. For example, Japanese multinational enterprise has tended to vertically integrate backwards into critical resource areas; Japan is relatively poor in natural resources, which makes it particularly vulnerable to opportunistic behaviour on the part of commodity suppliers. Backwards multinational integration is one means of increasing security.[16]

Although hedging and vertical integration represent alternative motives for technological transfer as far as multinational enterprise is concerned, they each have a common root source – bounded rationality. In the absence of bounded rationality considerations, there will be no problems of unexpected mugging or transaction costs such as opportunism. We have argued that strategies of hedging, vertical integration and horizontal multinational expansion depend on such bounded rationality considerations; if we have no information problems, we have no justification for multinational enterprise. Small wonder multinational enterprise has been neglected by mainstream neoclassical economies since bounded rationality problems are presumed to be eliminated by the price mechanism; so, also, is any justification for the creation of multinational enterprise. A corollary is that mere observation of the actual existence of multinational enterprises is in each case a signal that the price system does not eliminate all bounded rationality problems, and that associated information problems may be severe enough to require an organisational alternative to the market.

CONCLUSION

With the above analysis in mind, we can now summarise the rationale for multinational enterprise. Firstly, organising for economies from potential synergy rather than hedging is likely to be the preferred strategy for multinationals since hedging can usually be better achieved with domestically oriented strategies. We would expect multinational enterprise to pursue product-market links.

Secondly, firm-specific informational knowledge, especially in research and development, is the most likely source of economies for the multinational. In order for a multinational strategy to exist, the gains from these economies must overcome the inherent costs and potential vulnerabilities to technological 'mugging' a multinational enterprise faces. Other market-technological links, while exposing the multinational to threats, do not provide benefits from synergy.

Thirdly, if free trade exists, then exporting is the preferred strategy for international expansion. This allows for economies based on the consolidation of research, development, and production to be realised. If market imperfections exclude exporting as a viable strategic option, the exploitation of these firm-specific informational economies will depend on the extent to which these informational advantages are product-specific. If the informational content is completely product-specific, licensing technology is the preferred solution. If the informational content is non-product-specific, and easily transferred to other types of products and processes, exploitation of R & D economies can be most effectively realised by a domestic strategy of technological diversification without the need to allocate capital to multinational enterprise. It is the intermediate case of firm-specific/partially product-specific information that provides the rationale for multinational enterprise. Foreign location is necessary to exploit product-specific economies, while the multinational option internalises and guards the non-product-specific informational content of overseas investment.

Finally, other bounded rationality considerations may encourage country diversification to hedge against country-specific threats, while multinational vertical integration may be a consequence of transaction cost issues, such as potential opportunism.

It is illuminating to contrast this approach with that of Caves (1982), who develops a neoclassical critique of the multinational analysis in the spirit of his review of corporate strategy and structure discussed in Chapter 6 (it may appear unfair to keep picking on Caves, but it is a direct tribute to his clarity and consistency in pursuing the neoclassical grail). Caves comments in his preface:

An analytical survey of the MNE has trouble making peace with the vast literature on public policy. I know no subject in economic policy in which the issues that excite public discussion bear so little relation to the welfare issues identified by normative economists. Therefore, my strategy in chapters 1 through 9 is to take up the policy issues as they devolve from economic analysis rather than from governmental pronouncement and Sunday-supplement musings. (p. xi.)

In his final Chapter 10, Caves attempts to establish why politicians develop policies that frequently have little to do with maximising national (or anybody else's) economic welfare (p. xi). The underlying policy framework in Caves' book is that of neoclassical welfare economics in which actors, institutions and governments are able to optimise their respective objective functions. Thus, before page 1, Caves has obscured and distorted the whole purpose and character of the multinational enterprise; IBM, ITT and Exxon exist *because* the world of neoclassical theory is unattainable, and as a direct consequence of the bounded rationality problems discussed here. The irrelevancy of the ideal world of traditional welfare economics does not stop Caves imagining (p. 296) such institutions as 'an international forum that would bargain toward global-welfare-maximising arrangements toward MNEs (though he does recognise the practical improbability of such a body) but it does prevent him from considering the possibility that the gulf between the 'issues that excite public discussion' and neoclassical welfare economics may be more a reflection of the inadequacy of welfare economics than of misplaced public concern.[17]

Such tragic professional myopia has led neoclassical theorists to fail to identify the single ultimate factor underlying the variety of phenomena and issues discussed in this and Chapter 6. That factor is bounded rationality, and as we have seen earlier, its exclusion in neoclassical theory is born of necessity and in turn guarantees the sterility and irrelevancy of derived policy prescriptions. If bounded rationality is ignored, then the analysis of this present chapter could not be written, and it is such neglect in formal theory that leads to Caves' failure to approach the issues that may be central preoccupations in government and the Sunday newspapers. Public policy and concern over multinationals tend to revolve around questions of *power* and *influence*, questions which do not appear on the neoclassical agenda. As we shall see in Chapter 8, bounded rationality is the key to understanding these fundamental determinants of public policy.

8 Public Policy and Bounded Rationality

Give us our daily bread,
in individual slices
Elvis Costello

The purpose of this chapter is to explore the role of bounded rationality in public policy issues. We could address this question in different ways. One way would be to conduct an audit of public policy issues and analyse the role of information problems in each case. No doubt there lurks a political Salome cousin to entrepreneurial Salome behind the public policy fog; but we shall leave the politicians with their veils.

Instead we shall examine specific public policy issues by considering three works that have made a contribution in this area in recent years. We shall be quite clear in our prime purpose in doing so; it is to examine the role of information problems in this area. We hope to show how in each case the substantive differences between the analyst and neoclassical theory are reducible to the existence of information problems.

We shall examine three theses in turn as represented by Galbraith (*The New Industrial State*), Servan Schreiber (*The American Challenge*), and Schumacher (*Small is Beautiful*).[1] We hope to demonstrate the common theme running through each before contrasting it with Friedman's analysis (*Free to Choose*) in Chapter 9.

THESIS 1: *THE NEW INDUSTRIAL STATE*

J.K. Galbraith's *The New Industrial State* is a text that has been widely commented on, both favourably and unfavourably. While the text employs a high level of academic discussion and rigorous argument it remains accessible to the general reader. Broadly, although it has been generally welcomed by lay readers,[2] it has met stiffer resistance from professional economists. As Meehan (1979) points out (p. 8), the *Social Sciences Citation Index* for 1979 lists more than 250 references to Galbraiths' publications, but only 20 appear in journals even remotely connected with academic economics, and about half of those are to be found in the *Journal of Economic Issues*, an outlet for institutional economists. This resistance has been recognised by Galbraith himself, who has responded vigorously to academic criticism. The popularity of Galbraith's works[3] itself represents a challenge to the economics establishment; such popularity is difficult to ignore and account must be taken of it. However, if mass-appeal was the only distinguishing characteristic of Galbraith's work, this should do little more than promote spasms of jealousy and occasional countervailing literary efforts on the part of other economists. The frequently vehement response to Galbraith's work has been founded on stronger, more rational grounds – Galbraith represents a real and potentially dangerous threat to economic orthodoxy. His analysis is offered and recognised as an alternative paradigm to neoclassical theory. When this intent is combined with popular appeal, passivity is not an option open to neoclassical economists. Counter-attack is required.

We shall examine Galbraith's arguments and set them against the neoclassical paradigm. We shall see that it bears the same features that discriminates much of the earlier analysis we have been concerned with – Galbraith is concerned with information problems.

Thesis

At an early stage in his analysis, Galbraith makes an interesting distinction between two types of planning:

> A firm can plan to serve the market more efficiently by anticipating market behavior and responding to the resulting prospect – the need for plant, raw materials, labour supply, product design – which will enable it better to meet market preferences. This firm can also plan in the sense of obtaining the prices, cost and consumer and producer response that it wants. There is a vital difference between the two kinds of planning; the first responds more effectively to the market. The second replaces the market. (pp. 17–18)

The first kind of planning is responsive; the second type of planning is manipulative. The first is consistent with the passive black-box role of the entrepreneurial firm in neoclassical theory, while the second is more liable to be associated with the 'real-world' corporation described in earlier chapters.

In a different context, Galbraith also distinguishes between the 'Entrepreneurial Corporation' in which one individual still has control of capital, and the 'mature corporation' in which the entrepreneur has been replaced by group decision-making. Again these distinctions closely parallel those made earlier here between the neoclassical firm and the 'real-world' firm.[4] In making these comparisons, Galbraith is setting the field for a contrasting analysis of neoclassical theory and information problems.

Galbraith identifies two main struts in the marginalist neoclassical defence of profit maximising when faced with unavoidable evidence that large corporations do exercise significant control over prices; firstly that consumers retain sovereignty or control over their preferences – the firm is assumed to be unable to exercise any significant influence over purchase plans; secondly, the assumption of profit maximisation is retained as the role objective of the firm. Retention of these assumptions means the firm can be treated as a responsive system, and the concept of the entrepreneurial firm in neoclassical theory does not have to be abandoned. Market conditions and state policy dictate corporate resource allocation.

However, Galbraith argues that these assumptions do not realistically describe actual behaviour. He identifies what he defines as the technostructure – an organised collection of individuals whose function is to bring to bear specialised knowledge in the development of corporate strategy. They[5] direct the corporation, decide its policy and replace the entrepreneur with management in the mature corporation. The technostructure typically exercises significant discretion over the goals to be set for the corporation and over resource allocation in pursuit of these goals. The technostructure does not have the subordinate role posited for employees *vis-à-vis* employer in neoclassical theory, but instead derives substantial collective freedom from direct stockholder discipline due to their individual expertise and professionalism compared to the common stockholders.

Galbraith outlines the accepted sequence of neoclassical theory in which the consumer independently establishes his preferences and instructs the producer by his pattern of purchases what goods should be produced and how resources should be allocated. The flow of instruction from consumer to market to producer describes the process of consumer sovereignty. Galbraith contrasts this with his 'revised sequence' in which power lies with the technostructure; they control the attitudes and goals of the firm, manage market behaviour, and persuade and manipulate consumer purchases. This sequence is achieved because the dominant position of the technostructure enables it to exercise control over the goals of the corporation, which in turn seeks to adapt the goals and attitudes of society as a whole, and the consumer in particular, to those of the corporation. Advertising is employed to create 'organised public bamboozlement' (p. 294) selling goods from soap powder to sliced bread.

The major goal pursued by the technostructure is growth of sales. Such an objective means expansion of the technostructure, which in turn means more responsibility, status and remuneration. It is a goal which directly furthers the interests of the technostructure itself. The revised sequence is accompanied by revised goals.

Galbraith also describes the role and function of 'the educational and scientific estate',[6] which has emerged in importance as suppliers of human capital to the large modern corporations. Professional and scientific expertise is provided by the network of colleges and institutions associated with the estate. The estate has been largely created by the informational and organisational needs of the technostructure.

The relationship between the technostructure and the educational and scientific estate is frequently complex and uncomfortable. The technostructure is dependent on the estate for a steady supply of trained personnel, while the technostructure offers potentially high material gains to those members of the estate who co-operate with it. On the other hand members of the estate may consciously distance themselves from what they perceive to be the process of trivialisation associated with the materialistic base of the revised sequence; the individualistic atmosphere of the estate conflicts with the spirit of consensus and compromise associated with the technostructure; and both technostructure and estate may conflict in the political arena where both compete for recognition and influence. There is ambivalence and variability in terms of the respective attitudes and behaviour of technostructure and estate towards one another.

Discussion

Galbraith is concerned with the individual and institutional aspects of information problems. His argument is too detailed and wide-ranging to give more than a brief outline of major points here, but as summarised above, there are three main informational issues in Galbraith's discussion. Firstly, consumers are relatively ignorant, ill-informed and malleable. Consequently they are vulnerable to manipulation by the technostructure. Secondly, the technostructure is dependent on the estate for provision of information-based resources. Therefore the estate is in a potentially powerful position of influence over the technostructure, even if this is not always taken advantage of. Thirdly, the separation of ownership from control allows the techno-structure to pursue its own interests, generally expressable in terms of growth maximisation, with minimal or token interference from owners.

In each case, knowledge is power; the group in the stronger informational position is in a position of actual or potential dominance over the other. The analysis is reducible to bounded rationality terms; all groups have limits on their decision-making ability, but the producer group as represented by the technostructure is in an extremely favourable information position when compared to owners and consumers.

Galbraith presents his thesis as contradicting traditional neoclassical theory and he is aware of the threat his arguments have to the status quo. The neoclassical house of cards rests on the shaky assumption that bounded rationality problems are eliminated by the price mechanism. The emptiness of this assumption has been argued here in previous chapters and Galbraith's work represents a detailed and exhaustive critique in the same spirit. If consumers are not perfectly informed, consumers sovereignty is attacked; if owners are not perfectly informed profit maximisation is attacked. Galbraith's argument is a systemic and sustained attack on the concept of the entrepreneurial economy.

Many of the individual points made by Galbraith have been noted or developed by other theorists. For example the separation of ownership and control in the modern corporation has been widely commented on, while theories of managerial discretion have been put forward by a number of theorists. Whether or not Galbraith's thesis is correct point by point is not important, his work stands by its focus on the centrality of information in determining resource allocation. Bounded rational-ity occupies centre stage in Galbraith's argument in contrast to neoclassical theory. That is the significance of Galbraith's work, the foundation on which his real and important contribution to economics is based.[7]

THESIS 2: *THE AMERICAN CHALLENGE*

Servan-Schreiber's text was first published in 1967, the same year in which Galbraith's *The New Industrial State* was published. Like the American text, Servan-Schreiber's is concerned with the economic implications of the development of the modern corporation. There are similarities in the substance of the argument in the respective cases, the main difference being the European orientation of Servan-Schreiber's compared to Galbraith's essentially US perspective. As in the case of Galbraith's text, *The American Challenge* received widespread publicity and public interest.

Thesis

Servan-Schreiber's analysis was concerned with the growing US domination of European industry in the post-war period with the 'invasion' of European markets by US firms. US subsidiaries, technology and management style rapidly began to make major inroads into many markets and industries. There was much widespread public criticism of the growing control and 'Americanisation' of large sectors of European economies, with particular concern being expressed with respect to the economic, social and cultural dangers of such development.[8]

Servan-Schreiber argued that the main reason for American industries success in competition against their European counterparts was not due to any innate financial, scientific, technological or political superiority, but was instead a consequence of superior methods of *organisation*. A 'managerial gap' existed between the advanced institutions and methods adopted by the Americans and the inferior techniques of their European brethren. This managerial gap, together with a comparative weakness in the education sectors, accounted for the more visible and widely recognised 'technological gap' between the level of technological advancement possessed by the United States and that of European nations.

The basic organisational advantage possessed by the US firms was the multi-division form structure with its superior control and strategy-formulating properties. By way of contrast, compared to the flexible and adaptable US firms, European institutions were identified as being bureaucratic, overly structured, and rigid. Decision-makers were distanced from their problem areas, and preoccupied with routine, low level problems. The analysis here is consistent with the earlier comparison of the efficiency advantages of M-form structures over the control and strategy formulating faced by large, diversified and overstretched U-form corporations.

Specific solutions proposed by Servan-Schreiber are:

1. Creation of large industrial units capable of competition with the American giants, both by their size and their management.
2. Carrying out 'major operations' of advanced technology that will insure an independent future for Europe.
3. At least a minimum of federal power to protect and promote European industry.
4. Transforming the relation between business, the university and the government.
5. Broader and more intensive education for young people, specialized and continuing education for adults.
6. Finally, as the key to everything else, the liberation of imprisoned energies by a revolution in our social methods – a revolution to revitalize the elites and even relations between men. (Servan-Schreiber 1968, pp. 125)

Effectively, what Servan-Schreiber is proposing is the adoption of the M-form structure and philosophy, a sufficiently strong level of government involvement in shaping industry policy at EEC level, and a reshaping of social, commercial and cultural attitudes in which formal education would have a strong role to play.

Discussion

Since the publication of Servan-Schreiber's text in 1967 there has been significant changes in the structure and functioning of the EEC not the least of which has resulted from Great Britain entering the Common Market. Some of the policy recommendations have been overtaken by events, while others retain as much relevance today as when they were written. The Common Market still suffers from a lack of effective decision-making at top level; the protection and furtherance of national interests has tended to inhibit the development of a strong, coherent industrial strategy for Europe. On the other hand the post-war period has seen the rapid diffusion of the M-form structure amongst large European corporations as some recent studies have confirmed.

While the obsolesence or continuing relevance of the policy recommendations is of course of interest here, our main concern is with the analytical content of Servan-Schreiber's work. In particular, we shall consider whether the view of the world drawn by Servan-Schreiber can be related to our earlier analysis.

The first point to note is that Servan-Schreiber's concern is mainly institutional reform. Of the three forms of economic organisation discussed earlier he concentrates on firm and state structure and functioning. Market behaviour is treated in less detail, not because the role of market exchange is regarded as unimportant, but because Servan-Schreiber argues that controls or restrictions on market behaviour are undesirable. He concentrates his analysis on improving the efficiency of organisations operating in the context of a freely operating international market system.

In this respect the foundations of Servan-Schreiber's analysis are explicitly developed on an informational base. He argues that the technological gap between America and Europe is a consequence of the relative weakness of science and research in European countries. This weakness in turn derives from two sources; the lack of adequate and comprehensive higher education in Europe, and the apparent inability or inertia on the part of European institutions to adopt modern methods of management. Educational, organisational and managerial weaknesses generate weakness in technological innovation. Each of these factors represent information problems for the appropriate decision-makers. The message of Servan-Schreiber's text is that America has coped with its information problems rather better than European countries. Servan-Schreiber views American success as resulting from a symbiotic relationship between state and corporations, each operating systems of decentralised decision-making but with effective strategy formulating powers retained at respective boardroom and federal levels.

How does this relate to the tools and concepts provided by the neoclassical framework? The simple answer is that Servan-Schreiber's analysis bears no direct relationship to neoclassical analysis and theory, and for similar reasons to those that differentiated our analysis from neoclassical theory. We used the illustration of 'entrepreneurial Salome' to demonstrate how neoclassical theory stripped the corporation of all but capital, direct labour and entrepreneurial resources, and argued that informational roles and functions were incompatible with neoclassical theory. The capital and direct labour resources producing physical product were consistent with the neoclassical model. These were contrasted with resources which generated informational output and which contradicted the neoclassical model.

Interestingly, Servan-Schreiber's analysis makes the same distinction between resources for physical output and resources for informational output as we did earlier, and, as in our case, emphasises the greater importance of the latter area as a set of problems for economic analysis and policy making. He employs evidence supplied by Denison (1967) in which twentieth century economic development in the US was seen as following two distinct phases. The first growth phase from 1909 to 1929 was seen as being largely due to the expansion in the labour force and invested capital. Given the character and associated output of these resources we could legitimately describe this as the neoclassical phase. After 1929 the most important factors underlying economic growth were identified as education and technological innovation; from our analysis this might be described as the information based growth phase. Educational improvement and technological change are two fundamental informational outputs in the resource allocation process. Denison's analysis suggests a diminished relevancy for even the limited remit possessed by the neoclassical model as these qualitative changes in the factors underlying US economic growth occurred.

Denison's analysis is used as supporting evidence for Servan-Schreiber's argument. As Servan-Schreiber comments, 'the power to create wealth is the power to make decisions' (p. 45). It could also be said that the role of education, technological innovation and improved organisational structures is to increase the quality of this factor underlying the power to create wealth.

In one of the concluding paragraphs in the book, Servan-Schreiber expressively summarises the core factors underlying the American challenge represented by their 'conquest' of advanced technology:

> This new conquest is the perfect definition of 'intangible'. This no doubt explains why it has been misunderstood by leaders accustomed to think in terms of tons of steel, machinery and capital. The signs and instruments of power are no longer armed legions or raw materials or capital. Even factories are only an external symbol. Modern power is based on the capacity for innovation, which is research, and the capacity to transform inventions into finished products, which is technology. The wealth we seek does not lie in the

earth or in numbers of men or in machines, but in the human spirit. And particularly in the ability of men to think and to create. (p. 211)

Substitute 'neoclassical economists' for leaders in the above passage and we have an exact expression of the criticism of neoclassical theory which is a major theme of this present book. Servan-Schreiber continues; 'the training, development and exploitation of human intelligence – these are the real resources and there are no others' (p. 212). Information problems lie at the heart of the American challenge.

What is especially interesting about this is the demonstrable relevance of the dichotomy between the neoclassical framework and information problems that we developed earlier. Servan-Schreiber's analysis can be read at one level as a set of logically argued prescriptions for improvements in economic welfare. It can also be read at a higher, more abstract level as a critique of neoclassical theory and a vividly argued case that neoclassical theory should be set aside as the major diagnostic tool of present day economic analysis. This is all the more remarkable since such a critique was not an explicit objective of the analysis; it only becomes apparent when we fit our earlier analysis of neoclassical and information problems around it. The fit is clean, and our earlier analysis comfortably accommodates Servan-Schreiber's arguments and ideas. Just as the identification of information problems helped us split the economic world cleanly into two qualitatively distinctive hemispheres in Chapters 3 and 4, so the same distinction here helps to classify and highlight the basis of the arguments put forward by Servan-Schreiber in *The American Challenge*.

As far as the more obvious purpose of the book in developing policy recommendations is concerned, this is an area requiring careful consideration and empirical investigation. The analysis is too simplistic and polemical in many respects to serve as an entirely adequate means for strategic decision-making; it is, as the final sentence (p. 213) suggests, a 'call to action'. It is not a scientifically constructed treatise. To take one central example, the decentralised M-form structure is indeed a formula for efficient decision making – but only in certain circumstances. The more primitive U-form structure is to be preferred for small and/or specialised firms. Details of policy application such as these are glossed over by the broad brush strokes of Servan-Schreiber's assessment of the central problem.

However, the precise details of specific policy recommendations are not really our concern here in the first place. Properly constructed empirical investigation of the merits and demerits of the respective recommendations would require a book to itself. What we are more concerned with here is the substantive content of Servan-Schreiber's prescriptions, but with the diagnostic principles underlying it. These diagnostic principles are diametrically opposed to the guidelines provided by neoclassical theory. It is this conflict which is the central point of interest to us as far as Servan-Schreiber's work is concerned.

THESIS 3: *SMALL IS BEAUTIFUL*

Schumacher's *Small Is Beautiful* is an unusual economic text insofar as it blends social, ethical and religious principles with its economic analysis. Like the other theses discussed here it is written in a style accessible to the lay reader, and it has achieved best seller status after a slow start. At the risk of presenting a narrow perspective of Schumacher's work we shall concentrate on his economic analyses of choice of technology, around which his work revolves.

Thesis

Schumacher is primarily concerned with third-world problems, though his philosophy potentially encompasses all societies and economies. He identifies the basic problem of the dual economy in third-world countries in which the majority are poor, rural dwellers operating traditional industries coexisting beside a rich urban élite who have adopted modern attitudes and values. This latter group are more likely to introduce and operate modern technological techniques in industry. Schumacher argues that aid tends to go to this rich minority, the poor remaining unemployed, underfinanced and ignored since it is easier to establish new industries in the educated modern sector. Urban slums are created by poor rural workers who migrate to the cities in search of work (pp. 171–2).

Schumacher sees the prime task and responsibility of planners and policy-makers in those economies as being to create work opportunities around the existing system and through maintenance of the society and culture. In this context he identifies four propositions as being central to the achievement of the objective; (1) workplaces should be created where people are living, (2) workplaces should be cheap and not involve high capital demands, (3) technology should be simple with low skill demands, and (4) local inputs and markets should be sought wherever possible. Schumacher emphasises that industries should be chosen on the basis of available raw materials and potential markets. Technology should be chosen *after* the decision as to what industries should be introduced or supported (pp. 174–6).

The question of choice of technology lies at the core of Schumacher's analysis. Schumacher argues that the most appropriate technology for less developed countries is not the sophisticated and expensive modern technology of developed countries, nor the traditional indigenous technology of these countries, but instead a technology in between these extremes in terms of complexity and expense – intermediate technology. An example might be a light aluminium alloy, ox-drawn plough compared to developed countries tractors or the traditional technology of wooden ploughs. Schumacher describes intermediate technology 'symbolically' as £100 technology compared to the £1000 technology of developed countries and the £1 technology of developing countries. Not only would it be easier to raise – and spread – the capital required to improve productivity and growth, but also this technology would be more easily assimilated, operated and maintained by the less educated and relatively unsophisticated local workforce chain than if complex western technology was to be used (pp. 180–1).

Although Schumacher dislikes use of the terms labour and capital intensive because he believes it clouds discussion of the nature of technology, he concedes that intermediate technology would be labour intensive (pp. 178–9). He argues that these technologies should be generated by national and supernational research efforts, and that politicians and policy-makers should be less concerned with the grandiose and expensive projects that have characterised much of third-world development.

Schumacher identifies some objections to intermediate technology he suggests are commonly raised against it. Firstly, intermediate technology lacks the apparent glamour and sophistication of western technology and may have an aura of inferiority and second best. He discusses this objection as irrelevant to the needs and conditions of the rural poor in the third world. Secondly he quotes Kaldor as claiming that the high productivity of western and modern technology would improve growth in any particular context, and that alternative technologies involving less output per worker (as is associated with intermediate technology) waste scarce and limited capital. Schumacher argues that overall productivity may in fact be higher under intermediate technology; we shall discuss this point further below. Further, Schumacher argues against the proposition that entrepreneurial ability is a scarce commodity that would be spread thin by small scale, intermediate technology. Finally, Schumacher identifies two other objections to intermediate technology that products of intermediate technology would require protection from outside competition and would not be suitable for export. He dismisses both arguments as conjectural.

Discussion

The case for intermediate technology is the basis of Schumacher's argument, and it is on this which his work stands or falls.[9] In this respect there are two main aspects which will concern us here; firstly, Schumacher's claim that conventional economics can provide an inappropriate solution as far as technological choice is concerned, and secondly, the sources of failure to apply intermediate technology.

Firstly, as far as Schumacher's implication that conventional economics may support an inappropriate 'sophisticated' technology is concerned, this overlooks the point that if a standard prescription could be said to exist in conventional economics, it is one consistent with Schumacher's general position. It is a neoclassical argument that choice of technology is determined by relative prices of resources which in turn is determined by relative scarcity of those resources. To take the latter link in the chain first; economies differ to the extent they are endowed with respective capital land and labour resources. For example, Hong Kong has a scarcity of land relative to other resources, the Republic of China has a relative scarcity of capital, while in the US labour is in many areas a relatively scarce resource compared to many other economies. Relative scarcity is typically reflected in relative prices; land commands a high price in Hong Kong, labour is relatively cheap in China, while labour is relatively well paid in the United States. The relative price of the resource is reflected in the choice of technology – if a range of technologies are available to provide a given product, the relatively cheaper a resource is, the greater the incentive to use it intensively in the production of a given product. Consequently, economies that are relatively rich in capital will tend to use capital intensive techniques, those that are relatively well endowed in labour will tend to use labour intensive techniques, and so on. The third world countries should therefore tend to adopt techniques that utilise their relatively abundant and cheaper resource most intensively; in other words they should *naturally* adopt labour intensive techniques. Simple transfer of capital intensive technology from developed countries to developing countries runs counter to the conventional wisdom of received neoclassical theory as well as the recommendations of *Small Is Beautiful*.

This leads to consideration of the second question we shall be concerned with here, why intermediate technology does not evolve naturally in third world countries. Consideration of the neoclassical analysis above raises the obvious question of why outside intervention should be necessary to create intermediate technology in the first place and then stimulate its adoption.

We can characterise the problem in this fashion by continuing our example of the tractor and the plough. The wooden plough may be assumed to be the indigenous technology of a specific developing country. Let us suppose that tractor technology is introduced into this basically agrarian economy, increasing overall productivity and reducing costs of production and associated crop prices; the indigenous technology will be driven out by natural selection of the more highly productive technology.

However, the invading technology involves capital expenditures and technical sophistication outwith the range of most peasant farmers; failure of the traditional technology to match the high technology alternative in terms of cost and output price may increase failures among traditional farmers, increase rural poverty and encourage a further drift to the towns from the villages.

This scenario is consistent with the type of process described by Schumacher and its results. The rich urban élite have the level of education and the access to finance required to introduce the new technology, while the rural poor are unable to compete on equal terms. It is worth noting, however, that unless the western technology does reduce overall costs of production, it will not represent an effective threat to the traditional technology – in this respect it must be more efficient than the traditional technology even though it may have adverse effects on distribution of income as well as community and regional life.

Suppose now our third alternative of light aluminium alloy ploughs would result in the highest level of cost effectiveness for crop production in our developing country. This possibility is consistent

both with Schumacher's general prescription of intermediate technology for developing countries and the neoclassical solution of labour
intensive technology in those countries. In this case, what might inhibit
adoption of this alternative?

Schumacher argues that financial and educational informational
limitations on the part of the traditional farmers may have effective
barriers to the generation and spread of the intermediate technology.
However, if intermediate technology is indeed superior in productivity
terms to the extreme alternatives, financial inadequacies should
present no barriers as long as the capital market is working effectively
in the neoclassical perspective. As long as labour intensive technology
is less costly per unit of output than the developed country technology
(as we would expect from the neoclassical argument above), financial
intermediaries should be prepared to bankroll small farmers to adopt
the more efficient intermediate technology. Therefore capital expenditure should not pose barriers to entry as long as the market system is
working effectively.

In other words, the puzzle is why the market system in third world
countries does not provide intermediate technology solutions of its
own accord. It is in this context that Schumacher's argument must be
set.

Schumacher provides a solution himself. He identifies two sources
of market failure in not providing intermediate technology – financial
and informational (educational, organising) barriers, p. 180). However, if the capital market is perfectly informed, it should be prepared
to provide more labour intensive technology in the neoclassical view.
The fact that it does not may be taken as a reflection of informational
deficiencies in this sector also. Such informational deficiencies are
ignored in the neoclassical analysis which presumes perfect knowledge. The barriers to generation and adoption of intermediate
technology boil down to bounded rationality on the part of the rural
farmers and the capital market (to the extent the latter exists in
developing countries).

In the absence of information problems, we would not expect the
problem of lack of appropriate technology to exist. The unqualified
transfer of advanced inappropriate technology to developing countries
reflects severe *informational* deficiencies in those economies. Those
who possess the level of education, training and knowledge are
unlikely to be motivated to change this state of affairs; the very
characteristics of technical complexity and sophistication that inhibit
the spread of the advanced technology are the same characteristics that

concentrate profits in the few hands possessing the knowledge required to handle the technology. Knowledge constitutes an effective barrier to entry increasing monopoly power on the part of users of the high technology. Thus, even though the capital intensive technology may not be the most efficient from the view of the country as a whole, associated barriers to entry may concentrate the available profits in few hands. The very advantages of technology identified by Schumacher (relative simplicity, cheapness, ease of adoption and maintenance) are also liable to greatly reduce barriers to entry and spread potential profit amongst the rural majority away from the rich urban elite.

In those circumstances the rich are unlikely to be motivated to change the status quo and the poor will be unable to. Thus when Schumacher asks the question, 'Why is it so difficult for the rich to help the poor?' (p. 203), the short answer is, why should they? Knowledge is power – and wealth.[10]

CONCLUSION

The subject of Schumacher's thesis reduces to information problems just as did Galbraith and Servan Schreiber's theses. Bounded rationality problems on the part of certain major groups in the economic system put them at a disadvantage compared to relatively knowledge-rich groups – knowledge is power. There is an interesting similarity in each work in terms of the core theme. It is impossible to understate the significance of the fact that the predominant paradigm in conventional economics, neoclassical theory, assumes that such problems do not exist. The economic worlds of Galbraith, Schumacher and Servan-Schreiber are foreign to neoclassical theory, and their associated policy conclusions are based on premises inconsistent with the assumptions of that framework. We shall see in Chapter 9 what happens when a theorist attempts policy making using a neoclassical framework.

9   Synthesis and Antithesis

Orr was crazy and could be grounded. All he had to do was ask; and as soon as he did, he would no longer be crazy and would have to fly more missions. Orr would be crazy to fly more missions and sane if he didn't, but if he was sane he had to fly them. If he flew them he was crazy and didn't have to; but if he didn't want to he was sane and had to. Yossarian was moved very deeply by the absolute simplicity of this clause of Catch-22 and let out a respectful whistle.

'That's some catch, that Catch-22', he observed.

'It's the best there is', Doc Daneeka agreed.

Joseph Heller, *Catch 22*

Public policy in neoclassical theory has an appealing and elegant simplicity. The policy or normative branch of conventional economics is termed welfare economics and has attracted the close attention of the mathematical technicians in recent years. The two major preoccupations of welfare economists are efficiency and equity; roughly how to make the cake as big as possible and how to slice the cake, respectively.

As far as equity is concerned, a major issue has been the terms and conditions surrounding the supposed efficiency/equity trade-off. We shall reserve further discussion on this topic for Chapter 10. The major thrust of welfare economics has, however, been concerned with efficiency conditions, and the concept of Pareto-optimality is central in this area. Pareto-optimality is associated with a particular allocation if reallocation cannot take place without making at least one party worse off. Technical conditions for efficiency in exchange and production are derivable using Pareto-optimal criteria and a fundamental principle of welfare economics is that a perfectly competitive economy is Pareto-efficient. Welfare economics provides simple, clear guidelines for public policy.

The good news for welfare economics is that there is only one really major catch to this view of the world. The bad news is that this catch has a Catch-22 quality which makes it irrevocably damaging, indeed fatal, for welfare economics. Catch-22 is a strange loop, and it is strange loops deriving from bounded rationality problems that caves in the sophisticated superstructure of welfare economics.

These strange loops manifest themselves in a variety of ways, but there are two major levels of effect. At the level of the individual decision-maker bounded rationality creates substantial transactional and organisational costs which makes the attainment of the perfectly competitive ideal completely unrealistic. We have observed in previous chapters how such problems impinge on actual behaviour. In fact, the argument of Chapter 2 developed points made by Coase, Demsetz and others which can be summarised in the message that non-Pareto-optimal allocations are unstable in the absence of information problems. If there are no information problems there are no transaction costs. If there are no transactions costs, then in any non-Pareto-optimal situation in which at least one party could be made better off without others being made worse off, spontaneous bargaining should move economy and society towards Pareto-optimality through the striking of mutually or commonly advantageous agreements. Thus, any efficiency problems identified by neoclassical welfare theory (e.g. externality, public goods, monopoly) leading to non-Pareto-optimality through market failure, are automatically correctable through market transactions. The neoclassical basis of welfare economics circumscribes the kind of problem that may be identified and in turn provides the solution to these problems. Thus, it is the readily observable fact that the world is not characterised by atomistic markets populated by entrepreneurial Salomes that stands testament to the irrelevancy of welfare economics.

The second level at which strange loops are to be found is at the level of the policy maker. Before policy problems can be resolved, they have to be identified properly, and welfare economics assumes away the information based costs or impracticalities involved in specifying the conditions of optimality. Demsetz (1969) conducts a comprehensive survey of such problems in a critique of an article by Arrow, but the problems can be simply identified: for example, if a policy maker can costlessly identify a profit maximising output, why do decision-makers frequently find this costly or impossible? If the policy maker can freely identify a non-Pareto-optimal allocation, why do decision-makers not get together to do something about it? In practice policy makers are bound by the same information problems and strange loops of which Arrows information paradox is a central example.

In this chapter we move beyond the absurdities of neoclassical welfare economics. We approach the problem by drawing together the threads of Galbraith, Servan-Shreiber and Schumacher's argument in a synthesis of their related views of the larger modern corporation, and contrast it with Friedman's view of the firm and the role of the price mechanism.

The synthesis is illustrated with the aid of Figure 9.1. The arrows in each case represent an information impactedness condition; the source of the arrow possesses more information than the group at which the arrow is directed. This asymmetric information condition means the information-rich party has the ability to control or affect the behaviour of the information-poor party through selective provision or opportunistic misrepresentation of information. In short, knowledge is power. Galbraith, Servan-Schreiber and Schumacher all advocate alternative versions of this thesis as we shall see below.

Figure 9.1 is split into three main segments; the US, Europe and the

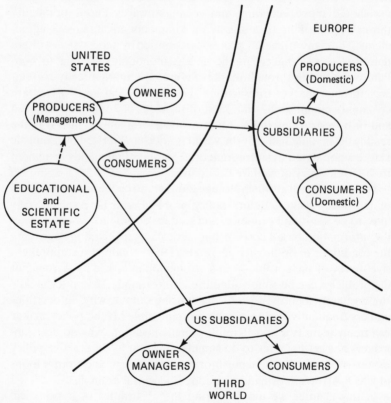

FIGURE 9.1 *Galbraith, Servan-Shreiber and Schumacher*

third world. In the US segment, the ultimate source of information – and consequently power – is the educational and scientific estate who have the potential to influence producer decisions. This latter group in turn has substantial discretion to pursue its goals and manipulate owner agreement and consumer preferences due to its advantageous information condition. This is the essence of the Galbraithian argument. The dotted line between the educational and scientific estate and the producers indicates that the first group may use its potential power only occasionally and in a limited fashion.

Servan-Schreiber's analysis of the relation between US multinationals and indigenous French industry is also illustrated in Figure 9.1. The arrow between US producers and subsidiaries in France illustrates the information relation in this analysis. The details and blueprints for the effective working of the multidivisional structure were transmitted along this channel in the course of *The American Challenge* to the exclusion of domestic French firms as indicated in the diagram.

A similar informational relation between US producers and well-placed third world capitalists exists in Schumacher's analysis, though here the information transferred is technological rather than organisational. We identify the simpler owner-managed firm as the basic element of Schumacher's system in contrast to the larger managerially controlled corporations of Galbraith and Servan-Schreiber. As in the Galbraithian case, Schumacher's third world consumers are disadvantaged informationally compared to the more powerful third world owners and US subsidiaries based on US technology. The poor and badly educated sections of the communities are isolated from competing on equal terms with the capital-intensive technology due to inherent informational deficiencies. A capitalist or entrepreneurial class may even fail to develop properly in this case; the 'owners' box may be poorly populated or effectively empty.

This summarises fairly simply, and integrates the three arguments discussed in the preceding chapters. As has been mentioned before, these arguments do not have a monopoly of interpretation of social and economic issues in their respective areas, and to some extent they have been at least partially overtaken by events. The Japanese challenge and European revival (based on multidivisional organisation) are examples of significant recent developments that might qualify any current updates of the respective books. Nevertheless they are interesting to the extent that each of the works coalesce into a central unifying theme; knowledge is power. The pattern of power and control is a consequence of the prevailing information impactedness conditions and relations illustrated in Figure 9.1.

By way of contrast, neoclassical analyses of the price mechanism are incapable of coping with this important – indeed central – determinant of resource allocation. The price system *eliminates* information problems in neoclassical analysis and therefore there exists no information impactedness conditions to give rise to entrenched powerful élites. Consumer sovereignty is based on the concept of perfect knowledge. Consumer ignorance provides the circumstances that may create the opportunity for Galbraithian producer's sovereignty.

This illustrates a central and crucial difference between the political notion of power and the treatment of the same concept in economic theory. Power in economics has typically been treated as a question of property rights (e.g., monopoly power) and associated ability to provide inducements or sanctions in the market exchange process (e.g., bargaining power). However, power contingent on bounded rationality problems may also fundamentally affect the resource allocation process. Possession of knowledge may be one source of power and influence as in the three theses just discussed. Also, power and authority may flow from hierarchical position and status within an organisation; since hierarchy is redundant in a system free of bounded rationality problems (such as the neoclassical price system), power arising from such positional factors is also excluded from discussion in neoclassical theory. In such fashion is the interpretation of power in mainstream economics reduced and limited to property rights questions.[1]

Far from just representing abstract academic points, such issues impinge directly on actual public policy. Though advisers to the Reagan administration may have differed on macroeconomic policy, they showed a common belief in the effectiveness of the price mechanism, finding intellectual support in mainstream neoclassical theory. Consistent with this philosophy, the Reagan administration introduced an approach to government which offered a delightfully rich menu of puzzles and paradoxes reminiscent of some of Hofstadter's problems discussed earlier.[2] For example, the Secretary of the Interior, James Watt, whose remit covered the development and conservation of the environment promulgated commercial exploitation of public lands with the greatest alacrity. His philosophy echoed that of the first UK Industry Secretary in Margaret Thatcher's administration who espoused a 'hands-off' approach characterised by an (intended) absence of government intervention. In the limit this creates the interesting possibility of an Industry non-Secretary (paradox; can *A* be *A* and not *A*?). In a less apocalyptic context it has echoes of Orwell's ministries of Love and Peace (I have a personal theory such linguistic confusion all started with the religious orders of crusading knights in the 11th–13th centuries, such as the Hospitallers who set about sending people to hospital with devout enthusiasm, and their co-missionaries the Poor Knights of Christ who dedicated themselves to rectifying the adjective in their title with acquisitive zeal).

A special case of these bureaucrats of non-bureaucracy was represented by those in the Reagan administration, such as the Secretary of Education, whose remit was to preside over and facilitate the elimination of their own jobs and departments. Such bureaucratic self-immolation recalls the paradox of the self devouring dragon depicted by Escher (see Hofstadter, p. 474). However, the existence of such paradoxes at political level should not be regarded as a coincidence since conventional economic theory often provides intellectual justification for these contemporary political philosophies.

Friedman's position, consistent with neoclassical interpretation, is that bounded rationality problems are handled effectively by the price mechanism. However, it is difficult to pin down exactly his view of the price system as a method of handling information. This is because he has traditionally invoked three alternative defences of the price mechanism, discussed below. The defences are arranged in order of strength of information requirements.

Defence (1): The price system automatically solves bounded rationality problems

This is the defence utilised in Friedman's pencil example discussed earlier. The price mechanism 'automatically' provides all necessary information. Though bounded rationality exists, the price system ensures that the bounds are not reached. For analytical purposes there is no distinction between unbounded rationality and non-binding bounded rationality constraints, and therefore the omniscience assumption may as well be made explicit. This is the defence with the strongest information requirement.

Defence (2): Bounded rationality problems exist, but repetition allows decision-makers to behave 'as if' they possess perfect knowledge

Friedman (1953) and Machlup (1946) provide similar analogies in a defence of the price mechanism that is less stringent in information terms than the first. Thus, Machlup uses the analogy of a car driver who can smoothly and effectively overtake a truck without consciously computing all the relevant physical considerations of velocity, acceleration, gear and direction changes, and so on. Friedman uses the similar analogy of a snooker player who can execute an optimal shot without resorting to the complex mathematical analysis involved in the physical dynamics of the situation. Friedman argues that habitual reaction and/or random choice leads to the natural selection of the optimal billiard shot (1953, pp. 21–2).

This defence is less restrictive in its information requirements than the first since it recognises the possibility of initial error in decision-making that may be corrected by an iterative process of learning through interaction with the environment. Through trial and error the 'correct' behaviour pattern is learned and the respective decision-makers behave 'as if' they were following some ideal or optimal formula. The special nature of such repetitious and standardised decision-making situations were well discussed in our earlier chapters, though both analysts interpret their analogies as being of general relevance.

Defence (3): The price system handles bounded rationality problems better than alternatives

This defence does not require the price mechanism to eliminate all information problems, only that it should handle it rather better than other forms of economic organisation. Thus, Friedman recognises that free markets might produce inferior or dangerous drugs, but argues that these potential defects are less important than the possible sacrifice in benefits arising from state suppression of novel drugs (1980, pp. 248–50). Similarly; 'Perfection is not of this world. There will always be shoddy products, quacks, con artists. But on the whole, market competition, when it is permitted to work, protects the consumer better than do the alternative government mechanisms that have been increasingly superimposed on the market' (Friedman and Friedman, 1980, pp. 263–4).

It should be noted that each defence of the price mechanism not only involves very different assumptions regarding the information characteristics and requirements of the price system, they also imply different behavioural and resource allocation characteristics. For example, suppose a new drug, neoclassomine, appears on the market advertised as a particularly effective tranquillizer. Defence (1) presumes that all I need is the price to make an optimal decision immediately on whether – and how much – of neoclassomine to purchase. Defence (2) presumes that if I experiment sufficiently with tranquillizer purchases I will approximate an optimal choice. Defence (3) makes no claim that I will make the best possible choice, only that an unregulated price system would allow me to make a better choice than if state intervention existed. Friedman hauls in each of these levels of defence to buttress his *laissez-faire* philosophy depending on circumstances but is not consistent in utilising any particular defence. Yet Defence (1) in the case of pencil analogy and Defence (2) in the case of the billiards analogy are both presented as *general* defences of the price system in their respective contexts. These two defences have the added advantage of still leaving the door open for the potential application of formal neoclassical theory to resource allocation questions, while the third – and inconsistent – Defence helps communicate a spirit of realism to the analysis.

Friedman's narrow view of the working of the price system also illustrates his analysis of the ills resulting from inflation. In the same section on 'Transmission of Information' in which the price system was regarded as automatically solving the problem of communicating all important information to decision-makers, the Friedmans argue that:

> One of the major adverse effects of erratic inflation is the introduction of static, as it were, into the transmission of information through prices. If the price of wood goes up, for example, producers cannot know whether that is because inflation is raising all prices or because wood is now in greater demand or lower supply to other products before the price hike. The information that is important for the organization of production is primarily about *relative* prices. High inflation, and particularly highly variable inflation, drowns that information in meaningless static. (1980, pp. 36–7)

First of all, a first year student of economics should be able to negate the claim that producers *cannot* distinguish between inflationary and real price increases. A simple piece of information – change in the current appropriate price index – is sufficient to provide a basis for such discrimination. However, let us be charitable and put the statement down to Friedman's over-enthusiasm for their case. The Friedmanite argument then boils down a defence of the price system in which the consumer is assumed to have the astonishing mental capacity of possessing *all* relevant information concerning the relative values of products in the absence of inflation – yet in the presence of inflation he or she cannot perform the elementary task of maintaining relative prices by deflating using a price index. The first is a daunting information gathering task of truly monumental proportions, in comparison the second is a simple information processing problem. The Friedmanite consumer is at once a mastermind and a simpleton.

Friedman generally claims that the price system eliminates bounded rationality problems – a claim which we have discussed earlier as implicitly involving highly restrictive and special assumptions concerning the market exchange situation. His statements regarding inflation are in fact the more reasonable since they recognise the existence of bounded rationality on the part of the consumer. It is a pity that such recognition is not extended to the price system in general except in isolated and unrelated contexts. In practice, both inflation *and* product market characteristics are liable to pose severe information problems for the consumer.

Friedman's example of the price system and the pencil, discussed in detail in Chapter 4, serves as the keynote for the arguments in favour of free markets in *Free to Choose.* In fact the recent appearance of a potential substitute for pencils may usefully help illustrate our criticism of Friedman's analysis in this respect.

The potential substitute is erasable pens, which have been recently introduced onto the market by Gillette and Scripto. The ink contains a chemical that prevents it from sinking into the paper. When the chemical evaporates, the ink is absorbed and becomes permanent. Gillette produces a refillable version, Scripto a disposable version. Gillette is a large diversified corporation with sales of $2 billion in 1981 and 31 700 employees. It produces razor and blades, toiletries and grooming aids, writing instruments, electric shavers and lighters. Scripto has sales of $4.1 million and 1018 employees in 1981, and produces mechanical pencils, ball pens, china marking pencils, cigarette lighters and fibre tips. Gillette spent $10 million on R & D and new equipment and $5.2 million on advertising to introduce their new product while Scripto spent $4 million to introduce their version. Scripto in fact possessed a patent on erasable ink for over ten years but delayed introduction because of uncertainty as to demand. Future developments are uncertain but the disposable market has been identified as a likely growth area.

The characteristics of this sector of the writing instruments industry are quite different from that of pencils. We can reasonably expect continuing development and change in this segment based on chemical technology. By way of contrast, traditional pencils are a stable and simple technology. We can contrast below present and projected developments in the erasable pen market with that of traditional pencils; in doing so we associate the transaction cost and product life cycle analysis of Chapter 6 with erasable pens, and associate the unqualified market system analysis of Friedman with his pencil example. While we could undoubtedly qualify Friedman's example with problems arising from questions of bounded rationality, we accept his example of a pure entrepreneurial system to aid comparison with our interpretation of the erasable pen substitute in Table 9.1 below.

TABLE 9.1 *Friedman's pencils, Gillette and Scripto's erasable pens*

Product	Pencil	Erasable pen
Technological description	Stable, simple	Dynamic, relatively complex
	↓	↓
Product life cycle	Long, slow changing	Short, rapidly changing
	↓	↓
Information on market and technology	Familiar, repetitious, simple information	Novel, uncertain, complex information
	↓	↓
Role of price	Price sufficient information	Price only one aspect of information requirements
	↓	↓
Economic organisation	Market sufficient	Firm may replace market in certain cases and organise information based activities
	↓	↓
Description of firm	Entrepreneurial	Managed, hierarchical, functional
	↓	↓
Example of activities	Physical production, market exchange of inputs and outputs	As left, plus R & D, advertising, diversification, vertical integration

The life cycle and informational aspects that create an entrepreneurial system on the one hand, and a managed corporate system on the other, have been well discussed in Chapter 6 and elsewhere. Consequently we shall leave Table 9.1 as being a largely self-explanatory summary of the informational determinants of market and corporate systems. It is interesting to compare the two sets of conditions and relationships contained in Figure 9.1 and consider how much of the description of Gillette and Scripto's corporate activities below could be analysed using a simple price theoretic model of the type associated with Friedman's market exchange analysis. For example, patenting, researching, diversifying, marketing and vertically integrating have all been analysed here as information based activities – therefore we should not be surprised to discover that while Friedman's defence of the price system appears reasonable in the context of the relatively safe example of pencils, it is not sufficient to analyse the more complex characteristics of resource allocation in the case of erasable pens. It requires an approach based on bounded rationality considerations such as transaction cost analysis to cope with the informational issues arising from the erasable pen industry – and as we have argued earlier it is informational issues such as these that represent the core of the problem of resource allocation. Price theory can analyse only a special, limited, indeed trivial, set of problems. Yet Friedman's adherence to the supremacy of the price mechanism in the context of a market exchange system is firm and unyielding. Samuelson (1980) summarises Friedman's philosophy:

> Can a human being today seriously be against social security? Against flood relief? Farm legislation? Pure food and drug regulation? Compulsory licensing and qualifying of doctors? And of auto drivers? Be against foreign aid? Against public utility and SEC regulation?
>
> Against the post office monopoly? Minimum wages? The draft? Price and wage controls? Anticyclical fiscal and monetary policies? Auto-safety standards? Compulsory and free public schooling? Prohibition of heroin sales? Stricter federal and state housing standards for migrant workers? Maximum interest-rate ceilings on usurious lenders? Truth-in-lending laws? Government planning? Pope Paul VI's encyclical naming central economic planning as the key to economic development? (p. 791)

As Samuelson points out, each of the negations above have been argued by Friedman in his works or *Newsweek* columns. Each issue is reducible to Friedman's beliefs that the individual is the best judge of his own welfare, the market is an efficient allocator of resources and government intervention is undesirable. Such beliefs mesh neatly with the neoclassical principles of perfect knowledge and constrained maximisation. However, it is one thing to produce a simple neoclassical model to illustrate a classroom point – it is quite another to believe the economic world would really *behave* that way if only government would stop interfering. Repeated lecturing in neoclassical theory in the benevolent environment of the University of Chicago may be conducive to a growing belief that the associated abstractions would be the blueprints for the emergence of society based on entrepreneurship with no residual information problems; however such beliefs require wider receptivity if its proponent is not to be labelled eccentric. To a large extent, the US economic and political system provides such an environment. The US cultural values tend to be represented by qualities such as individualism, initiative, self-interest and competitiveness, possibly the result of supply factors resulting from what it takes to create an emigrant from the old world in the first place, and demand factors resulting from the characteristics required to create a new country.

This social ethos differs significantly from that prevailing in Britain which is generally categorised as class ridden with at least three status levels – upper, middle, and working class. By way of contrast the US, being classless, only has as many status levels as there are income brackets. The entrepreneurial ethic, the profit motive, and individualistic self interest is a product of psychological, social and cultural forces. The fact that Friedman plied his trade in the city of Capone and Daley is unlikely to have dented his faith in the generality of aggressive and ruthless competitiveness.

The statement that Friedman's book makes is that 'government' intervention does not work'. It is a statement that would be echoed by a reasonably large consensus of US economists, though in terms ranging from the enthusiastic to the grudging. It is a statement which requires the implicit to be made explicit however; what Friedman is concerned with is how *US* government intervention does not work. Given the cultural emphasis on independence and individualism in the US it would not be surprising if the actual application of public policies should be characterised to an uncommon degree by self serving bureaucracies and a lack of sensitivity to community or social interests. In fact, for a US politician wishing to demonstrate the perfidy of state intervention, a sensible strategy might be to set up one state corporation, call it the US post office, and to do his best to make sure it did not work as a continuing reminder of socialist and collectivist inefficiency. To the extent that any state controlled body is efficient in the US, it runs counter to the natural grain of the socio-political system.

Friedman's market-oriented myopia may be seen as both partially resulting from, and sustained by, its particular cultural context. As we have seen from previous chapters the defects of a pure market analysis are glaring enough even in this area; they are exacerbated when Friedman extends his analysis beyond US frontiers. For example, Friedman summarises the Swedish experience:

> It too has recently been experiencing the same difficulties as Britain; high inflation and high unemployment; opposition to high taxes, resulting in the emigration of some of its most talented people; dissatisfaction with social programs. (1980, p. 124)

Friedman concedes that the Swedish economy has done much better than Britain but attributes that to Swedish neutrality. The ills of the Swedish economy are seen as a direct consequence of heavy government involvement in industry and the setting up of a welfare state.[3]

A man from Mars reading Friedman's analysis would glean correctly the high level of state involvement in Swedish economic life but would also gain an impression of dramatic economic failure. The visitor would not learn that this poorly endowed country[4] that industrialised relatively recently ranks amongst the highest in the world in terms of standard of living.[5] In economic terms a strange failure indeed.[6]

On the case of the remarkable post-war growth of the Japanese economy, Friedman is strangely silent. It is perhaps relevant that the Japanese performance can in no way be judged a failure, and the economy can in no way be characterised as entrepreneurial and *laissez-faire*. It is composed of giant Zaibatsu conglomerate empires which compete – and cooperate – across their respective frontiers.[7] Government involvement is deep and extensive. 'Japan's historical experience and value system have resulted in an economic ideology supportive of close and harmonious government-business relations. One thing immediately obvious is emphasis on group rather than individual, on cooperation and conciliation aimed at harmony, on national rather than personal welfare' (Patrick and Rosovsky, 1976, p. 53). As these authors of a Brookings Institute study imply, Japanese industry is based on principles antithetical to that of the individualistic, competitive, self-interested entrepreneur. It is difficult to see how

Friedman could begin to analyse the Japanese challenge using his framework, and he does not try, despite its emergence as one of the most significant economic phenomenon of the post-war period. Friedman's entrepreneur would be as comfortable in a Japanese corporation as a madame in a nunnery.

Hong Kong is chosen by Friedman to represent the ideal entrepreneurial economy. This nation of 4.5 million people built up entrepot trade due to its strategic situation on the rump of China. Its peculiar situational advantages created a trading economy in which domestic exports composed 69 per cent of GDP in 1976 and the ratio of total trade to GDP was 1.8. Despite its small population, Hong Kong ranked eighteenth in the world in terms of total trade in 1976 (Beazer, 1978).

Market exchange may well be identified as the dominant organisational form in this economy. However, a case could equally be made for corporate Zaibatsu organisation being the most significant determinant of Japanese economic growth, and for state direction as the source of Swedish success. Hong Kong is a special case created by history and geography and hardly an automatic model for the rest of the world. The market, the firm and the state may contribute to economic success in different measure in different economies.[8]

Friedman's obsession with the price mechanism cannot provide for more than a superficial and distorted explanation of economic activity both at an explanatory and normative level. The neoclassical approach does not enlighten economic analysis in the areas discussed above; an alternative route is required and, as we have suggested, useful signposts have been provided, perhaps most notably by Simon and Williamson. In Friedman's analysis the US is the land of opportunity, in Williamson, it is the land of opportunism. There is probably truth in both interpretations; neither are inconsistent, but both may lead to a differing set of policy conclusions.

A final but crucial issue arising from Friedman's philosophy is the political inference drawn by Friedman. Although *Free to Choose* and its precursor *Capitalism and Freedom* (1982, second edition) are ostensibly tracts in political economy, there is little attention to the workings of the political system in this context. Instead, economic freedom and political freedom are treated virtually identically – the state is the aggregate of individual voters just as the economy is the aggregate of individual firms and consumers in Friedman's philosophy. In *Free to Choose*, Friedman explicitly ties in political freedom to economic freedom (pp. 2–3). However, political freedom occupies an even more vague and polemical role in Friedman's analysis than does economic freedom. The principle of political freedom is frequently stated, but the practice is little examined.

The neglect extends to the role of party politics of the US. As Galbraith (1971, p. 60) points out, the economic concept of consumer sovereignty is closely associated with the political concept of citizen sovereignty. We have argued that bounded rationality considerations may impair the effectiveness of consumer sovereignty; similar arguments hold for citizen sovereignty. It is unlikely that abolition of political regulation and bureaucracy would eliminate abuses of political power and the monopoly power of the Democrats and Republicans any more than abolition of economic regulation and bureaucracy would eliminate abuses of economic power and the monopoly power of ITT and General Electric. A system designed to ensure that almost anybody can be president must find ways of dealing with the possibility that almost anybody will be.

Of course, if Friedman is correct in assuming all bounded rationality to be effectively handled by the price mechanism, and that all actors are the best judges of their own welfare, then his analysis is an extremely reasonable treatise. Food stamps, consumer protection legislation, licensure of doctors, and regulation of drugs would be abandoned as unnecessary and inefficient barriers to free choice. Why not? Amateur brain surgery can be fun. Support your local lemming.

However the Friedmans' analysis is neither quackery nor eccentric, it is one of the few analyses which makes explicit the policy conclusions following from the neoclassical paradigm. It is in this light that it must be judged, and it is its pure neoclassical character that makes it an invaluable exercise. It also precludes direct consideration of bounded rationality issues which means there exists no common language through which the public policy issues raised by Galbraith, Servan-Schreiber and Schumacher can be discussed; public policy contingent on bounded rationality has no place in neoclassical theory. Yet as we have seen at the beginning of this work, unless neoclassical theory explicitly invokes bounded rationality considerations there is no need for public policy since market exchange will solve all problems of externalities and economies. Neoclassical theory cannot bring in bounded rationality considerations explicitly – to do so means subverting the role of the price mechanism and abandoning the constrained optimisation basis of neoclassical theory since it is incompatible with conditions of true uncertainty and bounded rationality. So bounded rationality issues sneak into neoclassical analysis (as discussed in the externality generating monopoly in chapter 2) without being explicitly discussed; to do so would be to demonstrate the internally contradictory nature of neoclassical analysis. Thus it is left to Friedman and sympathisers to pursue neoclassical analysis to its logical conclusion. In doing so, entrepreneurial Salome identified in Chapter 3 reappears but from a different route. In pursuing such a path Friedman excludes from his analysis the substantive issues discussed here earlier – such as all industrial organisation issues in Chapter 6, multinationals in Chapter 7, public policy in Chapter 8. Such exclusion is born of necessity. Bounded rationality is at the heart of each of these issues, as we have argued. Since bounded rationality is handled by prices in Friedman's analysis, none of these can be discussed in neoclassical theory.

10 Ingredients and Recipes

> In capitalist reality as distinguished from its textbook picture, it is not (price) competition which counts but the competition from the new commodity, the new technology, the new source of supply, the new type of organization ... competition which commands a decisive cost or quality advantage and which strikes not at the margins of the profits and outputs of the existing firms but at their foundations and their very lives.
>
> Joseph Schumpeter, *Capitalism, Socialism and Democracy*

> The innovator makes enemies of all who prospered under the old order, and only lukewarm support is forthcoming from those who would prosper under the new. Their support is lukewarm partly from fear of their adversaries, who have the existing laws on their side, and partly because men are generally incredulous, never really trusting new things unless they have tested them by experience.
>
> Niccolo Machiavelli, *The Prince*

In this chapter we consider policy implications arising from our analysis. We shall deal with this aspect in four stages. Firstly, we shall consider the role of technological change in creating information problems. Secondly, we shall consider the implications of technological change for the operation of capital, labour and product markets by the firm. Thirdly, we shall briefly assess alternative institutional forms in terms of their ability to facilitate or inhibit the adjustment of these markets in conditions of rapid technological change. Finally, we shall discuss some implications for macroeconomic analysis and economic analysis in general. Our purpose will be to examine the implications of economic organisation for economic policy, particularly in small economies.

Each stage builds on the arguments of the previous stages. We shall conclude that technological change is the fundamental source of information problems, and that it may create adjustment frictions in capital, labour, and product-markets which may suggest alternative forms of economic organisation to handle these difficulties.

THE SIGNIFICANCE OF INNOVATION

Technological change is the major root source of information problems. Bounded rationality does not present severe difficulties in conditions of static technology. The neoclassical profit maximising model may be generally applicable in the absence of innovation.

We shall attempt to justify these statements then by resorting to the same form of mental experiment that earlier produced entrepreneurial Salome. In this case, instead of considering the implications of removing information problems, we shall remove innovation from our corporate economy and examine the possible consequences. In doing so, we picture the corporate economy as being originally composed of the mixture of corporate strategies and internal organisational forms that characterise large developed economies; conglomerate, related–linked and specialised strategies, and their associated structures, all have a place.

We assume that technological change has been removed from the economy. No innovation takes place and existing product life cycles continue indefinitely.[1] Further, the economy has had time to settle down and adjust to these circumstances. Below we suggest major adjustments on the part of firms in our technologically frozen corporate economy.

(1) *No corporate strategy*. In our discussion of industrial organisation in Chapter 6 we identified two major effects of bounded rationality. Bounded rationality in transactions created incentives to specialise; in the limit, single product firms reduce these costs to minimal levels. Bounded rationality in terms of the mugging potential of technological change leads to tendencies in the opposite direction; related–linked and conglomerate strategies are designed to limit links and their associated dangers.

If we eliminate technological change, we also eliminate the second source of bounded rationality. Bounded rationality in transactions becomes the sole determinant of the boundaries of firms. In this respect corporate strategy can be reasonably said to be eliminated since firms will divest or merge to create systems that are largely internally homogenous. The single product firm is the limit case of this process and natural pressures will lead firms to converge on this limit. In practice, complications such as antitrust policy and limited market demand for a given product may create diversification tendencies – to the extent that this occurs, firms will still operate on a principle of minimal differentiation by exploiting as many market and/or technological links as possible. With these qualifications in mind, the diverse molecules of the corporate economy are reduced to their constituent atoms.

(2) *No R & D function.* No innovation, no R & D.

(3) *Skeletal marketing function.* Firstly, there would be only a single product, or limited range of closely related products to market compared to the potential cats cradle of relationships involved in diversified firms. Secondly, the need for informative advertising is greatly reduced since consumer familiarity and knowledgeability would be much greater under conditions of static technology; the characteristics of available alternatives are invariant and permanent. Thirdly, these same information advantages should reduce the vulnerability and susceptibility of consumers to persuasive advertising.[2] The consequence of these factors is to reduce the breadth and depth of marketing activity at individual firm level.

(4) *Skeletal finance function.* As for the marketing function, the complexity of information requirements for the finance function are greatly reduced by the tendency of firms to operate single or limited and closely related product-markets. Also static technology eliminates much of the bounded rationality problems facing financial analysis of product-markets; the firm needs only repetitive and replicable cost and revenue information on existing products rather than highly uncertain and conjectural information on novel product-markets. The absence of innovation reduces the finance decision to a limited and neoclassical set of standard operating procedures.

(5) *Reduced possibilities for non-profit maximising behaviour.* Managerial discretion is a consequence of bounded rationality in the capital market. Information impactedness in favour of management facilitates the opportunistic pursuit of managerial objectives. However, in the absence of technological change we would expect the information impactedness condition to be substantially eliminated. Firstly, the capital market will have time and opportunity to gather information on market and technical characteristics of individual product-markets; indefinite product life cycles create continuing learning opportunities as well as the security involved in the elimination of mugging. Secondly, past performance will be a generally much

more reliable basis for judging future performance since we now have an unchanging set of product-markets, and so detailed knowledge of technical characteristics may not even be necessary. For the capital market to evaluate a new technology such as, say, Xerox copiers, at the invention stage involves information problems of mammoth proportions; for the same capital market to evaluate the potential of the same technology once established, and with patent protection, is a far more manageable task. If we could further assume that technology is frozen at a specific state of the art, market analysts not only can regard technological characteristics as parameters,[3] but can ignore technological mugging as a market threat. The past becomes a much more useful guide to future problems, with appropriate modifications such as changes in input prices and demand conditions. Even these modifications would be expected to be less frequent and extensive in a world of static technology. Thus, the information impactedness bias that favours managers compared to owners in capital market transactions under conditions of dynamic technology is liable to be far weaker under static conditions. Correspondingly the opportunities for managerial discretion are reduced or eliminated.

A derivative effect would be to compound the tendencies towards single product or specialised operation at the level of the firm discussed above, since residual managerial motives for diversification to enhance status, prestige, etc., would be more easily identified and controlled by owners.

(6) *Simple and limited hierarchy*. Firstly, there would be widespread substitution of divisional structures by functional structures. The effective elimination of corporate strategy also removes the major justification for multidivisionalisation. Some M-form structures may remain; for example on a geographic basis to stimulate profit center competition, especially for firms that exhaust all technological and market economies within geographic regions. However, corporate specialisation would swing the pendulum towards a general preference for functional U-form structures. Secondly, elimination of the R & D function and the conversion of the other functions to simpler mechanistic decision-making areas considerably reduces information problems for a given product-market. To this extent, the need for hierarchy is also reduced.

What are we left with? The cumulative effects of freezing technology can be simply summarised. In Chapter 6 we argued that innovation countervened the replicability and homogeneity requirements that were necessary for neoclassical theory. Removing innovation removes the fundamental source of uncertainty. Conditions for utilising models based on perfect knowledge and risk are greatly facilitated by the existence of stable technology. Replicability and high levels of knowledge transfer from one decision-making situation to another may now be reasonable assumptions.

These features are reflected in our transformed corporate economy above. Our typical firm is highly specialised to the extent it operates a single product in the absence of government or demand constraints. It operates an elementary functional internal organisation whose associated functions are concerned with problems of a very low level of sophistication and complexity. Management may more reasonably be expected to achieve profit maximising. Further, profit maximising can be more nearly imposed by the capital market due to the easier identification of maverick managements pursuing managerial goals.

The typical firm is one step up from the entrepreneur in terms of levels of complexity. There are still simple operating problems at functional levels and bounded rationality on the part of labour still perpetuates heterogeneity of labour. However the black box of neoclassical theory has only been slightly modified.

We can demonstrate this by considering what problems are liable to be important in this transformed economy. Changes in availability of resources would affect technology and scale requirements for production. Switches in consumer preferences may necessitate corresponding production adjustments on the part of the firm.

These types of problems would dominate managerial decision-making in conditions of static technology. As such they could themselves pose information problems. Switches in supply and demand requirements may involve a great deal of information. However there is a solution which allows a great deal of complex but certain information to be handled in simple form such that producers and consumers can pursue profit and utility maximisation respectively. It is called the price system. We could pull *Wealth of Nations* or *Free to Choose* off the shelf as operating manuals for a technologically static economy. The fact that Adam Smith wrote his work at a time of simple, slow changing technology and long product life cycles should not be regarded as a coincidence. These conditions also add weight and credibility to Smith's arguments in favour of a near universal market exchange system as being appropriate to his time and circumstances.[4] There is less justification for an equally charitable view of the second text published more than 200 years later in very different circumstances.

The technological perspectives of the 18th and 20th centuries bear little resemblance to each other. In economics, the very long run is the time taken for technology to change, while the long run is the period required for all costs to become variable. As Keynes observed, in the long run we are all dead; however in certain areas of high technology, product life cycles today are measured in months not years. In some cases the temporal dimensions of the Keynesian long run now lie closer to the life and times of the common or garden fruit fly than the traditional three score and ten of the human condition.

This point is reinforced by recent empirical analyses which have identified the central role of technological change in economic growth. Kuznets (1979) argues that technological innovations constitute the major source of modern economic growth (p. 11), while Denison (1967 and 1974) suggests that advances in technological and managerial knowledge were a fundamental source of economic growth in the US (1974 study) and in other major developed countries (1967 study). Denison and Chung (1976) support this claim for the Japanese economy.

However, circumstances may change more rapidly than philosophies. Keynes also remarked on the tendency of policy makers to become slaves to the ideas of some dead economist, and it is true that many ideas in economics do display the discomforting properties of exhumation.

INNOVATION AND MARKET ADJUSTMENT

In considering the effect of innovation and shortening product life cycles have on corporate behaviour, we shall start by holding onto our stripped-down version of the corporation in the technologically frozen economy. The conventional supremacy of the large diversified, strategy formulating, structurally complex corporation has been replaced by the universality of single product or highly specialised firms with short simple hierarchies, limited functional activities apart from production, and a general preoccupation with routine standard operating problems. We are approximating the good old days of the dawn of the capitalist heaven.

We assume there are three major markets the management of the firm has to deal with: the product-market and the two major resource-markets of capital and labour as indicated in Figure 10.1 below.

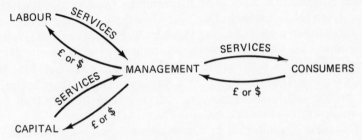

FIGURE 10.1   *The product- and resource-markets of the firm*

Consumers offer payment to the firm and the firm offers payment to the providers of capital and labour in return for services provided in each case. Management acts as the firms agents. In the product-market, the firm offers the consumer goods and services, in the labour-market the employee offers work services, while in the capital-market financial services are offered – dollars flow in both directions in this market.

The kind of information problems that transactors in these markets are likely to face in the technologically frozen economy are those which can be dealt with by the price system. Given stable technical characteristics, the content of services provided in the respective markets will be well known and established, and prices summarise the interaction of supply and demand conditions in the respective cases. Replicability, repetition and reputation all reduce bounded rationality to manageable proportions, when combined with the information handling properties of the price system.

Since bounded rationality is not liable to be a severe problem, transaction costs will be low. Since transaction costs are low, the respective markets will operate with minimal associated frictions. These conditions should permit the markets to converge on the economics of Nirvana associated with neoclassical theory. Owners, management, workers and consumers adopt their familiar assigned roles associated with standard price theory. If we want to associate a particular time and place with these circumstances, Adam Smith's Scotland might represent a reasonable approximation, as argued in the previous section. The *Wealth of Nations* draws on the familiar products of the butcher, baker and brewer as illustrative examples of market exchanges, a world removed from IBM, travel agents and R & D functions.

Now let us stir up this technologically sleepy economy by moving it forward two centuries or so to the present day. Firstly, let us assume that the institutional and transactional arrangements associated with Adam Smith's economy continue into our time; firms operate single products (or near enough), consumers continue to have the choice of familiar and well-known options, banks and shareholders can simply assess the performance and prospect of firms. However, we assume that these transactors now face the modern day realities of complex and dynamic technology and plague-ridden product life cycles. How would our market exchange system cope with those conditions?

The transactors would all face potentially severe information problems. The suppliers of capital are faced with highly specialised systems whose life expectancy is barely longer than it takes for the first substitute to appear in some cases. Consumers are typically faced with relatively novel unfamiliar products. Workers face the prospect of frequent periods of unemployment as firms are bankrupted by successive waves of innovation. Managers are in the strongest information position, but their existence as a team is terminated by outside innovation as a consequence of corporate specialisation.

In those circumstances bounded rationality poses problems for all transactors. For example, management can exploit the information impactedness condition operating in their favour to opportunistically mislead the capital-market on financial prospects, labour-market on job security and the consumer on product characteristics. Yet management themselves face the uninsurable prospect of technological catastrophe.

Given the pervasiveness of bounded rationality problems, complications appear in our market exchange system. Bounded rationality, information impactedness and opportunism may create a distorted misleading, and generally unsatisfactory context for trading. Either existing trades are conducted on a highly imperfect basis, or possible trades are abandoned or ignored; for example, consumers may cling to familiar products, workers may pursue job security, capital providers play safe and avoid uncertainty. However it is expressed, market exchange systems may face severe information problems in our technologically dynamic economy. These complications are not recognised in neoclassical theory since prices are presumed to eliminate bounded rationality problems.

In the next section we shall consider alternative forms of economic organisation in the light of these information problems faced by market exchange systems in conditions of technological change.

ECONOMIC SYSTEMS IN CONDITIONS OF TECHNOLOGICAL CHANGE

In Figure 10.1, our system is driven by the product-market. We assume here that the firm can exercise negligible control over the pace of technological change in a particular environment – it must swim with the tide of product-market change, get out of the water, or sink. The technological dynamics of the product-market feed back into resource-markets to dictate capital and labour-markets.

If these conditions hold, we have environmental incentive and stimulus for the firm to innovate. To the extent these circumstances take care of motivational aspects our problem is one of designing or encouraging systems of economic organisation that facilitate innovation. Incentive should be matched by ability.

The arguments of the preceding section can be summarised in one principle: *transactions inhibit innovation*. There are two main contributing reasons; firstly, innovation or the possibility of innovation, by its very nature creates high levels of information problems that are absent in standardised routine trading situations. These information problems cannot simply be handled through the price mechanism. Secondly, pure exchange systems create the circumstances in which transaction costs deriving from bounded rationality are liable to be pervasive and strong due to the separation of loyalty, allegiance and interest associated with the transacting parties. Some possible consequences of these circumstances were discussed in the previous section.

If this is the case, are there alternative forms of economic organisation that may prove superior to pure market exchange systems in dealing with regimes of rapidly changing technology? To deal with this question we have to consider what should ideally be achieved in any smoothing of the innovative process. These are three major markets that must be integrated in any adjustment in innovation in a pure exchange system – capital, labour, and product. Bounded rationality conditions may interfere in all three markets in innovative conditions. Yet the demands of the product-markets require that all three markets should be integrated and co-ordinated.

Management may exercise only limited control over the product-market in our system. It may vary the product characteristics within limits imposed by technical possibilities and market requirements. However, the rate of technical change is determined by the environment. To continue our swimming analogy, management can decide what stroke to use, but pace is largely determined by the tide. We can now suggest a principle on which economic organisation can be judged and compared in conditions of rapidly changing technology; economic organisation should effectively integrate resource and product market requirements and reduce costs associated with bounded rationality by internalising product and resource markets within as few system boundaries as possible. Such internalisation would substitute exchange relations with authority relations.[5] In doing so, the potentially high transaction costs associated with a market solution may be eliminated or at least mitigated.

We can consider how this may be achieved by first recalling that the form of transaction costs faced by the firm is liable to be discretionary to the extent they are substitutable within categories. The transactors may at least partially protect against opportunism by drawing up exhaustive and comprehensive contracts specifying respective actions, rights and responsibilities contingent on various states of the world occurring. However, these contracts would be by definition incomplete to the extent that they could not anticipate environmental 'surprises'. Alternatively, the parties could economise on contractual costs, widening the scope and discretion of potential opportunism which would be relatively high in uncertain, dynamic, rapidly changing environments. In a turbulent environment, transaction costs are liable to be expensive whatever form they are expressed in. Half a millenium ago, Machiavelli documented the combined power of vested interests and uncertainty in thwarting change, and these influences are still important today in determining transaction costs.

Authority relationships can economise on transaction costs in turbulent environments. The key lies in the systems treatment of opportunism and the ability to overrule sectional self interest. Opportunism may be more easily monitored and penalised in authority systems. Since the authority relation usually outlives the specific tasks which would be the subject of a market contract in an exchange relation, monitoring and auditing individual performance provides the possibility of *ex post* penalising of opportunism not feasible in a limited market contract. Internalisation of information flows increases ability to audit and monitor individual performance in this respect, and the continuance of relations over time serves to improve the quality of performance assessment.[6]

In a curious sense, authority relations may be perceived to be based on the same principles as the price mechanism; just as repetitious transactions allows the purchaser to build up a description of qualities of alternative commodities and their relative values in stable market conditions, so continuing employment allows a superior to build up a description of qualities of alternative subordinates and their respective values in both stable and changing conditions. Since opportunism may be more easily curbed within an organisation, employment contracts (the organisational parallel to market contractual costs) may be more loosely specified and cheaply constructed. The potentially high contractual costs of market exchange in turbulent environments are largely a response to potential opportunism.

Authority relations lose the information handling properties of price in market exchange. However, since transaction costs swamp the dubious signalling advantages of prices in highly uncertain environments, this is a minor consideration in regimes of rapidly changing technology.

Therefore, internalisation may smooth the process of change and adjustment that might otherwise be attainable only at high cost under a market regime. Information problems including fear of opportunism and misrepresentation may in some circumstances inhibit forging of market contracts in the first place,[7] as well as impede the operation of existing contracts. The organisational alternative can *integrate* and direct the changes required in turbulent environments.

However the integration possibilities afforded by organisation has limitations. If the system boundaries are thrown too far, protection and isolation from competitive pressures may dampen innovative incentive. The possibility is created of monopoly power over the environment,[8] and bureaucratic insularity of leaders or managers from external control, whether it be stockholder or political.[9] Inertia, apathy, risk avoidance and over-emphasis on vested interests and the status quo are well recognised problems of an insulated bureaucracy. If the system boundaries are pushed far enough, we encounter the dulled incentive system associated with the command economy.[10]

Our task therefore essentially involves creating systems which permit successive generations of innovations to go through their respective life cycles with minimal transactions at the transition stage of obsolescence and substitution. If we operate a pure market exchange system, the multiple transactions involved in replacing declining product-markets with a new phase of product-markets face the problems of pervasive bounded rationality constraints in all markets. If we operate a pure command economy, we lose the stimulus of market pressure. The problem becomes one of throwing system boundaries around potential transactors as far as possible to prevent the appearance of independent sub-systems with their attendant potential for sub-system allegiance, loyalty, identification and opportunistic treatment of other sub-systems – and yet system boundaries must not be thrown far enough to eliminate market incentives to compete, as in the case of monopoly and command systems.

The related–linked conglomerate and Japanese 'Zaibatsu' strategies all provide attractive integration characteristics, most notably in integrating capital- and product-market requirements. Williamson discusses the advantages of the conglomerate in terms of providing a mini-capital market (1975, ch. 9); internalisation of the capital-market reduces problems of bounded rationality, information impactedness and potential opportunism, while divisionalisation facilitates the operation of profit centres and performance assessment. Although Williamson does not explicitly discuss related–linked firms, they may also provide similar advantages, qualified to the extent market and technological links hinder separability of profit centres. A further possibility relates to internalising labour-markets in so far as product-market switches may be obtained by internally transferring labour as well as capital resources in highly diversified firms.

The Japanese Zaibatsu may merit an even higher rating on the integration test. Zaibatsu are generally large conglomerates which have shared ownership between the Zaibatsu manufacturing companies and the respective Zaibatsu bank. The depth of capital-market pocket is even greater than in the Western conglomerate case, with the consequent possibilities for capital-market integration with product-markets being strengthened. The integration of labour-markets with product-markets is also facilitated by the widespread adoption of life time employment in Japanese firms.[11]

In similar vein, state holding companies such as the United Kingdom's NEB and Italy's IRI have the potential to act as conglomerates with the capital-market advantage of close links with a government godfather. In practice, these institutions often face difficulties from inconsistent objectives and political interference.[12]

Another institutional form which has the potential to fare well on the integration test is industrial unionism, or amalgamation of all work groups in an industry under one umbrella negotiating body. Hardach

(1976, p. 158) discusses the role of industrial unions in West Germany:

> These industry based organisations, which represented all the workers in a particular industry (e.g. the metal industry) or related trade groups (e.g. construction and building materials), abolished the multiplicity and diffusion of the past and ended, or at least *internalised*[13] demarcation and comparability disputes. The new unions, built up from scratch, showed themselves incomparably better suited to the modern age than those inherited from the nineteenth century in some other European countries, since they facilitated a national wage policy and long term economic budgeting by management, expedited mediation, and reduced strikes and lockouts, apart from strengthening the bargaining position of the unions in the bilateral monopoly of countervailing power.

Instead of a plurality of union-management transactions when technological change requires re-negotiation of employment contracts, industrial unionism allows the integration and internalisation of differences and disputes concerning overlapping sectional interests. Such advantages have also been recognised in the UK context, which has been bedevilled by atomistic multiunionism.[14]

This is the advantage conferred at an even higher level by a further institutional alternative, the Labour-Market Board set up under the Rehn Plan in Sweden.[15] The Board is an amalgam of labour, government and employers representatives facilitating labour mobility and adjustment using investment funds and other incentives to promote change. The internalisation of potentially conflicting parties and interests within the Labour-Market Board has been successful in smoothing transition in labour-markets, and its achievements are at least partly due to the explicit recognition on all sides that change is a non-zero game from which all may benefit. As with industrial unionism, parties in the Labour-Market Board can take a long term, stable view compared to the short term perspective fostered by fragmented, pluralistic bargaining and the short term dog-eat-dog perspective it may generate.[16]

These, then, are some organisational alternatives which have the design capabilities to pass the integration test. We should beware, however, of the dangers of inferring behaviour from structure; for example, a conglomerate structure may hide neglect of capital-market opportunities, while individual industrial unions may be characterised by internecine fratricidial disputes. These institutional forms may be imbued with the potential for facilitating change but they do not guarantee it.

With these qualifications in mind, we may turn to the types of strategies that are likely to fail the integration test. To start with, specialised strategies are liable to fail in the face of rapid technological change; this is most evident in the extreme case of the single-product firm. As long as single product operation characterises the firm, the introduction of all innovation is characterised by new firms, new management contracts, new labour contracts and new capital contracts. Each innovation creates multiple transactions and corresponding high levels of transaction costs.

In theory firms could operate a specialised strategy by adopting the new technology as it appears and divesting the old. This would permit internalisation of transfer of capital and labour resources and would be consistent with the requirements of our integration test. In practice specialised systems are unlikely to be consistently successful in riding the product life cycle in this fashion. Specialisation by its very nature excludes the opportunity to learn the managerial skills necessary for product-market switching and resource transfers. Inflexibility and myopia are more easily developed. Also, if as we assumed earlier, technological change is swift and generally unexpected, there may not be time to adapt. Further, innovating systems are liable to have an information impactedness condition in their favour and in those circumstances would have a natural competitive advantage over the existing specialised system. Schumpeter's perennial gales of creative destruction generally involve an assumption of information impactedness.

Vertical integration is a particular type of specialised strategy which exacerbates the adaptiveness problems faced by such systems. The extension of corporate activity into vertically related stages of production increases the firms dependence on a single product and may create a cumbersome and conservative system. Vertically integrated systems typically are difficult to change or redirect; the sheer size of the vertically integrated set of operations frequently means that any attempts at diversification are liable to be regarded as peripheral or marginal in the corporate strategies with attendant prospects for being ignored or mismanaged. Also, once the decline phrase of the product-line cycle is entered, there is also the danger that the large capital commitment required to simply stay in a vertically integrated business will soak up the increasingly scarce funds available from internal and external sources, inhibiting the diversification escape route. Thus, vertical integration constitutes an extreme form of specialisation with special associated dangers in conditions of rapid technological change and leads to it being classified as a fail strategy in the integration test.

It is the specialisation/diversification split which also leads to the UK system of industrial nationalisation posing difficulties in terms of the integration principle. The UK nationalised industries are typically formed to exploit one basic material, product or function – such as gas, steel, electricity and rail.[17] Their strategy is specified and constrained by Act of Parliament, and consequently they are tied into a specific product life cycle. Adaptability and change is legislated away.[18]

Finally, multiunionism can create the fragmented collective bargaining system that requires multiple agreements and recontracting before change can take place. The evolution of UK trade unions along historic lines of craft and skill has resulted in multi-unionism in many areas and associated problems of demarcation, differentials and sectional interests.[19]

Just as *Wealth of Nations* and *Free to Choose* may be regarded as old-fashioned prescriptions more appropriate to 'Auld Lang Syne', so the fail strategies represent traditional solutions that are liable to inhibit innovation and change. By way of contrast, the pass list contains strategies which have evolved as demonstrably successful systems for encouraging growth and development in the respective countries. While the list was not drawn up to prove this point, it is interesting to note that the UK is characterised more by traditional fail solutions, such as nationalisation and multiunionism, than it is by the successful strategies associated with the integration test.[20] Designing strategies which carefully avoid the market transaction costs of innovation is not something at which the UK has been conspicuously successful. In those circumstances, it appears almost surprising that UK industry had the ability to be world leaders in the nineteenth and early twentieth centuries. However, the product-market characteristics of relatively simple technology and long product lines that characterised this period ensured that market transaction costs were generally low. For example, in the capital-market, these characteristics ensured that banks had the time and ability to evaluate the market potential of technologies; in the labour-market, craft based unionisation could be reasonably based round the relatively stable nature of most jobs and skills required by firms; in the product-market corporate specialisation was facilitated by the occasional nature of technological change. The

externally financed, craft unionised, specialised corporation constituted an appropriate system under those favourable product-market
conditions. Only when rapid technological change created substantial
transaction costs did these systems begin to encounter efficiency
problems. W.A. Lewis has also pointed out that Britain achieved her
early industrialisation through innovations in textiles and iron manufactures, and since cotton and iron factories were small, a belief in
individualism and atomistic competition was promoted and reinforced
(1957, p. 585). This was viable during the Industrial Revolution but
now betrays signs of obsolesence and integration problems.

In fact, this perspective on change and adjustment reverses the
emphasis placed on these issues in neoclassical theory. Instead of
'growth theory' we have 'retardation theory'.[21] Instead of looking at
the factors fostering growth, we focus on the features restricting or
inhibiting growth. In a sense it is not remarkable that some countries
have grown rapidly in the post-war period; the accumulation of
scientific and technical developments has continually enlarged production possibilities. What does require explanation is why some countries
have not taken advantage of technological change to pursue economic
growth.[22] It is the failure to realise the potential afforded by
technological progress that must be explained. Kuznets (1979)
expresses the problem clearly:

The various institutional adjustments and shifts in conditions of
work and life, required for effective channeling of the continuous
stream of technological innovations, were neither easy, nor costless.
The gap between the stock of knowledge and inventions as the
necessary condition, and the institutional and social adjustments
that would convert the former into a sufficient condition, is wide – as
past history of the economically developed countries and the current
history of the less developed amply show. (p. 12)

This interpretation is reinforced by Ayres (1944) earlier analysis of
the role of institutions in economic growth; 'Did institutions such as
those of business enterprise, democracy and the like 'make possible'
the development of the industrial economy? That has been the
traditional belief. There is a sense in which that belief is true. But there
is a more important sense in which it is quite false. The difference is
between active and passive agents. If the institutional structure which
prevailed in Western Europe prior to the industrial revolution of the
last five centuries or so had been sufficiently solid and rigid to inhibit

technological change, then it goes without saying that the change would not have occurred. Since the industrial revolution did occur, obviously the institutional structure which it confronted was insufficiently solid to prevent change. The structure was a causally significant part of the total situation; but its significance was – and consequently is still – permissive, not dynamic.'[23]

We can further express the significance of this perspective as follows; if we ignore institutional arrangements of the type discussed in this section, then rapid growth is the natural state of economies in the post-war period given the rapidity of technological change over that period, while slow growth appears puzzling if not downright inexplicable.

Economic stagnation cannot be explained without institutional analysis. As Olsen (1982) points out, resource endowment is not adequate to explain the growth of Japan[24] and an equally fallacious argument is that Japan and Germany were fortunate enough to be forced to reinvest due to war destruction of plant and equipment, while Britain was 'cursed' with inheritance of obsolescent capital.[25] Olsen argues that growth is more likely a consequence of destruction not of hardware, but of institutional rigidities in these countries. Kuznets (1959) and (1979), and Rosenberg (1982) have also emphasised the dual role of innovation and institutional flexibility in promoting growth; like Olsen's their analysis meshes with and complements the transaction cost analysis we have pursued here.

Neoclassical theory leads to growth theory, transaction cost analysis leads to retardation theory. The latter route appears to go further and ask the right questions. It implies that there is no one road to economic success. In Chapter 9 we examined how different countries saddled different economic horses for different courses; Japan is a country in which the giant Zaibatsu corporate empire represents the roots of rapid economic progress, Hong Kong is a living example of successful *laissez-faire* economics, Sweden is a socialist welfare state that ranks among the world leaders in terms of living standards. The firm, the market and the state have all contributed to the growth and living standards of each country, though in different measure in each case. Each has advantages and disadvantages depending on circumstances. Only dogmatists claim universal superiority for one or other system of economic organisation.

BROADER CONSIDERATIONS: DISTRIBUTION OF INCOME AND MACROECONOMICS

In this work we have been concerned with positive and normative issues in relation to the efficiency of economic organisation. We have concentrated on resource allocation and largely ignored questions of income distribution and macroeconomic behaviour. Rather than attempt a major extension of the work into these areas we shall give brief consideration to two related issues; the supposed efficiency/ equality trade-off in microeconomics and the role of aggregation and information problems in macroeconomics.

Firstly, the efficiency/equality trade-off is well enough established in the conventional wisdom of economics to rank alongside diminishing returns as one of the few economic laws; greater equality of distribution of income is only achievable at the expense of economic efficiency.

The efficiency/equality trade-off is something which every beginning student of economics leans to recite, whether taught by liberal or conservative oriented courses.[26] Measures to create a more equitable distribution of income in a market economy are seen as being at the expense of efficient resource allocation. The difference between liberal and conservative interpretations is typically reduced to *how much* efficiency should be traded for greater equity. The existence of the trade-off is never seriously challenged; 'Anyone who has passed a course in elementary economics can spout the right formal rule; promote equality[27] up to the point where the added benefits of more equality are matched by the added costs of greater inefficiency'[28] (Okun, 1973, p. 90).

The conventional wisdom is encompased by Okun's 'leaky bucket analogy' (Okun, 1975). In this analogy redistribution of water from water-rich to water-poor areas can be carried out using a leaky bucket – greater equality in water shares is thus achieved at the expense of overall water availability. The question posed by Okun is: how much of a leak should be tolerated before redistribution is no longer deemed worthwhile? A small leak results in a slight loss in efficiency due to redistribution, while a gaping hole in the bucket results in equality being achieved at the expense of a high cost in terms of sacrificed efficiency. The leaky bucket analogy is intended to elicit opinions and judgements on how much of a trade-off individuals are willing to tolerate in the context of dual efficiency/equality objectives.

The trouble with the 'leaky bucket analogy' is that it is of the 'when-did-you-stop-beating-your-wife' type; the question is loaded. Okuns' analogy presumes that a trade-off exists between efficiency and equality. Though the basis for the trade-off is usually not pursued in depth, it is in fact based on two propositions. They are both discussed below.

Proposition I: The free operation of the market leads to gross inequality of income

If all start with equal endowments of resources, survival of the fittest in the market-place will eventually create extreme inequality of income if left uncontrolled. Differences in luck, hard work and ability will create Carnegies, Rockefellers, skid row and the soup kitchen. The market is a hard – and generous – task master. As Nell (Bell and Kristol, 1981, p. 198) argues: 'The Invisible Hand, if it is to be found anywhere, is likely to be found picking the pockets of the poor.'

Proposition II: The free operation of the market leads to the highest attainable level of efficiency in the economy

Natural selection through the market mechanism of the most productive and profitable systems leads to maximum efficiency.[29] Monopoly is regarded as an aberration in this respect whose potential seriousness depends on whether a liberal or conservative perspective is adopted.

These two propositions together lead to a simple conclusion; the highest attainable level of efficiency in the economy is associated with gross inequality of income. This is the relationship at the core of the concept of the hypothesised efficiency/equality trade-off; if the free operation of the market is tinkered with to reduce inequities in income distribution, the Darwinist efficiency machine will cease to operate so smoothly and effectively. Reducing the pay-offs from luck, hardwork and ability will reduce the incentives that create maximum economic efficiency.

The efficiency/equality trade-off is founded on these two propositions. Therefore it would seem reasonable to give them rather closer scrutiny than is usually provided in this context. Proposition I is in fact entirely reasonable. The extreme income differentials associated with a pure market regime is generally recognised and rarely questioned. Liberals, conservatives, and Marxists generally agree on this relationship, differing only on their interpretation of the consequences of extreme inequity and associated solutions.[30]

The problem lies with Proposition II. In one sense this whole book could be regarded as an argument against Proposition II. Trading may incur transactions costs that create inefficiencies in market exchange systems. The market is only one of three forms of economic organisation each of which may provide the greatest level of attainable efficiency, depending on circumstances. In the absence of innovation, market exchange may well emerge as the most favoured system, but as we have seen technological change disrupts the signalling process of the price system.

Thus market exchange may lead to inefficiency. In these circumstances it may be that some measures contribute to both efficiency and equality. For example, education may be poorly and unevenly supported in an inequitable market system; state support for education may improve efficiency *and* equality. Similarly, state funding of alternative technologies in less developed countries may improve both overall productivity and the distribution of income. It is also worth noting that the successful Japanese and Swedish economies are amongst the most equitable for any of the OECD countries,[31] a phenomenon that is difficult to reconcile with any supposed efficiency/equality trade-off.

The efficiency/equality trade-off is generally stated as a truism. The examples above should not be interpreted to suggest that efficiency never trades-off against equality, only that the trade-off is not automatic. Whether a trade-off exists is an empirical question, and should be treated as such.

As far as the relevance of the analysis here to macroeconomics is concerned, we conclude by considering this question. Our concern in this book has been primarily microeconomic but it has macroeconomic implications by definition since macroeconomics is traditionally interpreted as aggregative economics. It is the economics of aggregate demand and aggregate supply and consequently the basic elements of any macroeconomic analysis are microeconomic, the individual consumer and product summed at the level of the economy.

Macroeconomic analysis does not usually concern itself with its microeconomic foundations. Such neglect is justifiable when assumptions regarding the behaviour and characteristics of the basic elements are reasonable. It is not when the assumptions are inappropriate. It will be recalled that separability of basic elements is an essential requirement of aggregation; we have argued that non-separability is a general feature of corporate behaviour and that simple aggregation of product-markets ignores this phenomenon. This argument has been pursued at the level of the corporation in this work and in Kay (1979 and 1982) and support provided to the extent derived theories have aided empirical explanation. The argument extends to macroeconomic levels; if aggregation is generally an inappropriate technique at intermediate levels (individual product-markets up to the level of the firm), how can it still be regarded as legitimate at macroeconomic levels (individual product-markets up to the level of the economy)? Chemical and biological systems are not analysed as simple aggregates of atoms and molecules, nor should corporations and economies be interpreted as the sum of individual product-markets. Instead a rich variety of structural models are available in chemistry and biology to analyse the behaviour of systems in which the *relationship* between basic elements is regarded as a central feature of the analysis.

As far as the implications for macroeconomic theory is concerned, this has to be left an open question. Traditionally economists have been notable for their laziness as far as empirical leg-work is concerned – even at micro level where a rich variety of system behaviours might be expected economists have basically relied on a handful of elementary models which typically differ from perfect competition only in one or two key assumptions. An anthropologist may spend years squating in the Upper Amazon establishing the basic kinship relationships operating in a single tribe, a chemist may spend long months deciphering the structural relationships for a single enzyme, yet a neoclassical economist has the comforting *a priori* knowledge that his probable basic relationship is that which exists between a downward sloping revenue curve and an upward sloping cost curve. The complexities of tribal networks and chemical molecules have no parallel in the simplistic world view of neoclassical theory. Aggregation perpetuates simplicity at macroeconomic level which operates at a level of abstraction some steps further divorced from microeconomic reality. How the macromachine could be refashioned is a highly speculative question since macroeconomics is a product of macroeconomists, and most macroeconomists do not have a mental set that easily accommodates nondecomposable systems. Monetarists and Keynesians still talk in terms of aggregate demand and aggregate supply.

It will be remembered that in Chapter 2 we identified a second major economic problem area in addition to aggregation, the neglect of information problems in economic theory building. In fact Keynes was fundamentally concerned with problems of uncertainty and information in constructing his General Theory. Such problems are difficult to accommodate within a formal analytical framework, and much revisionism of Keynesian theory has been concerned with attempting to squeeze it into a rigorous mathematical structure epitomised by Hicks development of the IS/LM framework. This difference between what Keynes said, and what subsequent analysts have remoulded as Keynesian economics led to Leijonhuvfuds *On Keynesian Economics and the Economics of Keynes*. In this respect, the suppressing of information problems may be also identified as a central problem of macroeconomic theory building also. In a sense we have already been concerned with macroeconomics in this chapter, or at least the microfoundations of economic growth. The microfoundations of macroeconomics have been a longstanding preoccupation of neoclassical theorists, understandably so, since the macroworld is perceived as the simple aggregate of microlevels in the paradigm. It is interesting that Hicks has recently (1979) testified to the difficulties encountered by neoclassical theory in this area, with specific reference to a conference on this topic which had generally adopted the unsatisfactory view that the microeconomics of the firm and the individual was a solid foundation on which to build (see pp. vii–viii).

The economics of stagflation (or simultaneity of low growth, high unemployment and inflation) is the central macroeconomic problem being faced by a number of western economies in the present day. It represents a novel post-war problem for government and its possible causes have been stimulated substantial discussion and controversy.

The emergence of stagflation can perhaps be better understood if we stand the problem on its head, much as we did in inverting growth questions into retardation questions. Instead of asking why stagflation has appeared recently in modern economies, it is useful to ask why it has not appeared before. As Samuelson (1980) points out (p. 780) the early days of capitalism was characterised by a 'cruel economy' in which unemployment carried a penalty which was enormous in human terms. Nowadays 'buddy can you spare a dime?' has been largely replaced by unemployment compensation, redundancy payments, welfare support and so the penalties of adventurous and inflationary wage and price increases have been greatly softened. The existence of safety nets encourages high flying on the wages and prices trapeze.

As Myrdal (1976) points out, conventional theory has contributed little to the analysis of such problems, not surprisingly since the problem is essentially institutional (pp. 88–9).[32] Myrdal's point is supported when we consider Veblens early interpretation of institutionalism;

An institution is of the nature of a usage which has become axiomatic and indispensable by habituation and general acceptance. Its physiological counterpart would presumably be any of those habitual conditions that are now attracting the attention of the experts in sobriety.

In this context, such an interpretation expresses well the characteristics of the wage round and wage and salaries differentials as a basis for beginning that have characterised UK collective bargaining. It is consistent with Hamiltons (1932) definition of 'institutions' as connoting 'a way of thought or action of some prevalence or permanence which is embedded in the habits of a group or the customs of a people' (p. 84).[33]

Indeed it is interesting to consider the solutions proposed to deal with stagflation; in many cases the tools suggested by in-principle neoclassicists have a strong institutional flavour. While such pragmatism indicates a creditable flexibility going beyond the limits of the neoclassical framework, it smacks of ad-hocery unless the solutions are placed in an appropriate theoretical context. Incomes policy, adoption of centralised bargaining as in Sweden, and Thatcher's hard line on wage and salaries increases, are all attempts to foster institutional change in the collective bargaining process in so far as they are intended to directly or indirectly create changes in habits and customs in the labour-market. Since such institutional questions do not appear on the neoclassical agenda of aggregate fiscal and monetary relationships, neoclassical theory is not an appropriate framework for looking at the sources of stagflation any more than it is suitable for examination of the sources of economic growth itself.

It is unlikely that any simple or single solution to stagflation is to be found. Remedies must be fitted to the special circumstances facing a particular economy at a given point in its historical development. What is essential is that the question must be framed correctly, and institutionally framed questions are more likely to be successful in this area.

Both aggregation and information problems are therefore liable to be of relevance at macroeconomic level as well as microeconomic. Problems of market, corporate and state behaviour are still important in this context as well as at microeconomic level. If our analysis has an implication for macroeconomic theory building at this juncture, it is that the market, the corporation and government intervention are only tools for economic decision-makers to utilise. They are not ends in themselves. These simple points tend to be obscured by the tendency of some economic analysis to elevate such tools to the level of political philosophy. They do of course have an integral part to play in this arena, the difficulties arise when philosophical arguments become firmed down into unscientific dogma and their functional roles become obscured. Just as technique has overrun economic science, so the means have become ends in themselves as far as choice of economic organisation is concerned in the perspective of some economists.

DIRECTIONS

Most critiques of neoclassical theory have been primarily concerned with the symptoms of neoclassical malfunctioning, less with possible avenues of escape from the neoclassical impasse. A reasonable defence by neoclassical theorists in such circumstances is that while neoclassical theory may be demonstrably defective, until something superior comes along it is the best we have. The major objective of this work has been to not only identify the source of problems in neoclassical theory, but to use this analysis as a stepping stone to fashioning an alternative approach. It is argued here that a viable and superior substitute for neoclassical theory may be developed and indeed that the basic materials for such an approach have already been laid out by behavioural and institutional economists and other social scientists. We have hopefully demonstrated in previous chapters how these foundations may be integrated into a workable framework and applied to actual problems of economic behaviour.

We can simply summarise the deficiencies with neoclassical theory before suggesting directions to be pursued by future investigations. As far as the firm is concerned, neoclassical theory is effectively built on one major decision-making problem – *optimal product-market price*. The optimal price may differ depending on whether we are looking at decision-making from the point of view of the entrepreneur, or society as a whole. However, the structure of the decision-making process is identical irrespective of the perspective of the decision-maker in neoclassical theory; *optimal* decisions are still expressed as problems in constrained maximisation, individual *products* are still the basic unit of analysis, *market* exchange is still the sole form of economic organisa-tion, while *prices* provide all necessary information.

Our analysis criticises each of these four components of neoclassical theory as being inadequate for the development of a reasonable theory of economic behaviour. We may consider each component in turn in the light of our analysis from previous chapters.

Optimal: the constrained maximisation approach requires perfect knowledge conditions to hold or be approximated (pure risk was seen earlier as being only marginally different from perfect knowledge in terms of requisite information conditions). Entrepreneurial Salome and related analysis demonstrated the sterility of such assumptions except in extremely limited circumstances. As has been discussed in this text, unless bounded rationality conditions are explicitly brought into consideration, neoclassical theory *must* remain internally self contradictory or be unable to deal with the rich variety of economic issues that has been our concern in this book. However, bounded rationality cannot be assimilated within neoclassical theory since it implies conditions of true uncertainty that precludes optimisation. Faced with the fog of uncertainty, the high precision zoom lens of neoclassical optimisation technique is rendered useless. Rather than pretend the fog does not exist, we suggest recognition of its existence is an essential precursor to theory building.

Product: as discussed here, particularly in Chapter 6, and in more detail in Kay (1982), the basic building blocks of corporate behaviour are constituent links rather than individual product-markets. Instead of being a collection of individual and isolated atoms, the corporation more resembles a complex molecule composed of product-markets linked by market and technological bonds. As discussed in Chapter 2, treating individual product-markets as separable, independent units facilitates the use of aggregation in neoclassical theory. However, the economic behaviour of the firm does not resemble the atomistic world of neoclassical theory. If economic scientists must draw on the natural sciences for inspiration and technique they might better study the chemistry of the firm rather than its physics. Portraying the economic world as a series of unrelated product-markets distorts and misleads rather than illuminates.

Market: as long as bounded rationality is not a problem, market exchange is an efficient method of economic organisation (indeed, one of the points made early in this work was that in the absence of information problems *any* form of economic organisation is efficient). As a consequence, neoclassical theory and the mainstream economic tradition has been solely concerned with the behaviour of markets. However, once bounded rationality problems in the form of trans-action costs are recognised in market behaviour, the economic problem becomes one of comparative institutional analysis in which the firm, the market, and the state each represent alternative mechanisms for organising resource allocation, each with their peculiar type of cost resulting from bounded rationality issues. Unless bounded rationality issues are explicitly discussed, no sensible analysis of forms of economic organisation other than market exchange can be developed. We have argued here that markets represent only one limited facet of economic organisation in modern developed economies, and consequently such neglect is serious. Most substantive issues in resource allocation cannot be addressed by attention to markets alone, yet in the days of ITT and General Electric we may still observe such neoclassical theorists as Gilder and Friedman purporting to provide a credible recipe for industrial organisation by using the entrepreneurial firm as their basic unit of analysis.[34]

Prices: in neoclassical theory, prices are the only relevant pieces of information. Such limitations are reasonable if bounded rationality problems are not significant in other areas. In such circumstances neoclassical theory can be applied to the behaviour of markets using constrained optimisation techniques. However, prices are only one limited class of information generally required in transactions and organisations. We have demonstrated the implications of introducing non-price information in economic organisation in Chapter 5, particularly the implication for the workings of the market mechanism and optimisation techniques. Not surprisingly, neoclassical theorists are reluctant to open the can of strange loops associated with information problems. However, we have argued that it is the existence of information problems in general that provides the rationale for such diverse phenomena as multinational enterprise, hierarchy, diversification, vertical integration, etc. If prices were the only category of information relevant to economic analysis then most of the economic phenomena and issues discussed in this book would not exist – indeed this, or any other book, would not exist in the perfect knowledge state of neoclassical Nirvana. It is the real world issues of bounded rationality, uncertainty and associated information problems that must feed into theory building. It is such a starting point that was adopted in this book.

Therefore the pursuit of the optimal product-market price in neoclassical theory is generally a faulty basis for consideration of resource allocation issues. On each count – the concept of optimality, the product level foundation, concentration on market exchange and the role of prices – neoclassical theory has been argued to be deficient for an adequate study of resource allocation issues.

The product level foundation is inadequate because product market linkages imply non-decomposable systems. Optimality is unattainable, except in certain restrictive circumstances, due to bounded rationality conditions; bounded rationality also severely qualifies the effectiveness of markets and prices. Thus, bounded rationality and the existence of product market linkages represent the two major sources of objection to neoclassical theory. It is therefore only reasonable that they should also form the basis for an alternative perspective as discussed here. We have argued that bounded rationality and product-market linkages serve as essential foundations for a workable theory of the firm, and discussed related principles and applications in the previous chapters.

Neoclassical theory has not found useful answers to resource allocation issues because it has posed the wrong question. If our concern is with the explanation of economic behaviour and with finding means to improve the welfare and standards of living in an economy, then the question of optimal product-market price and its variants is a cul de sac. Instead the fundamental economic question becomes 'what is the form of economic organisation that best facilitates innovation?' The question can be applied to firms, bureaucracies, and economies, singly or combination, for a specific society or a given point in its history. It is an institutional question.

The analysis here should not be regarded in isolation but in the spirit of well-developed traditions in economic theorising; behavioural theorists such as Simon, Cyert, and March, Institutionalists such as Galbraith and Williamson, and Post-Keynesians[35] such as Davidson and Shackle have all contributed to the literature on bounded rationality. Similarly, Ansoff has provided early analysis of the implications of product-market linkage; also in Kay (1982) it was pointed out that theorising based on system linkages has been a standard feature of other social sciences – Structuralists such as Chomsky, Piaget and Lévi-Strauss, have all based their theories on such interrelationships.

Given the breadth and depth of studies such as the above that may be interpreted as consistent with the principles underlying this work, it appears surprising that mainstream economics has not been significantly affected (or infected, depending on one's perspective). In fact, the theories, models, and textbooks that a contemporary student of economics is exposed to typically reflects a strong neoclassical basis with little, if any, recognition of alternative approaches. The constrained maximisation approach is still the basic technique employed in economic model building.

The insulation of neoclassical theory from empirical reality and competing paradigms has been virtually complete. It is interesting to consider how such insulation has been effected. Economists who have been concerned with bounded rationality issues have tended to be ignored, or assimilated and neutralised. The treatment of Keynes work is an interesting example of the latter process; the IS/LM system developed by Hicks as a framework to accommodate Keynesian analysis was a system of determinate equilibrium relationships.

Keynes' analysis of the implications of uncertainty was fundamental to his interpretation of economic behaviour, but it was squeezed out of the formal system of the IS/LM framework. Modern decision theorists concerned with decision-making under uncertainty tend to interpret Knight's distinction between risk and uncertainty as being an unnecessary complication. Williamson's early analysis on management utility maximisation is well known and still exhaustively discussed through his later work on transaction cost analysis is rarely referred to.[36] In one sense this appears surprising since Williamson now regards his early models as special cases of his more general later work; in another sense it is perfectly understandable since his early work uses constrained maximisation techniques associated with neoclassical theory, while his later work adopts an entirely different perspective. The similarities between managerial utility maximisation and neoclassical theory are greater than the differences. And, as we have seen earlier, Galbraith has been fairly briskly dismissed by mainstream economists as being concerned with non-economic matters such as power and institutional behaviour. Even the latest macroeconomic 'revolution' to deal with problems of information, Rational Expectations theory, is based firmly on traditional foundations of optimising and aggregation (see Willes (1981) and Maddock and Carter (1982)). Rational expectations, or 'Ratex' (further discussion in the readings edited by Dell and Kristol, 1981) is based on the presumption that the decision-maker has complete knowledge of the parameters of the real economic world, including government policy effects (see Davidson (1981) p. 162 for contrast with the post Keynesian philosophy). There are no surprises in Rational Expectations.

In this manner, mainstream economics has continued to be a fertile source of sterile theories, protected and buttressed by such defences. It represents an intellectual tragedy of the first order. The waste of potential academic talent, the premature hardening of cerebral arteries bred by repetitive neoclassical modelling, and the filtering out of bright, deviant students who regard neoclassical theory as irrelevant or unrealistic, all these factors perpetuate the neoclassical paradigm as the basic framework for economic analysis. The process starts with first year economics textbook; once the *tabula rasa* of beginning students has been filled in with neoclassical theory and IS/LM macromodels, it creates a deterministic equilibrium mental set by which future analysis is judged, accommodated, or rejected. Irrevocable damage is done in the first few terms of economic teaching experienced by a new student. Once started, the process is depressingly self-perpetuating; the individual intent on pursuing a career as economist has to be bright enough to understand the abstract ramifications of neoclassical theory and dumb enough to have faith in them. The profession of economics self selects a special breed of intellectual schizophrenic.

While we have not been directly concerned with macroeconomics in this work there are implications which may be of interest for future analysis. Bounded rationality and non-decomposable systems contradict the deterministic aggregate basis of conventional macroeconomic framework epitomised by the IS/LM framework. The economic engine may be tuned by monetary and fiscal policy, but the fundamentals of engine design are more likely to be dependent on institutional, psychological, social and cultural factors. The Post-Keynesians represent a school expressly concerned with bounded rationality considerations in macroeconomic analysis and there may be interesting connections between this school and the microeconomics of transaction cost analysis that merit further exploration.[37] At microeconomic levels, the Institutional economists have traditionally recognised both the importance of unpredictable 'uncertain change' (Commons, 1961) and the centrality of technological change in this process (see Gordon, 1980 pp. 10–16), though until Williamson's development it lacked an integrated framework.[38] It is reassuring to recognise that other economists have diagnosed the problem correctly in the past, and it is on their insights that this work has been developed. We hope that the analysis in this book has helped to support the contention made at the beginning, that economics is about information problems.

CONCLUSION

If, today, a relaxant was introduced that was physiologically addictive and could be expected to cause considerable numbers of deaths from cancer, drug regulations in most countries would inevitably prohibit it. Yet we have tobacco. If anybody today invented a sport which ritualised physical assault intended to concuss an opponent, and which resulted in cumulative brain damage and occasional deaths, there would be a public outcry. Yet we have boxing. If the neoclassical theory of the firm had remained in Nirvana, and somebody today published a proposal for a theory of the firm based on omniscient owner-managers of single product firms, the absurdity of this concept would guarantee it a brief life cycle. Yet we have the neoclassical theory of the firm. In these examples, origins predate modern times. Vested interests and habit perpetuate obsolescence and create a more favourable climate for acceptance than would be the case if each issue was introduced fresh today. Each in its own way represents an anachronism left over from a more primitive age, though each is still very much alive and kicking. Perhaps we should learn from the other two cases and tack a government health warning onto neoclassical models or require a doctor to be present whenever neoclassical theorising is to be practiced.

To the extent the language of this text has appeared intemperate at times, it reflects exasperation that current economic theory contains too much bad science and too little of relevance to real world problems. At policy level the level of potential human misery or happiness that hangs on the foundations of economic recommendations makes empirical relevance a critical feature of economic debate. Yet professionalism in economics is still equated with technical discussions around such problems as uniqueness solutions for general equilibrium systems. Even Gullivers Lilliputians, who spent many happy hours in debate over whether eggs should be opened at the narrow end or the broad end, did not go so far; at least eggs exist. Yet economic policies today affecting millions of people are frequently based on non-existent firms and imaginary economic systems bearing no relationship to economic reality. The stakes are high and the theoretical perspective is crucial in dictating policy analysis.

Diagnosis must precede prescription. Explanation of economic behaviour is a necessary prerequisite for normative policy-making. Rather than starting from an idealised view of how the world should be, economic analysis should adopt the iterative relationship between theory and observation generally pursued by the other sciences, both natural and social. Only in those circumstances can economic theory contribute to understanding and to policy.

Notes

CHAPTER 1: INTRODUCTION

1. 'There is much of economic theory which is pursued for no better reason than its intellectual attraction; it is a good game' (Hicks, 1979, pp. viii).
2. See Spadaro ed. (1978) for recent perspectives on Austrian economics, especially the articles by Lachman and Egger.
3. We shall be discussing post-Keynesian theory in more detail later. In some cases behavioural theorists have also tended to leave the centrality of product-market price undisturbed.
4. The contestable markets literature suggests that linkages between product-markets are a useful basis for theory development, rather than individual products.
5. Transfer pricing could be said to still deal with markets in an internal sense. The standard analyses of transfer pricing problems are Hirshleifer (1956) and (1957).
6. See Chamberlin (1933) and Robinson (1933).
7. A good example of how such insularity and internal consistency is maintained is evidenced by the severity of the hatchet job conducted on J.K. Galbraith from within the profession (see, for example, Scott Gordon, 1968 and Solow, 1967) compared to the general acceptance of Milton Friedman *qua* economist within the economics establishment. Galbraith attacks the basic foundations of conventional economic theory, and to my mind, attempts a skilled and thoughtful analysis of real-world problems and their theoretical implications in his various writings. Friedman's analysis is simplistic and dogmatic by comparison and compromised to the extent that his analysis typically involves a solution (free markets) looking for a problem. Despite Galbraith's more balanced approach, Friedman has been generally treated as the more respectable economist since his work can be accommodated within the traditional neoclassical framework attacked by Galbraith.
8. Bell and Kristol, eds (1981).
9. Ward (1972).
10. Balogh (1982).
11. See, for example, Blaug (1980, ch. 15), Davidson (1978, esp. ch. 16), Hutchison (1977), Bell and Kristol, eds (1981), Loasby (1976), and Balogh (1982).
12. Structuralism in this context is associated with the analysis developed by other social scientists such as Chomsky, Piaget, and Lévi-Strauss. For a fuller discussion, see Kay (1982, esp. pp. 11–29).
13. Decomposability is a corollary of aggregation. If systems can be treated as

composed of *separable* elements then aggregation and disaggregation (or decomposability) of system characteristics can be conducted without distorting the description of the system. The existence of *linkages* interferes with aggregation and may be associated with non-decomposability.

CHAPTER 2: THE PROBLEM

1. Examples of such approaches include the Behavioural School (associated most particularly with H.A. Simon as well as R.M. Cyert and J.G. March, 1963) and the Transaction Cost school (recently resurrected by O.E. Williamson, 1975).
2. Davidson (1978) points out that money only matters in a world of uncertainty; money's special properties as a store of wealth is due to its ability to postpone rigid and far reaching resource commitments (p. 16).
3. See Loasby (1967) for discussion in this spirit.
4. As Robert Solow (1967) remarks in a review of Galbraith's *The New Industrial State*, if Galbraith's approach works, then 'Apres moi la sociologie.'
5. Kay (1982) discusses these problems in more detail and builds an economic theory of diversification around the concepts of product market linkages and bounded rationality.
6. Though we shall be mentioning some relevant macroeconomic considerations in later comments on Keynes and Friedman's analysis.
7. However, some income distribution problems will be alluded to later, particularly in discussion of public policy questions.
8. Katouzian (1980) and Loasby (1976) present two contemporary critiques.
9. For further analysis of behavioural theory and its implications, see Cyert and March (1963), Day (1967) Day and Tinney (1968), Baumol and Stewart (1971), Cyert and Hedrick (1972) and Kay (1979).
10. For further analysis using evolutionary theory in economics, see Alchian (1950), Winter (1964), Winter (1971), Nelson and Winter (1973), Nelson *et al.* (1976).
11. See Hirshleifer and Riley (1979) for a survey of recent literature in this area.
12. The work on contestable markets has from the beginning been heavily concerned with economies of scope which derive from 'strict subadditivity of the cost function, meaning that the cost of the sum of any M output vectors is less than the sum of the costs of producing them separately' (Baumol, 1977, p. 801).

   The concept is in fact a formalisation of the concept of synergy introduced into the corporate strategy literature by Ansoff (1965). Other works looking at the implications of economies of scope for multi-product firms include Baumol, Bailey and Willig (1977), Baumol and Braunstein (1977), Baumol and Fischer (1978) and Willig (1979). Recent surveys are provided by Baumol, Panzer and Willig (1982) and Bailey and Friedlander

(1982). As the latter work makes clear (p. 1025), this literature is intended as an extension of the existing structure–conduct–performance paradigm of industrial organisation.

13. This is a crude summary of neoclassical efficiency conditions. Numerous elaborations of the derived conditions are available. A good straightforward coverage is provided by Hirshleifer (1980).

14. Bearing in mind that the efficiency rules must still invoke strong assumptions such as divisibility, perfect knowledge, etc. in their formal development.

15. This is a development of an example introduced in Kay (1982).

16. See McGuigan and Moyer (1976, pp. 582–5) for a deeper analysis of this basic argument.

17. For examples, see Hirshleifer (1980, pp. 534–5) and McGuigan and Moyer (1975, pp. 586–41).

18. Even if all externalities were not internalised by nationalisation, appropriate pricing policies would adjust output of the nationalised industry to the optimum level for that industry. Here we are presuming the nationalised industry pursues the national interest and does not limit itself to promoting its own sectional interest.

19. There is now a voluminous literature on the Coase Theorem and its implications. For an exhaustive analysis and coverage, see Hoffman and Spitzer (1982, pp. 73–5).

20. This obviously begs the question of who *should* pay. All that is being analysed here is whether an efficient allocation of resources would obtain. Two texts already referred to, Hirshleifer (1980, ch. 17), and McGuigan and Moyer (1975, ch. 20), provide extensive analysis of these points discussed here.

    The arguments underlying trading of property rights also holds for the auxiliary industry externality. While this may offer an unnatural or unlikely example for property rights trading, the principle of the Coase Theorem is still applicable in this case.

21. We should also add, for sake of completeness, that we have not exhausted the variety of forms that control of externalities may take. For example, government regulation, taxation or subsidy may provide methods of correction even when other institutional arrangements do not adequately internalise the externality.

22. In case this conclusion should be thought to be obvious, it is worth pointing out that Ansoff (1965) conducts an extensive analysis of the implications of intra-firm exploitation of economies of this type without systematically exploring the possibility that they may be traded in the market-place.

23. If anyone is uncomfortable with the generality 'some neoclassical theorists', for this phrase read 'Milton Friedman'.

24. Although some large divisionalised firms can create internal quasi-markets by using transfer pricing systems.

25. Analysis in the spirit of this section is developed in more detail in my forthcoming paper in the *Journal of Economic Studies* under the title 'Optimal Size of Firm as a Problem in Transaction Costs and Property Rights'.

26. These are as set out by Koch (1980).
27. Kalder (1934) developed his argument to demonstrate the inconsistency between the assumption of perfect foresight in perfect competition and the necessity to identify managerial co-ordination as the sole firm specific limited factor in the long run. It could also be added that if it is assumed scarcity of resources is the source of increased prices of resources (and the firms U-shaped cost curve), then partial equilibrium analysis breaks down (Sraffa, 1926).
28. As will be discussed in Chapter 3, advertising depends on the existence of information problems.

CHAPTER 3: ENTREPRENEURIAL SALOME

1. Useful audits of neoclassical theory and its empirical implications are conducted by Shackle (1967), Hay and Morris (1979) and Loasby (1971), the latter being contained in the broader ranging Loasby (1976) which is also of relevance to this issue.
2. See Winter (1964) and Scherer (1980, p. 38) for related discussions.
3. A good present-day example of the dangers of specialisation is that of the endangered species of Koala bears in Australia. Their diet is highly idiosyncratic, specialising in a limited type of eucalyptus leaves found only in a restricted number of places.
4. We could have chosen the more complex divisionalised form for our example but this does not add to the illustrative usefulness of the example.
5. An extensive literature on managerial theory sprang up in the sixties, but since then there have been few developments of real significance. Baumol (1958 and 1959), Williamson (1964), Marris (1963 and 1966) represent the standard contributions to this area. In recent years, Williamson has reinterpreted his earlier managerial theory in the 1964 work as being a special case and turned to the more general transaction cost analysis as represented by his 1975 work, abandoning constrained maximisation techniques in the process.

    See also Penrose (1959), J. Williamson (1966), Machlup (1967), Lackman and Craycroft (1974), Ng (1974), Wong (1975) and Yarrow (1976).
6. The dilution of ownership amongst numerous stockholders and the possibility of this leading to separation of ownership and control was the subject of Berle and Mean's work (1932).
7. For empirical analyses of the implications of managerial theories, see McGuire et al (1962), Lewellyn (1969), Masson (1971), Cosh (1975), McEachern (1975), Meeks and Whittington (1975).
8. This is similar to arguments put forward by Cyert and March (1963).
9. Advertising as both an informational and persuasive device has been well analysed in the economic literature. See, especially, Ozga (1960), Stigler (1961), Telser (1964), Doyle (1968), Nelson (1974 and 1975) and Schmalensee (1978).
10. There remains the possibility that 'image' advertising may change the

characteristics of the good consumed; the consumer buys a fast sports car because advertising successfully provides it with a macho image, or a certain washing powder because TV adverts link it with a contented domestic life. While such advertising is still, strictly speaking, concerned with the provision of information there are grounds for arguing that such information is concerned with changing the nature of the good consumed and not with compensating for informational inadequacies about the good consumed. Therefore, while difficult to differentiate in practice from simple persuasive advertising based on obvious informational inadequacies ('Zazo is better'), such image advertising does appear to be distinctive from advertising of the simple persuasive and informational types.

In fact, as far as our analysis is concerned, the distinctiveness of image advertising is illusory. If we push our perfect knowledge assumption far enough it becomes apparent that the sports car fan would know in advance of the advertising whether or not purchase of the sports car would change his image – the actual advert is redundant in this respect. Similarly the purchaser of the washing powder does not need the TV advert to inform them that the powder is associated with a happy home life – the truth or otherwise of this message would be known in advance of the advert. Therefore if perfect knowledge exists, advertising should not change preferences. In such circumstances changing of consumption patterns would be irrational, and as with all good economists such behaviour is outside the sphere of our analysis.

11. There is now a voluminous literature on the economics of innovation and R & D. For a summary of the literature and emphasis on the role of information and uncertainty in R & D, see Kay (1979) and Freeman (1982).

12. Here we go further than neoclassical theory which is concerned only with knowledge of *existing* products and processes. To this extent a neoclassical theorist might argue that we are taking the perfect knowledge assumption further than was intended in the neoclassical approach. However our analysis highlights the parallel information base of the marketing, finance and R & D functions.

13. The informational basis of differences in labour has been recognised by human capital theorists (see, for example, Schultz, 1969 and Becker, 1975).

14. The experiment itself was inspired by Pirsig (1974) who looked at the implications of removing the concept of quality from our interpretation of the world. Here we remove another concept, information problems.

15. For useful recent coverages, see Devine *et al.* (1979, pp. 259–62), Shepherd (1979, ch. 19), Koutsoyiannis (1982, ch. 2), and Scherer (1980, ch. 14).

16. For a summary of the literature, see Devine *et al.* (1979, pp. 214–25), Shepherd (1979, pp. 397–402) and Scherer (1980, ch. 15).

17. As Nordhaus argues, risk conditions in which the firm can form reliable estimates of the probability distributions of future states of the world allow expected utility maximisation procedures to be adopted. However, he concedes these circumstances may not typify technological change

circumstances. We shall return to analyse these problems of risk and uncertainty more fully in Chapter 5.

18. The persistent reader will find an adequate catalogue in Koutsoyiannis (1982, ch. 2) and Hay and Morris (1979, ch. 12 for advertising, and ch. 13 for R & D).

19. However, even this limited intention carries with it the danger that production resources would be analysed in isolation, when in fact they will have important linkages with the other resources of the firm, such as R & D, marketing and finance.

CHAPTER 4: MORE SALOME

1. We shall discuss shortly *how* policy may be decided, but leave this as an open question just now.

2. Davidson (1978) and other post-Keynesian macroeconomists make this point.

3. We leave open the question of election or selection, and related problems of weighting voter preferences etc.

4. See Koestler (1964) for an analysis of the role of surprise in humour. However, even though surprise is normally an essential element in humour, anticipation of known events can be still entertaining, as is evidenced by the popularity of re-runs of old Charlie Chaplin movies.

5. There are, of course, the possibly apocryphal stories of devotees who have seen *The Sound of Music* 100 times. We treat this as a special case.

6. Since our perfect knowledge assumption encompasses all potential technologies, then of course functions like train drivers might be automated and eliminated also.

7. The Friedmans make occasional token acknowledgments of, for example, risk-taking, opportunism and deceit (see for example, their pp. 170–1).

8. As Bell and Kristol point out, entrepreneurial decision-making under uncertainty has been discussed by J. Schumpeter, F.H. Knight and G.L.S. Shackle but do not appear in the formal models of economic theory (Bell and Kristol, eds., 1981, p. x).

9. In recent years economists have looked at bureaucracy using techniques and concepts adopted from economic theory. See especially, Downs (1967), Tullock (1965), Niskanen (1971) and Peacock (1979, ch. 17). However, the interested reader should be warned of the missionary zeal with which economics dogma has been imported for the benefits of the natives of this area.

10. Essentially maintenance, policing and protection of the public's rights, and certain public works that could not be provided out of private funds (see Friedman and Friedman, 1980, pp. 28–9).

11. This is a question we will be examining in more detail in Chapter 6.

12. One defence that the Friedmans could make, while still defending the superiority of the market system, is that firm monopolies may drive out more efficient market exchange. There is, however, no suggestion by the

Friedmans that this is regarded as a *general* reason for the existence of firms.

CHAPTER 5: RISK, UNCERTAINTY AND CHANCE

1. In his 'Chance and Necessity' (1972), Jacques Monod, the Nobel prize winning biochemist, takes an extreme reductionist perspective arguing that 'chance *alone* is at the source of every innovation, of all creation in the biosphere' (p. 110) and suggests that even ideas or cognitive innovation can be analysed in such terms (pp. 143–9, 154–5). He argues against the holistic perspectives of such system theorists as Von Bertalanffy and Koestler. Koestler's attack on materialist, reductionist, neo-Darwinism (see, for example, Koestler, 1980, which also refers specifically to Monod, p. 476), has also been criticised by Gould, a Harvard Scientist, in his extremely readable Darwinist essays on natural history (1977, p. 27 and 1980, pp. 80–4). In turn, Hofstadter (1980) on whose analysis a great deal of the development of this chapter depends, finds anti-reductionism of the Koestler type intrinsically fallacious although in a 'hard-to-pin-down way' (p. 751), and found Monod's analysis 'fertile' and 'exciting' (p. 752). On the other side, Lewis (ed.) 1974 is a collection of readings criticising *Chance and Necessity*.

   Thus we appear to have the evolutionary microanalytic approach of Hofstadter and Darwinism ranged against the systemic holistic approach of Koestler and Von Bertalanffy. Since all four theories are important to the arguments of this and the previous two books (Kay 1979 and 1982) it would seem that our analysis runs the danger of being based on inconsistent and conflicting philosophies.

   I have dealt at length with the reductionist vs. system/structure debate elsewhere in Kay (1979 and 1982). I believe a great deal of potential controversy can be resolved when it is noted that concepts such as natural selection in Darwinism, stimulus-response in behaviourism and price changes in neoclassical theory are all *causal* mechanisms. Like gravity they may contribute to a description of how systems change, but also like gravity they do not provide a description of systems characteristics. In structuralist terms these mechanisms are diachronic (involving relations over time), rather than synchronic (involving relations at a point in time).

   I believe the synchronic systems approach of Von Bertalanffy and Koestler (and of the Structuralists Piaget, Lévi-Strauss and Chomsky as discussed in Kay 1982) can be usefully meshed with the diachronic causal mechanisms of Darwinism and behaviourism, and much of my previous work (1979 and 1982) as well as the present work can be interpreted in this light.

2. Behavioural theory in economics is most strongly associated with Cyert and March (1963) who drew on H.A. Simon's work (see esp. Simon, 1961).

3. See Kay (1979), ch. 3 for a discussion of behavioural theory in this context.

4. See Friedman (1953) and Machlup (1946).
5. Shackle (1970) distinguishes between the surprise value of two types of events: 'a hypothetical event or class of events can have been envisaged and excluded, can have been dismissed in the sense of being assigned a high degree of potential surprise. The actual occurrence of such an event would then occasion great surprise, and ought to be the signal for reconsideration of the whole system of assumptions on which high potential surprise had been assigned to it. But the over-turn of assumptions and beliefs would be greater still, if the actual event were of a character which had in no way entered into any reckoning or been even remotely imagined. The former class we may call counter-expected events, and the latter class unexpected events' (p. 151).

As Lamberton (1972) points out (p. 197) the distinction between expected events and Shackle's counter-expected or unexpected events also highlights the distinction between mechanistic, administrative, standardised, programmed, optimal decision, and organic, strategic, complex, non-programmed, innovative decision respectively. Surprise is of relevance to the latter category of decision-making, which is also the area we are concerned with here.
6. Strictly speaking, practical ignorance includes risk also. Since we argue that risk is a minor qualification of perfect knowledge conditions, degree of partial ignorance in risk situations is low or trivial.
7. It should be noted that we have not demonstrated that neoclassical analysis is applicable even in this restricted context. The benefit of doubt is conceded in this case, though the example of quality control in the case of the pencil should be remembered as an example of risk in production.
8. For Williamson's approach to transaction cost analysis, see Williamson (1975) for a systematic development of his framework. See Williamson (1979) and (1980) for extensions. For other recent developments, see Calabresi (1968), Klein *et al.* (1978), Dahlman (1979) and Teece (1980).
9. Alchian and Demsetz (1972) discuss a number of methods by which opportunism and the adverse effects of surprises can be dealt with; warranties, guarantees, collateral, return privileges and penalty clauses are all examples. However, as they point out, almost every contract is open-ended in that many contingencies (surprises) are not covered.
10. Arrow (1973) has suggested regulation, taxes, legal liability, and ethical codes are possible remedies in situations where the seller knows more about quality effects than the buyer. While they might improve the ability of buyers to evaluate transactions, they are likely to be imperfect solutions in most cases.
11. See also Akerlof (1970) for another perspective on how information impactedness may affect market transactions.
12. For an analysis of political considerations in institutional behaviour that parallels and complements Williamson's analysis, see Hirshman (1970).
13. Quoted in Jensen and Meckling (1976).

CHAPTER 6: INDUSTRIAL ORGANISATION AND BOUNDED RATIONALITY

1. A relevant argument has been made by Hay and Morris (1979). In a review of neoclassical studies of vertical integration they conclude there are no cost savings which could not be obtained by a strictly market solution (p. 58).

   We make the stronger point that vertical integration is inexplicable unless information problems and transaction costs are brought directly into the analysis.

2. See Nelson (1959), Gort (1962), Laffer (1969), Livesay and Porter (1969) and Tucker and Wilder (1977) for studies of trends in vertical integration in the US.

3. For studies of diversification in the US, see Gort (1962), Rumelt (1974) and Berry (1975) and for the UK see Amey (1964), Gorecki (1975), Hassid (1975), Prais (1976) and Utton (1977).

4. Horizontal mergers of like product-markets would appear to be an exception to this argument in so far as they do not imply either diversification or vertical integration; however it was argued in Kay (1982) that they represent a limit case of perfect or complete links between product-markets. As such, the gains from merger are also potentially realisable through market trading in the absence of transaction costs, and therefore bounded rationality in market exchange may serve as a basis for analysing horizontal merger also.

5. A number of studies have looked at the effects of mergers and take-overs. See especially, Kelly (1967), Reid (1968), Gort (1969), Hogarty (1970), Gort and Hogarty (1970), Ansoff *et al.* (1971), Singh (1971), Lev and Mandelker (1972), Utton (1974) and Meeks (1977). The consensus in the literature is that there is no strong evidence that mergers and takeovers contribute to efficiency and profitability in the firm. In Kay (1982) it was argued that long term survival (and the avoidance of product-market linkages) was a likely major corporate objective in the post-war period of accelerating technological change and turbulent environments. This would partly explain the absence of strong evidence of short run profitability gains from synergistic product-market combination, and we develop this argument further in this chapter.

6. Monopoly and antitrust are problems of long standing in the economics literature. Scherer (1980) and Armentino (1982) give useful summaries of the theory of monopoly and the history of antitrust policy, Armentino looking at the latter from a critical point of view. Williamson (1975, ch. 11), looks at the problem from an institutionalist perspective.

7. There is an inelastic demand.

8. Problems of X-inefficiency (Leibenstein, 1966) and dynamic inefficiency (inefficiency in developing and innovating over time) are also contingent on bounded rationality problems.

9. The standard statement of second best issues is Lipsey and Lancaster (1956).

10. Notable contributions to the literature on the evolution of corporate

strategy have been made by Ansoff (1965), Chandler (1966), Rumelt (1974), Channon (1973) and Dyas and Thanheiser (1976).

11. For a variety of interpretations of the conglomerate phenomenon, see Alberts (1966), Smith and Schreiner (1969), Mueller (1969), Boyle (1970), Lorie and Helpern (1970), Lewellen (1971), Levy and Sarnat (1970) Higgins and Schall (1975). Of special interest is Williamson's transaction cost analysis of the conglomerate strategy (1975, ch. 9), while another transaction cost interpretation is provided in Kay (1982, ch. 6).

12. Major studies of the relationship between strategy and structure have been made by Chandler (1966), Markham (1973), Rumelt (1974), Channon (1973) and Dyas and Thanheiser (1976). The relationship between technology and organisational relationships was also studied by Burns and Stalker (1961) and Woodward (1965). Other studies of interest for analysis of hierarchy include Simon (1969, ch. 4), Spence (1975), Armour and Teece (1978), and Chandler and Daems, eds (1980).

13. Williamson (1975) adds the further consideration that divisionalisation may have superior strategy-formulating and control advantages. These include the separation of strategic from operating decisions, separation of functional interests from long term strategy and the competitive profit centre status of divisions.

14. Another possibility would be a vertical relationship with manure serving as an input in seed production. We ignore the possibility of an aesthetic link between manure and plastic garden gnomes.

15. It is interesting that General Electric encountered strategic planning problems with this system in the early seventies and attempted to overcome this by overlaying the concept of 'strategic business units' (SBUs) on top of the existing structure. SBUs were a collection of related businesses whose properties included sufficient absence of linkages with other SBUs for strategic planning to be conducted independently for each unit (see Springer and Hofer, 1980, and Hofer and Schendel, 1978).

CHAPTER 7: MULTINATIONAL ENTERPRISE

1. This chapter is based on 'The Nature of Multinational Enterprise' by N. Kay and C. Galbraith (discussion paper, University of California, 1982). My thanks to Craig Galbraith for permission to publish here.

2. For recent studies of the development of multinational enterprise, see especially Vernon (1971), Horst (1972), Dunning ed. (1974) and Caves (1974).

3. Buckley and Casson (1976) found that US multinationalism tended to be predominantly in high technology industry (pp. 15–16).

4. There is strong empirical support for the hypothesis that there is a relationship between multinational enterprise and R & D intensity. Caves (1974) found industry level R & D spending as a percentage of sales was significantly related to foreign firm share of Canadian and UK industry. Horst (1972) found that industrial R & D intensity was directly related to the likelihood of establishing an overseas subsidiary. However, within

industries firm size was found to be more closely related to the likelihood of multinational expansion and was interpreted as a superior measure of marketing and technical abilities at this level.

Horst suggests that this is not inconsistent with the R & D hypothesis, and this is indeed the case; our basic argument for foreign location relates to potential informational economies of R & D competing against the costs of informational diseconomies from operating in a different country. To the extent that potential informational economies are liable to be directly related to *absolute* size of R & D effort, size of firm is likely to operate as crude indicator of this variable *within* industries. R & D intensity is likely to be a better indicator of this variable between industries.

Wolf (1977) also found a direct relationship between the proportion of QSEs employment at industry level (an indicator of technical skills) and the proportion of industry sales accounted for by foreign subsidiaries in a sample of 95 US industries.

Mansfield *et al.* (1979) found for a sample of US multinationals that approximately a third of profit return from R & D projects came from overseas subsidiaries.

5. A useful distinction between software and hardware is made by Hofstader (1979, pp. 301–2) who defines software as 'anything you could send over the telephone lines' and hardware as 'anything else'. Technology transfer by a multinational exploits software economies.

6. The concept of internalisation has been taken up in recent years by analysts of multinational enterprise, and Buckley and Casson (1976), Dunning (1981) and Rugman (1981) all present various developments of this thesis from which the arguments in this chapter have benefited.

However, there is an uncomfortable tendency for some proponents of internalisation to couch their analysis in the context of market structure and profit maximisation. While they trace their arguments back to Coase as root source of the internalisation concept there are grounds for suspecting closet neoclassism lurking in the background.

In fact, reversion to neoclassical concepts such as maximisation of profit and market imperfections (which carries with it the corollary that market *perfection* might be a relevant concept, at least in a notional sense) is unnecessary. These works can be usefully referred to without the need to encumber interpretation with neoclassical shackles.

7. Buckley and Casson (1976) identify four main groups of factors as being important to the internalisation decision: industry-specific region-specific, nation-specific and firm-specific factors. While we discuss nation-(or country)-specific and firm-specific factors above, our interpretation of the basis of these factors is not equivalent to Buckley and Cassons. We also add product-specific factors as a critical determinant of multi-nationalism.

8. Rugman (1981, pp. 70–2) points out the dangers of opportunistic utilisation of information provided by the licensing option.

9. The possibility of licensees opportunistically appropriating the firm specific advantages of a non-standardised product is a recognised problem

in the multinational literature (see Rugman, 1980(a)). Rugman interprets the danger as being the loss of a knowledge monopoly through licensing. Our contribution above is to regard the technological transfer problem as involving a package of elements, some of which are product-specific and some of which are not.

10. Examples of highly product-specific information would tend to constitute technical recipes which could not be usefully broken down into components, as in many food and drink examples. Thus, Kentucky Fried Chicken may be more suitable for licensing whereas, Polaroid would be more likely to pursue the multinational route in the face of trade impediments.

11. Peno (1975) argues that concentration of expatriates in top engineering and technical posts have been frequently adopted to protect the firms market position and slow down leakage of firm-specific technical knowledge, a position supported by Shearer's earlier analysis (1960), while Kidron (1965) argued that British and US investment in India was characterised by expatriate control, reluctance to import knowledge to local personnel, and highly restricted R & D, all measures designed to continue home company control of know-how.

12. Dymsza (1977) argues that centralisation of R & D may have the obvious advantage of exploiting informational synergies, but may also have the side effect of inhibiting potential opportunism.

13. Therefore, firm-, country- and product-specific factors are each important in determining multinationalism. The concept of resources and skills being specific to a particular domain (e.g. product, firm and nation) is fundamental to the concept of idiosyncratic tasks as described by Williamson (1975, pp. 62–3) though our interpretation is wider than that utilised by Williamson.

14. Buckley and Casson (1976) found evidence to suggest that multinationals tended to be highly diversified in terms of products (pp. 20–1).

15. For example, if we treat such environmental threats in standard risk terms, shareholders could achieve the benefit of portfolio diversification by diversifying ownership and stockholdings without the need for the corporation to move out into other areas. This is similar to the argument against a portfolio theory analysis of domestic diversification.

16. See Hood and Young (1979, pp. 67–8) for discussion of Japanese multinationalism into extractive industries in this light.

17. The curious feature of Cave's analysis is that he begins by recognising that the determinants of multinational enterprise are essentially transactional, involving the internalisation of intangible assets of knowledge in one form or other. He recognises the centrality of transaction costs in this area, including problems of opportunism, uncertainty, information impactedness and so on. Yet he proceeds to analyse the multinational in an essentially neoclassical framework, without considering the possible inconsistency of an alternatively transactional and neoclassical perspective.

Read as a literature survey and textbook, Cave's analysis is readable and useful; it is only the strange hybrid nature of the underlying transactional/neoclassical framework which creates some difficulty and confusion.

CHAPTER 8: PUBLIC POLICY AND BOUNDED RATIONALITY

1. The texts were chosen partly because each attained a certain cult status on the periphery of economics while I was a student, yet each tended to be excluded from any more than casual attention or passing mention in standard degree courses. Since each was involved in different ways with the economics of knowledge and power, protection through caveat or neglect from such disturbing influences could frequently be deemed to be in the best interests of the student. Preoccupation with such alien philosophies were quite liable to distract from the main purpose of an economics degree which was to satisfy external examiners as to a student's facility as a player of the neoclassical game. Consequently 'sociological' was a frequent epithet used in conjunction with the dismissal of each author or text.

2. *The New Industrial State* followed *The Affluent Society* which was also a best-seller.

3. Galbraith has produced a number of books and articles, but his best known include *American Capitalism*, *The Affluent Society* and *The New Industrial State*. In *American Capitalism* (1952) the concept of counter-vailing power was introduced. Strong monopolistic buyers or sellers were seen as breeding a countervailing response on the other side of the market – e.g. trade unions as a response to monopolistic employers. *The Affluent Society*, first published in 1958, was concerned with the subordination of consumers' interests to producers through advertising and marketing. The role of the large corporation was developed and elaborated further as discussed above in *The New Industrial State*.

   In Galbraith's latest major work *Economics and the Public Purpose* he pursued conflicts between corporate and public objectives as well as rectifying the neglect of small business in his earlier work.

4. Galbraith has elsewhere pointed out the contrast between real world corporations and the homogeneous firms of Friedman's system (Galbraith, 1980).

5. Galbraith identifies the boundaries of the technostructure in the large corporation as containing all those who contribute information to corporate decision-making, from manager to blue collar worker (p. 85–6).

6. 'There is no good term for this large group which is associated with education and scientific research apart from that undertaken by the techno-structure. In political discourse they are grouped with writers and poets and referred to either as intellectuals or eggheads' (Galbraith, p. 283).

7. For an argument against Galbraith's vision of the death of the entre-preneurial economy, see Gilder (1981, esp. ch. 7).

8. Dyas and Thanheiser (1976) note the effect Servan-Shreiber's analysis had on policy makers and managers (pp. 5–6 and 266) and discuss subsequent changes in the strategy and structure of European firms.

9. See Dickson (1974) for an interesting, radical analysis of political

social and economic issues surrounding the role of intermediate technology.

10. In the context of Zambia, Borrell (1980) argues that political power is concentrated amongst 'the educated and their followers'. Calls for labour intensive technologies and small scale establishments made by Kaudas policy adviser faced these constraints to implementation.

CHAPTER 9: SYNTHESIS AND ANTITHESIS

1. In fact Commons (1924) can be interpreted as making an important early distinction between property rights and power according to Kanel (1979). However, Commons was interpreting the world through institutional spectacles rather than from the narrow neoclassical perspective. I believe highlighting the central role of information problems above helps illustrate the roots of the essential difference.

2. The Reagan administration in its first year advocated the market system as the ideal system of economic organisation and encouraged corporate merger to achieve economies and an advantageous international competitive position. As should be clear from earlier chapters, these are inconsistent policies since merger involves *replacing* the potential domain over which market exchange can operate with corporate systems. Any such set of economic policies contains the implicit premise that market exchange has efficiency limits and that an alternative form of economic organisation may be superior in certain cases.

3. Indeed, Sweden has had one of the highest levels of government spending amongst OECD countries in the post war period. See National Accounts of OECD countries published regularly by OECD, and also comparative data for 1962–75 in OECD (1978, p. 16). Sweden's income tax and social security contributions were also the highest as a proportion of gross income of any of the major European nations in the late seventies (*The Economist*, 1978, p. 26–7).

4. See Jones (1976, p. 3–13) and Lindbeck (1975, p. 5), for comments on Sweden's limited resource base.

5. Lindbeck (1975), using OECD statistics calculated that per capita income in Sweden was about 40% higher than the rest of Western Europe, and around the same level as the US 1972–4 (depending on a fluctuating exchange rate). Using the same sources, *The Economist* (1978) confirmed Sweden was still the richest of the major European nations in 1976.

6. An OECD survey of Sweden (OECD, 1981) does suggest that the country is facing economic difficulties in common with the majority of Western nations, but this does not diminish the Swedish achievement of a high standard of living for its people in conjunction with a high level of public spending and one of the most equitable distributions of income in the OECD.

7. See Caves and Uekusa (1976, pp. 494–502) for discussion of the characteristics of Zaibatsu enterprise.

8. An example of a local economy that provides numerous examples that

could support both Friedmanite and Galbraithian theses is Los Angeles. The area produces advertising kitsch that would provide supporting examples in any Galbraithian critique; the medical alert system which respirates sales on commercial radio by having an actor audibly simulate a cardiac arrest, and the used-car salesman who promises a donation to a children's home for each deal struck are especially notable.

However restaurant chains and service stations generally provide quick, efficient service compared with that available in the UK. In this respect, replicability and repetition facilitate the working of the market mechanism in such a mobile competitive society consistent with Friedman's interpretation of market operations.

CHAPTER 10: INGREDIENTS AND RECIPES

1. Other 'surprises' could still cause a decline in the product life cycle – for example, depletion of a natural resource, government edict, discovery of health hazards in the use of a particular product, etc. We assume that these can be represented by appropriate shifts in the supply and demand curves facing decision-makers since substitution of consumption and production can only take place from amongst well known established alternatives in our example.

2. In discussion, Carol Uhlaner pointed out to me an additional factor that would reduce the need for advertising; consumers will no longer be persuaded by genuine or deceptive claims that a product is 'new', 'improved', 'better', or 'has new ingredients' if innovation is not possible. Such advertising would become redundant since it is dependent on the *belief* that innovation can take place. Galbraith (1972, p. 208, footnote) makes a similar point when he argues that sales strategies may exploit the prescription that any 'new' product is inherently superior to an old one in cultures that place a high value on technological change.

3. The options are fixed, but of course changes in input prices or required scale of production may cause switches in technology used.

4. In this context it is interesting to note the examples of exchange used by Adam Smith. Trades are conducted by dyemakers, tailors and farmers, not consultants, IBM or advertising agencies. Familiar physical products constituted the typical market in Smith's world, in contrast to novel information-based commodities and services frequently associated with modern economies.

5. 'Authority' may be defined as the power to make decisions which guide the actions of another. It is a relationship between two individuals, one 'superior', the other 'subordinate'. The superior frames and transmits decisions with the expectation that they will be accepted by the subordinate. The subordinate expects such decisions, and his conduct is determined by them (Simon, 1965, p. 125).

6. Williamson (1975, pp. 53–4) discusses how hierarchy can curb opportunism

in such terms. It should be noted that Williamson criticises the distinction between authority and market relations as being simplistic. However it is sufficient for our purposes at this stage.

7. This phenomenon can be observed in a wide variety of contexts from the vending of matches on street corners, to second hand markets.

8. See Williamson (1975, ch. 10) for a discussion of the literature on monopoly control and its implication for innovativeness.

9. See Williamson (1975, p. 127) for a discussion of problems of bureaucratic insularity of managers arising from separation of ownership and control in large firms.

10. If the leap from considering individual bureaucracies to the level of the planned economy is thought too far fetched, it is worthwhile considering that in the US, the hundred largest corporations control approximately 1/3rd of national net output (the figure is even higher for most other countries). It would take only a few dozen selected mergers of existing bureaucracies coupled with an increased level of government intervention and protection to approximate the features of a planned economy.

11. See Caves and Uekusa (1976, pp. 189–9), Allen (1972), Bronfenbrenner (1970), Rotwein (1964), Halliday (1975, pp. 273–9) and Williamson (1975, p. 162), for useful analysis of the post-war Zaibatsu phenomenon.

12. State holding companies have been adopted as methods of promoting industrial efficiency and/or industrial reorganisation by a number of countries, notably Italy and Sweden; the UK National Enterprise Board was ostensibly viewed by its procreators as a potential means of pursuing such ends, though its birth in 1975 was attended by a number of political midwives with frequently differing and possibly inconsistent views as what the objectives should be; the N.E.B. as a tool for efficiency, state participation, or socialist control were each touted as desirable roles, and in turn treated difficulties in framing a coherent, consistent strategy for that body. See Parr (1979) and Grant (1982, ch. 5), for further discussion of these issues.

13. My italics.

14. The Donovan Report on UK trade unions summarised the advantages industrial unionism might provide; Sectional claims on behalf of different occupational groups within a particular factory could be more easily harmonised and it might be easier for the union concerned to conclude effective company and factory agreements. Demarcation problems between craft groups would be more easy to solve and the temptation for unions to seek to out-do each other in militancy or obduracy would be eliminated. There would also be no need for shop stewards from different unions within the same plant or company to form 'unofficial' or 'unconstitutional' joint shop stewards committees. All the unions members in a given factory could be organised into one branch with appropriate sections for different occupations and groups (Royal Commission on Trade Unions and Employers Associations, 1968, p. 179).

   Donovan also added that there was no guarantee that industrial unionism would eliminate sectional problems such as demarcation, and difficulties of informal organisation.

15. The Rehn Plan was named after Gustav Rehn, an economist who helped

shape Swedish economic policy in the post-war period and who has been credited by some as the architect of Sweden's industrial success.

16. For a description of the Labour Market Board and its workings, see Jones (1976, ch. 2). For criticisms of the Rehn Plan, see Lindbeck (1975, pp. 39–49).

17. For an analysis of UK nationalised industries viewed from the perspective of conventional economic theory, see Pryke (1971) and (1981). For a wide ranging analysis of organisational aspects of European state controlled enterprises, see Mazzolini (1979). Vernon and Aharoni, eds (1981) cover a wide ranging set of theoretical and empirical issues on different countries, while Prest and Coppock, eds, (1982) (ch. 4), look at current policy and problems in the UK nationalised sector.

18. Many US corporations in what are nationalised industries in the UK, have attempted to escape product cycle decline by diversification, US Steel's adventures in petroleum being a recent example, while Penn Centrals conglomerate diversification out of railroads represents a spectacular early case.

19. For a recent survey of inter-union and demarcation problems arising from multiunionism, see Brown, ed. (1981, pp. 59–61). See Hawkins (1981) for a good survey of recent UK trends in trade union structure and behaviour. Radice (1978) argues against industrial unionism as a panacea on the grounds that it ignores the historical perspective in the growth and evolution of British trade unions.

20. Samuel Brittan (1978) provides an interesting analysis that suggests the lag in the UK growth rate has not been directly attributable to state intervention and argues that there is no great evidence of a connection between growth rates and degree of state intervention (pp. 256–7). He attributes low growth to more complex institutional and political factors.

21. This term suggested itself through Olsen's use of the term 'retardants' of growth (1982, p. 4).

22. Some time ago (1957) Lewis pointed out with respect to Britain's poor performance in exports that original technological innovation is not necessary to create an export market and that rapid technological imitation would be sufficient, citing Japan, Belgium and Switzerland as successful examples of the latter tactic.

23. Ayres (1944, p. 95), also quoted and discussed in Seckler (1975, pp. 70–1).

24. Japan is sparsely endowed with natural resources including land and energy.

25. Olsen points out that a profit maximising firm that owns obsolete plant and equipment will be better off for owning the old capital, or alternatively no worse than if it had no capital left at all. The best that bombing could do is to save wrecking costs, which is hardly likely to be a major consideration.

26. Major first year texts inculcating the equality/efficiency trade-off include Wonnacott and Wonnacott (1979), Baumol and Blinder (1979), Samuelson (1980) and Mansfield (1980). Mansfield qualifies the trade-off as being a probable relationship.

27. Okun speaks of 'more or less equality as implying smaller or greater disparities among families in their maintainable standard of living'.

28. For Okun, efficiency means 'getting the most out of a given input' (p. 2).

29. Okun bases his case for efficiency of capitalism on Adam Smith's 'invisible hand' and cites the long term record of US growth and progress as justification (pp. 50–1). This is a rather surprising platform since the US growth record has been amongst the lowest of the OECD countries for some considerable time.

30. Okun points out (p. 92) that attitudes to the efficiency/equality issue range from Rawls (1971) who would give equality priority over efficiency, to Friedman (1982) who would give priority to efficiency.

31. Sawyer (1976) studied income distribution in the OECD countries using data from the late sixties and early seventies and found that three countries (Japan, Sweden and Australia) had the most equal distribution of post-tax income of 12 countries studied, depending on what measure of inequality was applied.

32. The *Journal of Economic Issues* is the major channel for institutional economists, and a good survey of the range of institutional thinking is provided in the two volume set of readings from the journal edited by W.J. Samuels (1979 (a) and (b)). Lekachman, in the foreword, identifies Veblen, Commons, Ayres, Galbraith, Gruchy and Gamb as leading institutional economists. To this list should certainly be added Oliver Williamson. For an entertaining 'Cook's Tour' of Institutionalism, see Boulding (1957) and also the mixed response to his personal view of Institutionalism in the discussion by Gruchy, Hill, Knight, Parsons and Ayres following his article (pp. 13–27).

33. See Seckler (1975) for these and other definitions of institution.

34. Given the emphasis on individual optimisation in mainstream economies, it is not surprising that liberalism constitutes a strong explicit or implicit theme in political economy since it is a political philosophy based on the human beings as individual rather than social animals. Mainstream economic theory and the political doctrine of liberalism are mutually reinforcing.

35. The post-Keynesians emphasise the role of time, uncertainty, surprise, institutions and power (see particularly Davidson (1981), for a discussion and an analysis of this school of thought in those terms). Davidson (1978) is a full elaboration of Davidson's post-Keynesian philosophy.

36. For examples of such treatment, see McCloskey (1982), Koch (1980), and Shepherd (1979).

37. Davidson argues 'when such pre-eminent scholars as Arrow, Hahn and Hicks have indicated the impossibility of modelling via traditional neoclassical concepts a real world economy where time, uncertainty, contracts, finance and market institutions are essential factors and that any serious monetary analyst must explicitly account for these factors, then it is time for many other fair-minded neoclassical economists to recognize there is a paradigm's worth of difference between the economics of Keynes and general equilibrium economics. It is only in the Keynes's framework that real world monetary·characteristics are promi-

nently and explicitly developed so that "money matters" ' (1978, pp. 367–8).

Davidson's analysis also builds on the Keynesian tradition maintained by Shackle, so we should not be surprised to find strong kinship between the post-Keynesian analysis and the approach to microeconomics developed here.

38. Brazelton (1981) has made the point that post-Keynesians and Institutionalists have a great deal in common.

References

Adams, D. (1979), *The Hitchhiker's Guide to the Galaxy* (NY: Simon & Schuster).

Akerlof, G.A. (1970), 'The Market for "Lemons": Quality, Uncertainty and the Market Mechanism', *Quarterly Journal of Economics*, 84, 488–500.

Alberts, W. (1966), 'The Profitability of Growth Through Merger', in Alberts, W. and Segall, J.E. (eds), *The Corporate Merger* (Chicago University Press).

Alchian, A.A. (1950), 'Uncertainty, Evolution and Economic Theory', *Journal of Political Economy*, 58, 211–21.

Alchian, A.A. and Demsetz, H. (1972), 'Production, Information Costs and Economic Organisation', *American Economic Review*, 62, 777–95.

Allen, G.C. (1972), *A Short Economic History of Modern Japan* (London: Allen & Unwin).

Amey, L.R. (1964), 'Diversified Manufacturing Business', *Journal of the Royal Statistical Society*, Series A, 127, 251–90.

Ansoff, H.I. (1965), *Corporate Strategy* (London: Penguin).

Ansoff, H.I., Brandenburg, R.G., Partner, F.E. and Radosevich (1971), *Acquisition Behaviour of U.S. Manufacturing Firms 1946–65* (Vanderbilt University Press).

Armentino, D.T. (1982), *Antitrust and Monopoly: Anatomy of a Policy Failure* (NY: John Wiley).

Armour, H.O. and Teece, D.J. (1978), 'Organisational Structure and Economic Performance: a Test of the Multidivisional Hypothesis', *Bell Journal of Economics*, 9, 106–22.

Arrow, K.J. (1962), 'Economic Welfare and the Allocation of Resources for Invention, in *The Rate and Direction of Economic Activity: Economic and Social Factors* (National Bureau of Economic Research, Princeton University Press) 609–26.

Arrow, K.J. (1973), 'Social Responsibility and Economic Efficiency', *Public Policy*, 21, 303–17.

Ayres, C.E. (1944), *The Theory of Economic Progress* (Chapel Hill: University of North Carolina Press).

Bailey, E.E. and Friedlander, A.F. (1982), 'Market Structure and Multiproduct Industries', *Journal of Economic Literature*, 20, 1024–48.

Balogh, T. (1982), *The Irrelevance of Conventional Economics* (NY: Liveright).

Baumol, W.J. (1958), 'On the Theory of Oligopoly', *Economica*, 26, 187–98.

Baumol, W.J. (1959), *Business Behaviour, Value and Growth* (NY: Harcourt Brace).

Baumol, W.J. (1977), 'On the Proper Cost Tests for Natural Monopoly in a Multiproduct Firm', *American Economic Review*, 67, 809–22.

Baumol, W.J., Bailey, E.E. and Willig, R.D. (1977), 'Weak Invisible Hand

Theorems on the Sustainability of Multiproduct Natural Monopoly', *American Economic Review*, 67, 350–65.

Baumol, W.J. and Blinder, A.S. (1979), *Economics, Principles and Policy* (NY: Harcourt Brace Jovanovich).

Baumol, W.J. and Braunstein, Y.M. (1977), 'Empirical Study of Scale Economies and Production Complementarity: the Case of Journal Publication', *Journal of Political Economy*, 85, 1937–48.

Baumol, W.J. and Fischer, D. (1978), 'Cost, Minimising Number of Firms and Determination of Industry Structure', *Quarterly Journal of Economics*, 92, 439–67.

Baumol, W.J., Panzar, J.C. and Willig, R.D. (1982), *Contestable Markets and the Theory of Industry Structure* (NY: Harcourt Brace Jovanovich).

Baumol, W.J. and Stewart, M. (1971), 'On the Behavioural Theory of the Firm', in Marris and Wood, eds (1971).

Beazer, W.F. (1978), *The Commercial Future of Hong Kong* (NY: Praeger).

Becker, G.S. (1975), *Human Capital: a Theoretical and Empirical Analysis with Special Reference to Education* (NY: National Bureau of Economic Research).

Bell, D. and Kristol, I., eds (1981) *The Crisis in Economic Theory* (NY: Basic Books).

Berle, A.A. and Means, G. (1932), *The Modern Corporation and Private Property* (NY: Macmillan).

Berry, C.H. (1975), *Corporate Growth and Diversification* (Princeton University Press).

Blaug, M. (1978), *Economic Theory in Retrospect*, 3rd edn (London: Cambridge University Press).

Blaug, M. (1980), *The Methodology of Economics: or How Economists Explain*, (London: Cambridge University Press).

Bohm, D. (1980), *Wholeness and the Implicate Order* (London: Routledge & Kegan Paul).

Borrel, J. (1980), 'Zambian Socialism's Failure Laid Bare', *Guardian*, 19 March.

Boulding, K.E. (1957), 'A New Look at Institutionalism', *American Economic Review, pap & proc*, 47, 1–12.

Boulding, K.E. (1968), *Beyond Economics* (University of Michigan Press).

Boyle, S.E. (1970), 'Pre-merger Growth and Profit Characteristics of Large Conglomerate Mergers in the United States', *St Johns Law Review*, 152–70.

Brazelton, W.R. (1981), 'Post Keynesian Economics: an Institutional Compatibility', *Journal of Economic Issues*, 15, 531–42.

Brittan, S. (1978), 'How British is the British Sickness', *Journal of Law and Economics*, 21, 254–68.

Bronfenbrenner, M. (1970), 'Japan's Galbraithian Economy', *Public Interest*, no. 21, 149–57.

Brown, W. ed. (1981), *The Changing Contours of British Industrial Relations*, (Oxford: Basil Blackwell).

Buckley, P.J. and Casson, M. (1976), *The Future of Multinational Enterprise*, (London: Longmans).

Burns, T. and Stalker, G.M. (1961), *The Management of Innovation* (London: Tavistock).

Calabresi, G. (1968), 'Transaction Costs, Resource Allocation, and Liability Rules – a Comment', *Journal of Law and Economics*, 11, 67–73.

Caves, R.E. (1974), 'Causes of Direct Investment: Foreign Firms' Shares in Canadian and United Kingdom Manufacturing Industries', *Review of Economics and Statistics*, 56, 279–93.

Caves, R.E. (1980), 'Industrial Organisation, Corporate Strategy and Structure', *Journal of Economic Literature*, 18, 64–92.

Caves, R.E. (1982), *Multinational Enterprise and Economic Analysis*, (London: Cambridge University Press).

Caves, R.E. and Uekusa, M. (1976), *Industrial Organisation*, in H. Patrick, and N. Rosovsky, eds (1976).

Chamberlin, E.H. (1933), *The Theory of Monopolistic Competition* (Boston: Harvard University Press).

Chandler, A.D. (1966), *Strategy and Structure* (NY: Doubleday).

Chandler, A.D. (1977), *The Visible Hand: the Managerial Revolution in American Business* (Cambridge: Harvard University Press).

Chandler, A.D. and Daems, M. (1980), *Managerial Hierarchies: Comparative Perspectives on the Rise of the Modern Industrial Enterprise* (Cambridge: Harvard University Press).

Channon, D.F. (1973), *The Strategy and Structure of British Enterprise* (Boston: Harvard University).

Coase, R.H. (1937), 'The Nature of the Firm', *Economica*, 4, 386–405.

Coase, R.H. (1960), 'The Problem of Social Cost', *Journal of Law and Economics*, 3, 1–44.

Commons, J.R. (1924), *Legal Foundations of Capitalism* (Madison: University of Wisconson).

Commons, J.R. (1961), *Institutional Economics* (Madison: University of Wisconson).

Cosh, A. (1975), 'The Remuneration of Chief Executives in the United Kingdom', *Economic Journal*, 85, 75–94.

Council of Economic Advisers (1982), *Economic Report of the President*, (Washington, DC: US Government Printing Office).

Cyert, R.M. and Hedrick, C.L. (1972), 'Theory of the Firm: Past, Present, and Future; an Interpretation', *Journal of Economic Literature* 10, 398–412.

Cyert, R.M. and March, J.G. (1963), *A Behavioral Theory of the Firm*, (Englewood Cliffs, NJ: Prentice Hall).

Dahlman, C.J. (1979), 'The Problem of Externality', *Journal of Law and Economics*, 22, 141–62.

Darwin, C. (1929), *The Origin of Species by Means of Natural Selection*, (London: Watts).

Davidson, P. (1978), *Money and the Real World*, 2nd edn (London: Macmillan).

Davidson, P. (1981), 'Post Keynesian Economics', in Bell and Kristol, eds (1981) 151–73.

Day, R.H. (1967), 'Profits, Learning and the Convergence of Satisficing to Marginalism', *Quarterly Journal of Economics*, 81, 302–11.

Day, R.H. and Tinney, E.H. (1968), 'How to Co-operate in Business without Really Trying: a Learning Model of Decentralised Decision Making', *Journal of Political Economy*, 76, 583–600.

Demsetz, H. (1968), 'Why Regulate Utilities?', *Journal of Law and Economics*, 11, 55–65.

Demsetz, H. (1969), 'Information and Efficiency: Another Viewpoint', *Journal of Law and Economics*, 12, 1–22.

Denison, E.F. (1967), *Why Growth Rates Differ* (Washington: Brookings Institution).

Denison, E.F. (1974), *Accounting for United States Economic Growth 1929–69* (Washington: Brookings Institution).

Denison, E.F. and Chung, W.K. (1976), *How Japan's Economy Grew so Fast*, (Washington: Brookings Institution).

Devine, P.J., Lee, N., Jones, R.M. and Tyson, W. (1979), *An Introduction to Industrial Economics*, 3rd edn (London: Allen & Unwin).

Dickson, D. (1974), *Alternative Technology and the Politics of Technical Change* (Glasgow: Collins).

Downs, A. (1967), *Inside Bureaucracy* (Boston: Little, Brown).

Doyle, P. (1968), 'Advertising Expenditure and Consumer Demand', *Oxford Economic Papers*, 20, 395–417.

Dunning, J.H., ed. (1974), *Economic Analysis and the Multinational Enterprise* (London: Allen & Unwin).

Dunning, J.H. (1981), *International Production and the Multinational Enterprise* (London: Allen & Unwin).

Dunsire, A. (1978a), *Implementation in a bureaucracy* (Oxford: Martin Robertson).

Dunsire, A. (1978b), *Control in a bureaucracy* (Oxford: Martin Robertson).

Dyas, G.P. and Thanheiser, H.T. (1976), *The Emerging European Enterprise, Strategy and Structure in French and German Industry* (London: Macmillan).

Dymsza, W.A. (1977), 'Regional Strategies of U.S. Multinational Firms that Affect Transfers of Technology to Developing Countries', in Germides, D. (ed.), *Transfer of Technology by Multinational Corporations*, vol. II (Paris: OECD) 93–114.

Economist, The (1978), *The Structure and Management of Europe's Ten Largest Economies* (London).

Egger, J.B. (1978), 'The Austrian Method', in Spadaro, ed. (1978) 19–39.

Freeman, C. (1982), *The Economics of Industrial Innovation*, 2nd edn (London: Francis Pinter).

Friedman, M. (1953), *Essays in Positive Economics* (University of Chicago Press).

Friedman, M. (1962), *Price Theory* (Chicago: Aldine).

Friedman, M. and Friedman, R. (1980), *Free to Choose* (London: Penguin).

Friedman, M. (1982), *Capitalism and Freedom*, 2nd edn (University of Chicago Press).

Galbraith, J.K. (1952), *American Capitalism: the Concept of Countervailing Power* (Boston: Houghton Mifflin).

Galbraith, J.K. (1971), *Economics, Peace and Laughter* (NJ: New American Library).

Galbraith, J.K. (1972), *New Industrial State*, 2nd edn (London: Penguin).

Galbraith, J.K. (1973), *Economics and the Public Purpose* (Boston: Houghton Mifflin).

Galbraith, J.K. (1976), *The Affluent Society*, 3rd edn (Boston: Houghton Mifflin).

Galbraith, J.K. (1980), 'Galbraith', *Observer*, 31 August, p. 15.

Gilder, G.F. (1981), *Wealth and Poverty* (NY: Basic Books).

Gold, B. (1982), 'Managerial Considerations in Evaluating, the Role of Licensing in Technological Development Strategies, *Managerial and Decision Economics*, 3, 213–17.

Gordon, S. (1968), 'The Close of the Galbraithian System', *Journal of Political Economy*, 76, 635–44.

Gordon, W.C. (1980), *Institutional Economics: the Changing System*, (University of Texas).

Gorecki, P.K. (1975), 'An Inter-industry Analysis of Diversification in the U.K. Manufacturing Sector', *Journal of Industrial Economics*, 26, 131–43.

Gorecki, P.K. (1976), 'The Determinants of Entry by Domestic and Foreign Enterprises in Canadian Manufacturing Industries', *Review of Economics and Statistics*, 58, 485–8.

Gort, M. (1962), *Diversification and Integration in American Industry* (Princeton University Press).

Gort, M. (1969), 'An Economic Disturbance Theory of Mergers', *Quarterly Journal of Economics*, 83, 624–42.

Gort, M. and Hogarty, T.F. (1970), 'New Evidence on Mergers', *Journal of Law and Economics*, 167–84.

Gould, S.J. (1979), *Ever Since Darwin* (NY: Norton).

Gould, S.J. (1980), *The Pandas Thumb* (NY: Norton).

Grant, W. (1982), *The Political Economy of Industrial Policy* (London: Butterworths).

Hahn, F. (1981), 'General Equilibrium Theory' in, Bell, D. and Kristol, I. (1981) 123–38.

Halliday, J. (1975), *A Political History of Japanese Capitalism*, (NY: Mon. Rev. Pr.).

Hamilton, W.H. (1932), 'Institution', *Encyclopaedia of the Social Sciences*, vol. 8, pp. 84–9 (London: Macmillan).

Hardach, K. (1976), *The Political Economy of Germany in the Twentieth Century* (University of California Press).

Hassid, J. (1975), 'Recent Evidence on Conglomerate Diversification in U.K. Manufacturing Industry', *The Manchester School of Economics and Social Studies*, 43, 372–95.

Hawkins, K. (1981), *Trade Unions* (London: Hutchison).

Hay, D.A. and Morris, D.J. (1979), *Industrial Economics: Theory and Evidence* (Oxford University Press).

Hayek, F. (1945), 'The Use of Knowledge in Society', *American Economic Review*, 35, 519–30.

Heller, J. (1961), *Catch-22* (NY: Simon & Schuster).

Hey, J.D. (1979), *Uncertainty in Microeconomics* (Oxford: Martin Robertson).

Hey, J.D. (1981), 'Are Optimal Search Rules Reasonable? And Vice Versa? And does it matter anyway?', *Journal of Economic Behaviour and Organisation*, 2, 47–70.

Hicks, J.R. (1979), *Causality in Economics* (Oxford: Blackwell).

Higgins, R.C. and Schall, L.P. (1975), 'Corporate Bankruptcy and Conglomerate Merger', *Journal of Finance*, 30, 93–113.

Hirshleifer, J. (1956), 'On the Economics of Transfer Pricing', *Journal of Business*, 29, 172–84.

Hirshleifer, J. (1957), 'Economics of the Divisionalised Firm', *Journal of Business*, 30, 96–108.

Hirshleifer, J. (1980), *Price Theory and Applications*, 2nd edn (Englewood Cliffs, NJ: Prentice-Hall).

Hirshleifer, J. and Riley, J.G. (1979), 'The Analytics of Uncertainty and Information – an Expository Survey, *Journal of Economic Literature*, 17, 1375–421.

Hirschman, A.O. (1970), *Exit Voice and Loyalty: Responses to Decline in Firms, Organisations and States* (Cambridge, Mass.: Harvard University Press).

Hofer, C.W. and Schendel, D. (1978), *Strategy Formulation: Analytical Concepts* (St Paul: West Publishing).

Hoffman, E. and Spitzer, M.L. (1982), 'The Coase Theory: Some Experimental Results', *Journal of Law and Economics*, 25, 73–98.

Hofstadter, D.R. (1979), *Godel, Escher, Bach: an Eternal Golden Braid*, (NY: Random House).

Hogarty, T.F. (1970), 'The Profitability of Corporate Mergers', *Journal of Business*, 43, 317–26.

Hood, N. and Young, S. (1979), *The Economics of Multinational Enterprise* (London: Longman).

Horst, T. (1972), 'Firms and Industry Determinants of the Decision to Invest Abroad', *Review of Economics and Statistics*, 22, 258–66.

Hutchison, T.W. (1977), *Knowledge and Ignorance in Economics* (London: Blackwell).

Hymer, S.H. (1976), *The International Operations of National Firms: a Study of Foreign Direct Investment* (MIT Press).

Jensen, M.C. and Meckling, W.H. (1976), 'Theory of the Firm: Managerial Behaviour, Agency Costs and Ownership Structure', *Journal of Financial Economics*, 3, 305–60.

Jones, H.G. (1976), *Planning and Productivity in Sweden* (London: Croom Helm).

Kaldor, N. (1934), 'The Equilibrium of the Firm', *Economic Journal*, 44, 60–76.

Kanel, D. (1979), 'Property and Economic Power as Issues in Institutional Economics', in, Samuels (1979a).

Katouzian, H. (1980), *Ideology and Method in Economics* (London: Macmillan).

Kay, N.M. (1979), *The Innovating Firm* (London: Macmillan).

Kay, N.M. (1982), *The Evolving Firm* (London: Macmillan).

Kelly, E. (1967), *The Profitability of Growth Through Mergers* (Pennsylvania State University Press).

Keynes, J.M. (1937), 'The General Theory of Employment', *Quarterly Journal of Economics*, 51, 209–23.

Kidron, M. (1965), *Foreign Investment in India* (London: Oxford University Press).

Klein, B., Crawford, R.G. and Alchian, A.A. (1978), 'Vertical Integration, Appropriable Rents, and the Competitive Contracting Process', *Journal of Law and Economics*, 21, 297–326.

Knight, F.H. (1921), *Risk Uncertainty and Profit* (NY: Harper & Row).

Koch, J.V. (1980), *Industrial Organisation and Prices*, 2nd edn (London: Prentice-Hall).

Koestler, A. (1964), *The Act of Creation* (London: Hutchison).

Koestler, A. (1980), *Bricks to Babel* (London: Hutchison).

Koutsoyiannis, A. (1982), *Non-Price Decisions: the Firm in a Modern Context* (London: Macmillan).

Kuznets, S. (1959), *Six Lectures on Economic Growth* (Glencoe, Free Press).

Kuznets, S. (1979), *Growth, Population and Income Distribution* (NY: Norton).

Lachman, L.M. (1978), 'An Austrian Stocktaking: Unsettled Questions and Tentative Answers', in, Spadaro, ed. (1978), 1–18.

Lackman, L.L. and Craycroft, J.L. (1974), 'Sales Maximization and Oligopoly: a Case Study', *Journal of Industrial Economics*, 23, 81–95.

Laffer, A.B. (1969), 'Vertical Integration by Corporations 1929–65', *Review of Economics and Statistics*, 51, 91–3.

Lamberton, D.M. (1972), 'Information and Profit', in Carter C.F. and Ford, J.L., (eds), *Uncertainty and Expectations in Economics* (Oxford: Basil Blackwell) 191–212.

Leibenstein, H. (1966), 'Allocative Efficiency vs. X-Efficiency', *American Economic Review*, 56, 392–415.

Leijonhufvud, A. (1968), *Keynesian Economics and the Economics of Keynes* (Oxford University Press).

Leontief, W. (1971), 'Theoretical Assumptions and Nonobserved Facts', *American Economic Review*, 61, 1–7.

Lev, B. and Handelker, G. (1972), 'The Microeconomic Consequences of Corporate Mergers', *Journal of Business*, 45, 85–104.

Levy, H. and Sarnat, M. (1970), 'Diversification, Portfolio Analysis and the Uneasy Case for the Conglomerate Merger', *Journal of Finance*, 25, 795–802.

Lewellyn, W. (1969), 'Management and Ownership in the Large Firm', *Journal of Finance*, 24, 299–322.

Lewellen, W. (1971), 'A Pure Financial Rationale for the Conglomerate Merger', *Journal of Finance, Papers & Proceedings*, 26, 521–37.

Lewellen, W. and Huntsman, B. (1970), 'Managerial Pay and Corporate Performance', *American Economic Review*, 60, 710–20.

Lewis, J., ed. (1974), *Beyond Chance and Necessity; a Critical Analysis into Professor Jacques Monod's Chance and Necessity* (London: Garnstone Press).

Lewis, W.A. (1957), 'International Competition in Manufactures', *American Economic Review, Papers & Proceedings*, 47, 578–87.

Lindbeck, A. (1975), *Swedish Economic Policy* (London: Macmillan).

Lipsey, R.G. and Lancaster, K. (1956), 'The General Theory of Second Best', *Review of Economic Studies*, 24, 11–32.

Livesay, H.C. and Porter, P.C. (1969), 'Vertical Integration in American Manufacturing 1899–1948', *Journal of Economic History*, 29, 494–500.

Loasby, B.J. (1967), 'Long Range Formal Planning in Perspective', *Journal of Management Studies*, 4, 300–8.

Loasby, B.J. (1971), 'Hypothesis and Paradigm in the Theory of the Firm', *Economic Journal*, 81, 863–85.

Loasby, B.J. (1976), *Choice, Complexity and Ignorance* (London: Cambridge University Press).

Lorie, J.H. and Helpern, P. (1970), 'Conglomerates: the Rhetoric and the Evidence', *Journal of Law and Economics*, 13, 149–66.

McCloskey, D.N. (1982), *The Applied Theory of Price* (NY: Macmillan).

McEachern, W.A. (1975), *Managerial Control and Performance* (Lexington: Heath).

McGuigan, J.R. and Moyer, R.C. (1975), *Managerial Economics* (Hinsdale: Dryden Press).

McGuire, J., Chiu, J. and Elbing, A. (1962), 'Executive Income, Sales and Profits', *American Economic Review*, 52, 753–61.

Machlup, F. (1946), 'Managerial Analysis and Empirical Research', *American Economic Review*, 36, 519–54.

Machlup, F. (1967), 'Theories of the Firm: Marginalist, Behavioural, Managerial', *American Economic Review*, 57, 1–33.

Maddock, R. and Carter, M. (1982), 'A Child's Guide to Rational Expectations', *Journal of Economic Literature*, 20, 39–51.

Mansfield, E., Romeo, A. and Wagner, S. (1979), 'Foreign Trade and U.S. Research and Development', *Review of Economics and Statistics*, 61, 49–57.

Mansfield, E. (1980), *Economics, Principles, Problems, Decisions*, 3rd edn (NY: Norton).

Markham, J.W. (1973), *Conglomerate Enterprise and Public Policy* (Boston: Harvard University).

Marris, R.L. (1963), 'A Model of the Managerial Enterprise', *Quarterly Journal of Economics*, 77, 185–209.

Marris, R.L. (1966), *The Economics of Managerial Capitalism* (London: Macmillan).

Marris, R.L. (1971), 'The Modern Corporation and Economic Theory', in, Marris & Wood, eds (1971) 270–317.

Marris, R.L. and Wood, A., eds (1971), *The Corporate Economy: Growth Competition and Innovative Power* (NY: Macmillan).

Marschak, J. (1968), 'Economics of Inquiring, Communicating, Deciding', *American Economic Review*, 58, 1–18.

Masson, R.T. (1971), 'Executive Motivations, Earnings and Consequent Equity Performance', *Journal of Political Economy*, 79, 1278–92.

Mazzolini, R. (1979), *Government Controlled Enterprises: International Strategic and Policy Dimensions* (Chichester: John Wiley).

Meehan, E.J. (1982), *Economics and Policymaking: the Tragic Illusion* (Connecticut: Greenwood).

Meeks, G. (1977), *Disappointing Marriage: a Study of the Gains from Merger* (Cambridge University Press).

Meeks, G. and Whittington, G. (1975), 'Directors' Pay, Growth and Profitability', *Journal of Industrial Economics*, 24, 1–14.

Mills, C.W. (1959), *The Sociological Imagination* (NY: Oxford University Press).

Mises, L., Von (1951), *Socialism – an Economic and Sociological Analysis* (Newhaven: Yale University Press).

Monod, J. (1972), *Chance and Necessity: an Essay on the Natural Philosophy of Modern Biology* (London: Collins).

Mueller, D.C. (1969), 'A Theory of Conglomerate Mergers', *Quarterly Journal of Economics*, 83, 643–59.

Myrdal, G. (1976), 'The Meaning and Validity of Institutional Economics', in, Dopfer, K., (ed.), *Economics in the Future: Towards a New Paradigm* (London: Macmillan).

Nelson, P. (1974), 'Advertising as Information', *Journal of Political Economy* 82, 729–54.

Nelson, P. (1975), 'The Economic Consequences of Advertising', *Journal of Business*, 48, 213–41.

Nelson, R.L. (1959), *Merger Movements in American Industry*, 1895–1956 (Princeton University Press).

Nelson, R.R. and Winter, S. (1973), 'Toward an Evolutionary Theory of Economic Capabilities', *American Economic Review*, 63, 440–9.

Nelson, R.R., Winter, S.G. and Schuette, H.L. (1976), 'Technical Change in an Evolutionary Economy', *Quarterly Journal of Economics*, 90, 90–118.

Ng, Y. (1974), 'Utility and Profit, Maximisation by an Owner-Manager: Towards a General Analysis', *Journal of Industrial Economics*, 23, 97–108.

Niskanen, W. (1971), *Bureaucracy and Representative Government* (Chicago: Aldine).

Nordhaus, W.D. (1969), *Invention, Growth and Welfare: a theoretical treatment of technological change* (MIT Press).

OECD (1978), *Public Expenditure Trends* (Paris: OECD).

OECD (1981), *Sweden* (Paris, OECD).

Okun, A.M. (1975), *Equality and Efficiency* (Washington, DC: Brookings Institution).

Olsen, M. (1982), *The Rise and Decline of Nations; Economic Growth, Stagflation and Social Rigidities* (Newhaven: Yale University Press).

Ozga, S.A. (1960), 'Imperfect Markets Through Lack of Knowledge', *Quarterly Journal of Economics*, 74, 29–52.

Parr, M. (1979), 'The National Enterprise Board', *National Westminster Bank Quarterly Review* (Feb.) 51–62.

Patrick, H. and Rosovsky, H. (1976), *Asias New Giant: How the Japanese Economy works* (Washington, DC: Brookings Institution).

Peacock, A. (1979), *The Economic Analysis of Government and Related Themes* (Oxford: Martin Robertson).

Peno, J.D. (1975), *Multinational Corporate Behaviour in Host Country High-Level Manpower Markets* (Paris: OECD).

Penrose, E.T. (1959), *The Theory of the Growth of the Firm* (Oxford: Blackwell).

Phelps-Brown, E.H. (1972), 'The Underdevelopment of Economics', *Economic Journal*, 82, 1–10.

Pirsig, R.M. (1974), *Zen and the Art of Motorcycle Maintenance* (NY: Bantam Books).

Prais, S. (1976), *The Evolution of Large Firms in Britain* (London: National Institute of Economics and Social Research).

Prest, A.R. and Coppock, D.J. (1982), *The U.K. Economy: a Manual of Applied Economics* (London: Weidenfeld & Nicolson).

Pryke, R. (1971), *Public Enterprise in Practice* (London: MacGibbon & Kee).

Pryke, R. (1981), *The Nationalised Industries: Policies and Performance Since 1968* (Oxford: Martin Robertson).

Radice, G., 1978, *The Industrial Democrats: trade unions in an uncertain world*, (London: Allen & Unwin).

Rawls, J. (1971), *A Theory of Justice* (London: Oxford).

Reid, S. (1968), *Mergers, Managers and the Economy* (NY: McGraw-Hill).

Robinson, J. (1933), *The Economics of Imperfect Competition* (London: Macmillan).

Rosenberg, N. (1982), 'The International Transfer of Industrial Technology: Past and Present', in, *North South Technology Transfers: the Adjustments Ahead* (Paris: OECD).

Rotwein, E. (1964), 'Economic Concentration and Monopoly in Japan', *Journal of Political Economy*, 72, 262–77.

Royal Commission on Trade Unions and Employer Associations (1968), *Report*, Cmnd 3623 (London: HMSO).

Rugman, A.M. (1980a), 'A New Theory of the Multinational Enterprise: Internationalization Versus Internalisation', *Columbia Review of World Business*, 14, 23–9.

Rugman, A.M. (1980b), 'Internationalization as a General Theory of Foreign Direct Investment: a Reappraisal of the Literature', *Weltwirtshaftliches Archiv*, iii, 365–79.

Rugman, A.M. (1981), *Inside the Multinationals: the Economics of Internal Markets* (London: Croom Helm).

Rumelt, R.P. (1974), *Strategy, Structure and Economic Performance* (Boston: Harvard University).

Samuels, W.J. ed. (1979a), *The Economy as a System of Power*, vol. I (New Jersey: Transaction Books).

Samuels, W.J. (1979b), *The Economy as a System of Power*, vol. II (New Jersey: Transaction Books).

Samuelson, P. (1961), *Foundations of Economic Analysis* (Cambridge: Harvard University Press).

Samuelson, P. (1980), *Economics*, 11th edn (NY: McGraw-Hill).

Sawyer, M. (1976), 'Income Distribution in O.E.C.D. Countries', *Economic Outlook*, occasional studies, July, 3–36.

Scherer, F.M. (1980), *Industrial Market Structure and Economic Performance* 2nd edn (Chicago: Rand McNally).

Schmalensee, R. (1978), 'A Model of Advertising and Product Quality', *Journal of Political Economy*, 86, 485–503.

Schultz, T.W. (1969) *Investment in Human Capital: the Role of Education and Research* (New York: Free Press).

Schumacher, E.F. (1973), *Small Is Beautiful: Economics as if People Mattered* (NY: Harper & Row).

Schumpeter, J.A. (1954) 4th edn, *Capitalism, Socialism, and Democracy*. (London: Allen & Unwin).

Seckler, D. (1975) *Thorstein Veblen and the Institutionalists* (London: Macmillan).

Servan-Shreiber, J.J. (1967), *The American Challenge* (London: Pelican).

Shackle, G.L.S. (1967), *The Years of High Theory* (Cambridge University Press).

Shackle, G.L.S. (1969), *Decision Order and Time*, 2nd edn (Cambridge University Press).

Shackle, G.L.S. (1970), *Expectation, Enterprise and Profit* (London: Allen & Unwin).

Shackle, G.L.S. (1972) *Epistemics and Economics* (London: Cambridge University Press).

Shearer, J.C. (1960), *High level Manpower in Overseas Subsidiaries* (Princeton University Press).

Shepherd, W.G. (1979), *The Economics of Industrial Organization* (Englewood Cliffs, NJ: Prentice-Hall).

Simon, H.A. (1955), 'A Behavioral Model of Rational Choice', *Quarterly Journal of Economics*, 69, 99–118.

Simon, H.A. (1961), *Administrative Behavior*, 2nd edn (NY: Macmillan).

Simon, H.A. (1969), *The Sciences of the Artificial* (MIT Press).

Singh, A. (1971), *Takeovers* (Cambridge University Press).

Smith, A. (1776), *The Wealth of Nations* (NY: Cannon; 1937 edn).

Smith, K.V. and Schreiner, J.C. (1969), 'A Portfolio Analysis of Conglomerate Diversification', *Journal of Finance*, 24, 413–29.

Solow, R.M. (1967), 'The New Industrial State of Son of Affluence', *Public Interest*, Fall, 100–8, 118–19.

Spadaro, L.M., ed. (1978), *New Directions in Austrian Economics* (Kansas: Sheed Andrews & McMeel).

Spence, A.M. (1975), 'The Economics of Internal Organisation: an Introduction', *Bell Journal of Economics*, 6, 163–72.

Springer, C. and Hofer, C.W. (1980), 'General Electrics Evolving Management System', in Hofer, C.W., Murray, E.A., Charan, R. and Pitts, R.A., *Strategic Management* (St Paul: West Publishing) 454–70.

Sraffa, P. (1926), 'The Laws of Returns under Competitive Conditions', *Economic Journal*, 36, 535–50.

Stigler, G.J. (1961), 'The Economics of Information', *Journal of Political Economy*, 69, 213–25.

Stoppard, T. (1968), *Rosencrantz and Guildenstern Are Dead* (London: Faber & Faber).

Teece, D.J. (1980), 'Economics of Scope and the Scope of the Enterprise', *Journal of Economic Behavior and Organisation*, 1, 223–47.

Telser, L.G. (1964), 'Advertising and Competition', *Journal of Political Economy*, 72, 537–62.

Telser, L.G. (1969), 'On the Regulation of Industry: a Note', *Journal of Political Economy*, 77, 937–52.

Tucker, I.B. and Wilder, R.P. (1977), 'Trends in Vertical Integration in the U.S. Manufacturing Sector', *Journal of Industrial Economics*, 26, 81–94.

Tullock, G. (1965), *The Politics of Bureaucracy* (Washington: Public Affairs Press).

Utton, M.A. (1974), 'On Measuring the Effects of Industrial Merger', *Scottish Journal of Political Economy*, 21, 13–28.

Utton, M.A. (1977), 'Large Firm Diversification in British Manufacturing Industry', *Economic Journal*, 87, 96–113.

Veblen, T. (1923), *Absentee Ownership* (NY: B.W. Huebsch).

Vernon, R. (1971), *Sovereignty at Bay: the Multinational Spread of U.S. Enterprises* (London: Basic Books).

Vernon, R. and Aharoni, Y. (1981), *State-Owned Enterprise in the Western Economies* (London: Croom Helm).

Ward, B. (1972), *Whats Wrong with Economics* (London: Macmillan).

Wiles, P.J.D. (1977), *Economic Institutions Compared* (Oxford: Blackwell).

Willes, M.H. (1981), ' "Rational Expectations" as a counterrevolution', in Bell and Kristol, eds (1981) 81–96.

Williamson, J. (1966), 'Profit Growth and Sales Maximisation', *Economica*, 34, 1–16.

Williamson, O.E. (1964), *Economics of Discretionary Behavior: Managerial Objectives in a Theory of the Firm* (Englewood Cliffs, NJ: Prentice-Hall).

Williamson, O.E. (1975), *Markets and Hierarchies: Analysis and Antitrust Implications* (NY: Free Press).

Williamson, O.E. (1979), 'Transaction Cost Economics: the Governance of Contractual Relations', *Journal of Law and Economics*, 22, 233–61.

Williamson, O.E., (1980), 'The Organisation of Work: a Comparative Institutional Assessment', *Journal of Economic Behavior and Organisation*, 1, 5–38.

Willig, R.D. (1979), 'Multiproduct Technology and Market Structure', *American Economic Review, papers and proceedings*, 49, 346–51.

Winter, S.G. (1964), 'Economic "Natural Selection" and the Theory of the Firm', *Yale Economic Essays*, 4, 225–72.

Winter, S.G. (1971), 'Satisficing, Selection, and the Innovating Remnant', *Quarterly Journal of Economics*, 85, 237–61.

Wolf, B.M. (1977), 'Industrial Diversification and Internalization: Some Empirical Evidence', *Journal of Industrial Economics*, 26, 177–91.

Wonnacott, P. and Wonnacott, R. (1979), *Economics* (NY: McGraw-Hill).

Wong, R.E. (1975), 'Profit Maximisation and Alternative Theories: a Dynamic Reconciliation', *American Economic Review*, 65, 689–94.

Woodward, J. (1965), *Industrial Organisation: Theory and Practice* (London: Oxford University Press).

Worswick, G.D.N. (1972), 'Is Progress in Economic Science Possible?', *Economic Journal*, 82, 73–86.

Yarrow, G. (1976), 'On the Predictions of the Managerial Theory of the Firm', *Journal of Industrial Economics*, 24, 267–79.

Index